Kate Bush and *Hounds of Love*

RON MOY
Liverpool John Moores University, UK

ASHGATE

Published by
Ashgate Publishing Limited
Gower House
Croft Road
Aldershot
Hampshire GU11 3HR
England

Ashgate Publishing Company
Suite 420
101 Cherry Street
Burlington, VT 05401-4405
USA

Ashgate website: http://www.ashgate.com

British Library Cataloguing in Publication Data
Moy, Ron, 1956–
   Kate Bush and the Hounds of love. – (Ashgate popular and folk music series)
   1. Bush, Kate – Criticism and interpretation 2. Bush, Kate. Hounds of love
   I. Title
   782.4'2164'092

Library of Congress Cataloging-in-Publication Data
Moy, Ron, 1956–
   Kate Bush and the Hounds of love / Ron Moy.
      p. cm. – (Ashgate popular and folk music series)
   Includes bibliographical references (p.   ) and index.
   ISBN-13: 978-0-7546-5791-0 (alk. paper)
   ISBN-13: 978-0-7546-5798-9 (alk. paper)
  1. Bush, Kate – Criticism and interpretation. 2. Rock music – England – History and criticism. I. Title.

   ML420.B897M69 2007
   782.42166092–dc22

                       2006032547

ISBN 978-0-7546-5791-0 HBK
ISBN 978-0-7546-5798-9 PBK

Printed and bound in Great Britain by MPG Books Ltd, Bodmin, Cornwall.

Contents

General Editor's Preface

The upheaval that occurred in musicology during the last two decades of the twentieth century has created a new urgency for the study of popular music alongside the development of new critical and theoretical models. A relativistic outlook has replaced the universal perspective of modernism (the international ambitions of the 12-note style); the grand narrative of the evolution and dissolution of tonality has been challenged, and emphasis has shifted to cultural context, reception and subject position. Together, these have conspired to eat away at the status of canonical composers and categories of high and low in music. A need has arisen, also, to recognize and address the emergence of crossovers, mixed and new genres, to engage in debates concerning the vexed problem of what constitutes authenticity in music and to offer a critique of musical practice as the product of free, individual expression.

Popular musicology is now a vital and exciting area of scholarship, and the *Ashgate Popular and Folk Music Series* aims to present the best research in the field. Authors will be concerned with locating musical practices, values and meanings in cultural context, and may draw upon methodologies and theories developed in cultural studies, semiotics, poststructuralism, psychology and sociology. The series will focus on popular musics of the twentieth and twenty-first centuries. It is designed to embrace the world's popular musics from Acid Jazz to Zydeco, whether high tech or low tech, commercial or non-commercial, contemporary or traditional.

Professor Derek B. Scott
Chair of Music
University of Leeds

Acknowledgements

Many people have actively helped me during the research and writing of this book. My initial thanks must go to Derek Scott, and the commissioning board at Ashgate, for their faith in this project. I must also thank my editor, Heidi May, for all her assistance. Several members of staff within the School of Media, Critical and Creative Arts at Liverpool John Moores University have taken the time to help me. I would particularly like to thank Jo Croft, Elspeth Graham, Ned Hassan and Gerry Smyth. Special thanks should go to my colleagues in Popular Music Studies: Stuart Borthwick and Tim Dalton. Tim has helped me with DTP issues on numerous occasions. Innumerable students have helped maintain my love and enthusiasm for popular music since I began teaching in 1992, and I thank them collectively. Particular mention should go to Jess Carver and David Kelly for their musicological assistance. Paul Andrade was kind enough to proofread a draft of this text, and offer valuable advice. Amongst the many writers whose work has helped in my research, I must single out Rob Jovanovic, Holly Kruse, Phil Sutcliffe and Sheila Whiteley, all of whom have written with particular insight about Kate Bush and her music. Many contributors to websites, some unknown, have also been a great help. The Gaffaweb site has been a rich mine of information and sources, as have the articles placed upon Rock's Back Pages.

Several friends have helped me over the course of many years to formulate opinions through discussions relating to popular music; my thanks go to Brian Dunne, Ian Runeckles and Brian Sharp.

My biggest thanks must go to Mike Brocken and David Buckley, long-standing friends and sources of musical knowledge, texts and advice, and to my family – Anne, Byron and Elena – who always make my favourite journey the one 'home'.

And finally, my thanks to Kate Bush herself, whose music has given me such pleasure over almost 30 years, and without whose inspiration this book would have no reason to exist. Others have already used this title as a 'sign-off', but I can't find a better one – be kind to my mistakes.

Ron Moy, Cheshire, England

Introduction

Biography

Kate Bush's biography has been exhaustively researched and repeated *ad nauseam* in countless music press articles and a few full-length works (see Juby, 1988; Sutcliffe, 2003; Jovanovic, 2005 by way of overview), so what follows cannot hope to be comprehensive, or little more than a retread (with a personal slant) of existing material. Biography can be as peripheral or as vital to forming an understanding of the work of an artist as the individual writer, reader, analyst or fan wants it to be. For every account claiming to be able to 'explain' a career path in biographical, sociological or psychological terms, there is a counter argument that such readings are over-deterministic, too reliant on hindsight or just plain opportunistic on behalf of the reader or writer, telling us more about their psyches than those of the subject under scrutiny. Not that this factor is unimportant; art is there to speak of us as much as we speak of it. Biography has its place, as long as we acknowledge its constructed nature and its partiality. It tells a story, as do all narratives, fictional or otherwise; but it doesn't tell 'the truth' or 'the whole story': nothing does, and no one can.

Catherine (Kate) Bush was born on the suburban fringes of southeast London on 30 July 1958. Her family background was comfortable, without being privileged. The home was shared with her mother, father and two older brothers, John and Paddy. Numerous accounts vouch for the unusually close emotional bonds between the Bush family members. Indeed, Paddy and her father lay claim to be her original musical mentors and her brother is one of only two musicians (along with drummer Stuart Elliott) to appear on all her albums. The family also exhibited talents in poetry, photography, design and musical instrument making. Kate Bush's mother, Hannah, was Irish, which many have seen as contributing to an environment filled with varied styles of music and amateur music making. Bush showed early talent, particularly in composition, and throughout her teens became a prolific writer of songs, and a competent self-taught pianist.

A family friend brought her to the attention of David Gilmour, of Pink Floyd. Her rough demos impressed him enough to finance some more professionally made recordings in June 1975 (these demos are now unofficially available online as MP3 files, although their legal status is problematic). Gilmour presented these recordings to his record company, EMI, who were particularly entranced with a song called 'The Man with the Child in his Eyes', reputedly written when the young writer was 13. In that same year, the 17-year-old was linked to the label on an 'apprenticeship' type contract, allowing her funds to pursue her career and another year to develop. Between that point and mid-1977, Kate Bush left school, moved into a flat with her brothers, took dance classes with the venerated Lindsay Kemp and gigged around London with the K T Bush Band, mostly performing cover versions.

In July and August 1977 Kate Bush recorded her first album, *The Kick Inside*, which was released in the UK in February 1978. The first single, 'Wuthering Heights', which reached the top of the UK singles chart in the same month, prefaced the album release. The album proved a great commercial and critical success, reaching number 3 in the UK chart. During the same year, the artist achieved more success in the singles chart, and also recorded her second album, *Lionheart*, which reached number 6 in the UK chart. In 1979, Kate Bush embarked upon her first, and likely to be her only concert tour, the *Tour of Life*. This featured numerous costume changes, elaborate staging and choreography, and the pioneering use of a 'hands-free' microphone, allowing the artist to make great use of her dance and mime training. However, being something of a perfectionist, Kate Bush found the whole experience exhausting and unsatisfying and the tour was marred by the death of lighting engineer Bill Duffield, who died after a fall. This was to be the first of several deaths of people closely associated with Kate Bush's career. Since this only major tour, she has subsequently put most of her creative energies into recording, producing, video and directing.

Since the exhaustive period culminating in her tour of 1979, Kate Bush has pursued a less high-profile career, with the periods between album releases growing successively longer. After 1980's *Never For Ever*, her first number 1 album in the UK, her next album, 1982's *The Dreaming*, was her first relative commercial failure in her homeland, reaching number 3 but selling only a fraction of previous releases. This album was noticeably less 'user friendly' than previous works, with even the choices for singles ('The Dreaming', 'Sat in your Lap' and 'There Goes a Tenner') demonstrating a more esoteric, experimental sensibility that resulted in generally poor sales. However, the album's very inaccessibility did change the critical perception of the artist, and she began to garner serious praise from the likes of the US college or 'alternative' market. At this point, there was a widespread perception in the media (aided by the subject matter of some of her songs, and her unusual album covers) that Kate Bush had 'lost it' or 'gone mad'.

The painstaking recording of *The Dreaming* in expensive studios had cost Kate Bush a great deal, in both financial and artistic terms. To overcome these issues she commissioned the construction of her own home studio, which was used to record her next album, 1985's *Hounds of Love*. This work is widely held to be her finest, and was both a critical and commercial success, giving her a second number 1 in the UK album chart and her first real breakthrough in the US, where it reached number 30. The album also spawned four hit singles. As late as 2004 it was voted 22nd best UK album of all time in the *Observer* music monthly poll – the highest by a solo female artist. In the same year, *Q* magazine's readers voted her 29th 'Greatest Music Star of All Time' (Jovanovic, 2005: 8). Since the release of *Hounds of Love*, the artist has pursued an ever more sedate career path, with just three albums of new material in getting on for 20 years. *The Sensual World* in 1989 and *The Red Shoes* in 1993 both reached number 2 in the UK charts. In the period since this last album Kate Bush has become a mother and done few interviews. Contrary to tabloid press reports she has not retired or become a recluse, but merely lives a private existence only notable as the result of the nature of her celebrity and great wealth. Rumours on fan websites stated that her next album was 'imminent' for about four years in the period following 2000. *Aerial* was finally released in the autumn of 2005.

Despite the paucity of recent recordings, and lack of personal appearances, her critical capital has remained high. Indeed, her privacy has inevitably helped fuel her 'cult status'. Many diverse artists have vouched for her influence, she has been given many 'landmark' type awards by the music industry (as well as turning at least one down), and a wide number of artists and acts have covered her songs.

Kate Bush is one of the most successful and influential female solo artists to have emerged in the UK. For journalist Jim Irvin, she 'is the greatest living British artist in song' (Irvin, 2005: 96). The feeling remains that, despite the slowdown in her musical output over the past 20 years, this woman's work is far from complete.

Rationale and Methodology

The main body of this book consists of a linear track-by-track musical analysis of Kate Bush's albums released between 1978 and 2005. In particular, it pays close attention to the 1985 album *Hounds of Love*, which forms the centrepiece of my musical analysis. The text will break from the constraints of chronology during this section in order to explore several important critical issues raised by the artist's work and position as a solo, female artist in an industry that still largely conforms to the stereotypes of patriarchy. In particular, I will be paying close attention to three aspects, under these headings:

1. 'A Daughter of Albion?' Issues of national and ethnic identity have been consistently brought to the fore by Kate Bush's genealogy, her musical influences, her collaborations and musical aspects centring on genre, style and the grain of the voice. This section will explore and problematise notions of ethnicity and identity via the artist's relationship to influences as diverse as Celtic folk, Bulgarian choral singing, British cinema and TV, and the classical pastoral tradition of Vaughan Williams, Delius and others.

2. 'Kate Bush and *Auteur* Theory.' Important work has been carried out, particularly in screen theory, relating to notions of authorship, authenticity, artistic intent, and to questions of where meaning and worth reside in a text. Film and music production share a common rationale of collaboration, and I will be applying *auteur* theory to a close analysis of the methodologies employed by Kate Bush as part of the gendered, creative process. In addition, comparative analysis with Madonna and Björk will shed further light on the nature and extent of authorial input into these artists' careers and on the concept itself.

3. 'Audio Texts, Video Texts: Extensions or Detractions?' will investigate the relationship between Kate Bush's musical and video performances. The artist's training in mime and expressive movement has clearly influenced the style of the pop videos that accompany large numbers of her songs. In addition, for *Hounds of Love* and *The Red Shoes*, audio-visual texts assume, or attempt to assume, the status of conceptual works. In this section I will be exploring

the relationship between the different music-based media and drawing wider conclusions about the nature of music in an increasingly specular age.

The book is not intended to be comprehensive or 'completist', so the many b-sides, alternative mixes and non-album tracks produced during the artist's career will not be part of the critical brief. Whilst openly admitting that I am a great fan of her music, I am not a fanatic with encyclopaedic knowledge about the artist's life, biography and works. This book will not be a hagiography or a celebration of the artist and her work and readers are advised to seek out more biographical or web-based sources for this kind of account. What I do bring to the project is a lifetime's interest in popular music as fan, and more latterly analyst, lecturer in the subject and author.

My own relationship to Kate Bush's music and career has been inconsistent. Her debut single, 'Wuthering Heights', and her first album initially entranced me. After the disappointment of her second album, I became a more detached fan of her music during the early to mid-1980s. With 'Running up that Hill (A Deal with God)' and *Hounds of Love*, in 1985, I again became a huge fan before my appreciation became more 'measured' in the following years. However, my interest and admiration for Kate Bush's music always endured. In particular, as a fellow southern English suburbanite, I have always identified with her ethnicity and accent, which closely matches my own. In around 1992, when somewhat belatedly moving into the CD era, *Hounds of Love* was my first purchase of the new format. In more recent years, partly as a result of this book project, I have reappraised her work, in the process retrospectively getting to know later albums such as *The Red Shoes*. In the final months of my research, her 2005 album *Aerial* was released. As will be stated in due course, this album can be seen as a successful return to form, with the music, as a complete entity, close to rivalling her best work

The issue of methodology is a particularly vexing one for popular music studies. Susan McClary and Robert Walser's essay (1990), aptly subtitled 'Musicology Wrestles with Rock', articulates many of the most important issues. This is best exemplified by a mythical exchange that the authors construct between symbolic representatives of the two opposing schools of music analysis – the sociological school and the musicological school. The sociologist asks the musicologist why a particular note has prompted such a powerful affective response. The musicologist replies:

> 'You were expecting an E-flat, and he sang an E-natural.' And the sociologist explodes because she knows perfectly well that she was not expecting an E-flat, that in fact she would not know an E-flat from a hole in the wall, and that the musicologist is once again taking a perfectly transparent phenomenon and obfuscating – flaunting specialized and apparently useless information. (McClary and Walser, 1990: 279).

The point is well made. Essentially abstract musicological terminology is of limited value because the issue lies not within the naming of the note, but within the fact that as members of a reading community, affective codes relating to the 'right' or 'wrong' note have been intuitively absorbed from an early, even pre-literate stage. Franco Fabbri makes the point that children can identify generic distinctions at a very young age (Fabbri, 1982: 55). Essentially, the dilemma lies in the methods and taxonomy used to articulate this kind of knowledge. For the purposes of this text, these methods must be inter-disciplinary, academic, yet at times openly emotive and affective – in essence, 'phenomenological', in critical terms.

The problem remains within the recognition that all linguistic sign systems contain a structural imperative, leading on to the situation within which 'academics – those who are uncomfortable with inexplicable sexual responses ... wish to be able to control those responses rationally' (McClary and Walser, 1990: 286). As is ever the case, this dilemma is not solvable, but merely needs to be stated – openly acknowledging all the inconsistencies that must inevitably result. However, no methodology should be discounted, but rather its hegemonic claims should be problematised. As the authors state, musicology has a contribution to make in:

> explaining how the powerful moments in music are accomplished, without discrediting the impression that they are exciting, disturbing, or pleasurable. The focus should be on constructing models that serve only as flexible backdrops, up against which the noise of the piece can reverberate. (McClary and Walser, 1990: 289).

Equally, sociological and ethnographic approaches have a value, but one whose limitations – and assumptions – must be acknowledged. Rehan Hyder's ethnographic study of the UK Asian music scene firmly states that 'Any study of musical meaning and cultural significance taken from a musical text must be counterbalanced by consideration of the avowed intentions of the artists themselves' (Hyder, 2004: 4). I would concur, although if this 'consideration' is intended in an essentialising or prescriptive manner, rather than as a potentially useful interpretive component, then it goes too far down the road leading to 'proof'. Hyder maintains that 'too often ... meanings ascribed to lyrical texts...are alien or even anathema to authors themselves' (ibid.). Here I do disagree with the notion that meaning resides (or *should* reside) within authorial intent rather than being a negotiation between author, text and modes of interpretation, but at this point, let me conclude by stating that questions of meaning and authorship will be extensively scrutinised in later chapters.

Despite some experience in music performance and digital composition, I have no formal playing or reading skills. I approach music as a socially mediated text that allows for a multitude of critical and aesthetical entry points to manifest themselves through individual interpretive strategies. These strategies are all equally justifiable insofar as they are self-consciously made evident. Thus, elements of musicology, sociology, ethnography, psychoanalytical and feminist theory, biography and iconography will all be brought to bear (as 'flexible backdrops'). In addition, it is important to situate the works within historical, industrial, commercial and technological contexts. Fundamental themes relating to issues such as gender, sexuality, ethnicity, authorship and aesthetics will also be explored – both interwoven into musical analysis and also as separate critical headings.

My approach will be academic, yet inter-disciplinary and is intended to be as accessible as the complexity of some of the analysis and debates allows – another unsolvable dilemma. Musicological terms will be employed sparingly, with a more inclusive taxonomy typically being employed to encourage a holistic humanities-based rationale. Readers are encouraged to augment this text with their own analysis of the musical texts themselves. Interpretive dilemmas relating to issues such as meaning's origination and residence will be made explicit in this book; not in order to solve these dilemmas, but rather to foreground and highlight the unique problems posed by music as a nebulous and 'objectless' text, one that is 'an especially resistant medium to write or speak about' (McClary and Walser, 1990: 278). Any musical text is the catalyst for the means by which self-analysis is manifested, rather than merely the end product in itself.

Literary Sources and Critical Context

In pragmatic terms, it is unreasonable to expect an artist such as Kate Bush to have provoked as much media and critical coverage as, say, Madonna. Madonna is a global pop star whose notoriety, performances and songs have rendered her one of the most recognisable human beings on the planet. In contrast Kate Bush is primarily a recording artist with a very low public profile. My contention is not that Madonna deserves less attention (although she herself might disagree!), but that Kate Bush deserves a little more.

Kate Bush has achieved both huge commercial success (by late 2005, this amounted to 20 top-30 chart singles, and nine top-10 chart albums in the UK, see Jovanovic, 2005: 220) and, broadly speaking, much critical acclaim. In the wake of these achievements the paucity of literary and academic sources devoted to Kate Bush is, on first glance, something of a mystery. By way of illustrating this point, Lori Burns and Melisse Lafrance's *Disruptive Divas: Feminism, Identity & Popular Music* (2002) contains not even a passing mention to the artist. Sheila Whiteley's *Women and Popular Music: Sexuality, Identity and Subjectivity* (2000) includes one brief mention of Kate Bush merely in terms of her influence upon k.d.lang (2000: 153). Whiteley's edited collection *Sexing The Groove: Popular Music and Gender* (1997) has no mentions. In the introductory section to *Women and Popular Music* the author states: 'I am concerned with female performers who can be considered catalysts within their respective genres – Janis Joplin, Joni Mitchell. Patti Smith, Madonna, k.d. lang, Tracy Chapman, Tori Amos' (Whiteley, 2000: 1). Perhaps Bush's work cannot be contained within one genre? I offer no criticism of any writer's choice of subject matter (indeed, Whiteley is a notable exception; I am indebted to her research on popular music, gender, youth and Kate Bush in particular), but the reasons for Kate Bush's near total absence are significant, and tell us a lot about both the nature of her success, and about how the critical climate, particularly relating to female performers, functions.

Amy Raphael's *Never Mind the Bollocks: Women Rewrite Rock* (Raphael, 1995), perhaps logically bearing in mind the title (for 'rock' read 'working-class authenticity' or 'marginality' or 'distorted guitars'), ignores Kate Bush in favour of performers such as Courtney Love of Hole, 'riot grrrl' act Huggy Bear and Pam Hogg, of Doll. Again, my point is not that female musicians that swear, take drugs and make a cacophony should not be granted critical space, but that equally so should polite, middle-class, female musicians that love their families and make their interviewers nice cups of tea. Furthermore, musicians that earnestly avoid the mainstream and commercially 'fail' deserve attention, but so do those that write seductive melodies and sell large quantities of their work to a varied, worldwide audience.

Whiteley's list of catalysts is worth deconstructing. Although many of the examples have achieved both acclaim and success, it can be argued that they all conform to the authenticity paradigm that grants status to those seen to be 'marginal', 'transgressive' or who have, in some way, 'suffered'. Curtis White refers to this interpretive fallacy as 'the…Church of the Commodified Vernacular' (White, 2005: 10). Thus, Janis Joplin lives a life of excess before succumbing to a drug overdose. Patti Smith works as a band leader in a masculine genre, and has uncoventional, 'unfeminine' looks. Madonna's many transgressions have been common currency for many years. k.d.lang is an 'out' lesbian working mainly within the conservative, patriarchal genre of country. Tracy Chapman is a black woman working within the mainly white, male genre of 'protest folk'. Tori Amos has a provocative style, both in terms of lyrics and performance, and brings biographical examples of sexual violation into her songwriting. Joni Mitchell's supposed 'promiscuity' and the way that love affairs were 'exploited' within songs garnered her critical approbation in a way that would not have been considered appropriate for a male equivalent (see Hinton, 2000).

In a paradoxical manner, I would argue that all the above-mentioned artists' 'transgressions' are actually recuperated within a critical popular music discourse. They conform to mythologies that place them within a counter-hegemonic analysis that essentially ends up as conformist – the 'tortured artist effect' beloved of bourgeois ideology, yet supposedly unfettered by it. Within this scenario, Kate Bush can actually be judged as the true outsider. Not only has she sold millions of records (itself a problem for some 'purist' critics) and led an unscandalous, bourgeois, 'non-celebrity' life that eshews drug-taking, promiscuity and homosexuality, but the vast majority of her creative time has been devoted to writing, recording and producing music in a private studio space. In addition, although (as I will proceed to argue in due course) her work is explicitly concerned with issues of gender and sexuality, her opinions relating to notions of feminism and masculinity can be read as 'unreconstructed' by those not sharing her values and views. This last factor may have a bearing on the observation that most of the critical attention paid to Bush has come from men, notable exceptions being Simon Reynolds and Joy Press's work (1995: 240–243), Whiteley's chapter on Bush, Tori Amos and Björk in *Too Much Too Young* (2005) and the essay 'In Praise of Kate Bush', by Holly Kruse (1990: 450–465).

The field of 'serious' music journalism is a far more fertile terrain for Kate Bush criticism. Many incisive articles exist in journals such as *Q*, *Mojo*, *New Musical Express*, *Melody Maker*, *Village Voice*, *Pulse*, *New York Times*, *The Guardian* and so on. However, the lack of biographical data – the artist essentially has had little or no 'public life' since about 1980 – does result in a large amount of duplication.

There have been, to date, only a small number of full-length biographies relating to the artist, for reasons outlined above. Fred (and Judy) Vermorel's two studies (1979, 1983) are both full of interest, particularly bearing in mind the authors' interest in fandom and star personae, but they can only cover a small part of Bush's career. Vermorel's 1983 biography is a strange text that largely overlooks the music in favour of some spurious investigations into the artist's genealogy that attempts to 'explain' her appeal in terms of her connections to myths surrounding 'Celtic mysticism'.

More recently, two texts have been published. John Mendelssohn's *Waiting For Kate Bush* (2004) is an imaginative reflection upon the nature of fan worship that details one man's obsession with the long hiatus in the artist's career, dovetailed into some tracts of straightforward biography and musical analysis. The fictional elements work much better than the writer's attempts to come to terms with the music and the book's brave attempt to straddle the genres of fiction and biography is not really successful. In 2005, Rob Jovanovic's *Kate Bush: The Biography* emerged – purely incidentally – simultaneously with the artist's first album in 12 years. It was thus both blessed and cursed in dealing with an artist concurrently re-emerging into the public eye, yet was rendered instantaneously in need of critical updating. It is a mark of the artist's 'unnewsworthy' nature that Jovanovic manages to successfully summarise some 47 years of Kate Bush's life in only 230-odd pages of double-spaced, large-fonted text. Although the main emphasis is on biography and new and existing interviews with collaborators, the limited amount of musical analysis is efficient and occasionally very illuminating. His work can be judged particularly useful in terms of the interviews with music and production partners. The artist herself was unwilling to participate in this process – as is her right. This poses any analyst of her music with something of a critical dilemma, yet to my mind actually frees the writer from the constraints of biography and rationality, granting the creative work the status it actually deserves.

No one has, to my way of thinking, yet engaged in an in-depth manner with the most fundamental aspect of Kate Bush's life – her music. As previously stated, this in itself raises another critical dilemma, as I possess no formal musicological skills, but my intention is to attempt to reconcile academic rigour and analytical complexity with an inter-disciplinary approach that is accessible, and combines the best facets of academic and journalistic methodology.

Despite the exponential growth in popular music studies in the UK post-16 education sector over the past 20 years, this period has seen something of a 'bunker mentality' develop in terms of the lack of dialogue between the spheres of academia and journalism. Not only is it almost impossible to obtain reviews for academic texts in commercial press journals, or for journalistic texts in academic circles, but the crossover potential for writings that attempt to straddle the two fields is very small. This seems a missed opportunity for a discipline such as popular music studies that is greatly concerned with notions of the popular, the commercial and 'crossover appeal'. In any case, some of the most successful examples of popular music are those that manage to straddle the commercial and the critical worlds. David Buckley, my erstwhile fellow postgraduate student and lecturer at Liverpool University's Institute of Popular Music, and now a sucessful music journalist and biographer, stated during a personal interview:

> back in the early 1990s, it seemed as if a new way within popular music studies was not only possible, but inevitable. Simon Frith, Jon Savage and Steve Redhead were producing

work that elided the safe boundaries between rock journalism and academic discourse, and, for those working in the field at the time it seemed ... that both ... would provide a space for a more personally engaging academic style to exist between both disciplines. However, today it seems that the two are as entrenched in their positions and as separatist in their views as ever. Academic writing appears to be almost wholly about speaking to the converted...and the target only ever appears to be to gain kudos and money in research assessment exercises rather than actually to connect with a wider readership. On the other side, music magazines give academic writing little or no coverage in their review pages, and tend to regard the whole academic project to 'take music and culture seriously', to be irrelevant and slightly mad. (Buckley, 2006).

This kind of attitude must be challenged, and is part of the polemical dimension implicit in this book. Its success in challenging and reconciling two very different critical methodologies is for others to judge.

Part One

Her Early Work

The Kick Inside

Music is often described in terms of its transcendent or timeless qualities. But we must acknowledge that music is also grounded in the concrete realities of time and space. What we bring to a piece of music, or an artist's career, should not be overlooked. I make these points to try to justify my longstanding opinion that Kate Bush's debut album is a great work, but only when viewed in the context of her own career, the music scene and my own personal biography. Had the same songs been placed on her third album, for example, they would not have provoked the same critical impact.

The cover artwork, rudimentary compared to later albums, features the artist flying gripping an oriental kite, exposing a little flesh, but demurely pulling her right leg across her body, suggesting modesty. Unlike most of her subsequent cover shots, she is one small feature in the overall design, rather than the centrepiece. It is an interesting design, but not really bold or provocative – as later artwork proved to be.

The album was an almost impossibly assured debut from an inexperienced female musician in the early stages of womanhood. It is often said that an artist has the whole of their life to write the songs on their first album, and usually only a few months to write the songs on the follow-up. Certainly, in Bush's case *Lionheart* struggles to fulfil the promise of *The Kick Inside*, but more on that issue below. *The Kick Inside* (henceforth *Kick*) was scheduled for release in late 1977, but was delayed until early 1978 because of disagreements over the cover design. In retrospect, this proved an astute commercial decision, allowing an unknown to make a bigger splash in a traditionally quiet part of the musical year, rather than having to battle to be seen and heard in the festive maelstrom of Christmas and New Year.

In the UK the extensive impact of punk was still rippling through the industry. 'Classic' punk music was still widespread, although the 'no-hopers' of 1976 and 1977 had mostly already disappeared back into obscurity after a handful of gigs and one or two singles released on an independent label. Punk 'royalty', such as the Sex Pistols, the Clash and the Buzzcocks had all released successful albums during 1977. The mainstream music industry was attempting to recuperate its market status by touting the less threatening generic term 'new wave' to try to encourage a mainstream crossover for the likes of the well-established Jam and the Stranglers, and as a new label for emerging artists such as Blondie, Elvis Costello and the Attractions and Ian Dury and the Blockheads. However, in terms of the UK charts, more traditional forms such as soul (mutating into disco), commercial pop, heavy metal and stadium rock still predominated. Reggae had also re-emerged in the punk era, and its rhythmic tendencies had a widespread impact.

Relative to today, female artists found themselves in an invidious position in the late 1970s – forced to conform either to the sensitive singer-songwriter model (Carole King, Joni Mitchell), or the torch-song balladeer (Barbra Streisand, Elaine Paige) or the sassy r'n'b diva (Tina Turner, Millie Jackson). Females operating in the rock idiom were relatively few and most women in band settings were there to provide vocals or sexy moves. Punk had allowed for the emergence of powerful female artists, such as Patti Smith and Siouxsie Sioux, but few women had managed to escape the stereotypes of angel, whore or witch that the industry has established in order to confine them. Despite all concerted efforts, Deborah Harry still has a mainly iconic status, over and above all her artistic or musical achievements. Into this fragmented world – on the cusp of moving beyond the values and styles laid down in the late 1960s, but not yet fully embracing the post-punk world of video, synthesisers and music programming – emerged a seemingly fully formed mature and unique artist.

Kate Bush had the backing of EMI behind her: a long-established patrician organisation a little too conservative to fully embrace punk. In October 1977 the Tom Robinson Band achieved their first hit with '2 4 6 8 Motorway'. Tom Robinson pressed the right buttons in terms of commitment without offending the musical sensibilities of the label that was also home to Cliff Richard (but no longer the Sex Pistols). EMI proved to be a sympathetic and nurturing label for Kate Bush, allowing the time and artistic control she and her family needed, and subsequently supporting her through relative commercial failures and long periods between releases. EMI also possessed the studio and marketing infrastructure of a global 'major', allowing for the extensive promotional push needed to present a new artist to the music world.

In 1978 the weekly music press and billboard advertising were far more important then today. An early provocative pose of the artist, all pouting lips and stiff nipples protruding through a skimpy vest, ensured that the artist's image was widespread in early 1978. More importantly, EMI had contacts with experienced musicians, producers and arrangers, and Kate Bush's debut pays tribute to their collective efforts. Most of the musicians on *Kick* had extensive experience, both as session musicians and as members of successful bands. From the group Pilot came bassist David Paton and guitarist Ian Bairnson. Pilot had had two hits with the singles 'Magic' and 'January' in 1974–75, but in common with the rock versus pop divide of the time had not made the transition to credibility or album sales despite the assurance and classiness of their material. From the group Cockney Rebel came drummer Stuart Elliott and keyboardist Duncan Mackay. This band (along with Pilot, an EMI act) had achieved wide success in the mid-1970s as both a single and album act, aided by their media-savvy front man, Steve Harley. Elliott had been a founder member, and Mackay joined later and played on the number 1 single 'Make Me Smile (Come Up and See Me)' in 1975. As with Pilot's music, Cockney Rebel's was bright, intelligent pop, in the latter's case topped by the exaggeratedly English vocals of Harley. These English traits, unusual for popular music as a whole, were also recognised by EMI staff. Terry Slater commented: 'Kate is a real English girl…She's from the roots of Great Britain. It's not a gimmick or produced. She's the first really English girl singer for some time' (Slater, in Jovanovic, 2005: 50).

These musicians, together with Bush herself on piano, jazz player Morris Pert on percussion, multi-instrumentalist Paddy Bush and EMI producer/arranger Andrew Powell on keyboards, formed the basis of the *Kick* sound. Powell had previously contributed the grandiose string arrangements to some Cockney Rebel tracks. Without seeming to fall into the polite sterility associated with some session playing, the backing musicians gave the inexperienced artist the firm platform from which to project her own musical vision. *Kick* was a truly polished and collaborative album, with Bush the creative pinnacle – rightly so as all the songs were self-composed. In addition, almost all main and backing vocals were Bush's sole responsibility, with her assured multi-tracking abilities evident from early in the very first track. Recording took place in AIR Studios' two principal spaces – Studio Two for the main band tracks, and the larger Studio One for the orchestral parts (Jovanovic, 2005: 57).

'Moving'

'Moving' does what any opening track on a debut album should do: it 'sets out the stall' and provides clear indications of artistic intent and style. In many cases this track also sets the musical tone for the subsequent album. On 'Moving' a slow fade-in of pre-recorded whale cries establishes an ambient and intriguing mood of anticipation. A more obvious opening track would possibly have been the already huge hit, 'Wuthering Heights'. Conversely, the mooted first single, 'James and the Cold Gun' (firmly rejected by the artist in the face of label opposition), would have provided a more forceful and high-energy beginning, but would have created a false impression – being the only real 'rock' number on the album. Instead, 'Moving' introduces us gently to the kind of slow- to mid-tempo balladic terrain that Kate Bush has returned to on numerous occasions, and one that forms the bulk of the tracks on her first two albums.

I can still remember the anticipation before playing this album, tinged with the fear of anti-climax. However, all fears were dispersed when the lushness of the chorus couched in Powell's sympathetic strings and topped by the artist's multi-track harmonies swept in at 50 seconds (around the time of the 'classic' chorus entry in most commercial pop). In terms of the often muddy and slapdash rock production of the time, the signature sound of *Kick* was bright, resonant and crisp. Unusually, no prominence was given to any frequency or element. The vocals were mixed up-front, but not too high and all instrumental elements could be identified. Most of the backing tracks were recorded 'live', adding to the brightness and room ambience offered by large studio spaces (Jovanovic, 2005: 62–3).

Lyrically, 'Moving' is one of the artist's 'inspiration' songs, in this case her dance mentor Lindsay Kemp. In terms of effect they also trace many of Kate's dominant concerns: love, relationships, sensuality and desire. As well as being direct and assertive ('touch me, hold me, how my aching arms ache') they also inhabit a more poetic and metaphorical terrain on occasions ('you crush the lilly [her spelling] in my soul'). In the narrative tensions between these two poles of activity and passive reflection rest many Kate Bush lyrics.

'Moving' ends as it starts, cyclically returning us to ambient sounds before a piano provides a segued link into the next track, 'Saxophone Song', one of two tracks dating from recording sessions with a different group of musicians in 1975.

'Saxophone Song'

This track again places the narrator in a relationship to a 'mover', yearning for connection. In the case of this track, this yearning is underpinned with a more overtly sexual undercurrent, expressed both lyrically and vocally in the urgency of 'it's in me, it's in me'. Although written in a directly autobiographical sense, the artist maintained that it was a fictional narrative; she had never been in a Berlin bar listening to a saxophonist. This exemplifies both the positive nature of biographical evidence, and also its limitations. Once we know that the lyric is essentially a fiction, or a fantasy, we can never again discount this information 'from the horse's mouth'. It thus satisfyingly 'closes' the text to an extent (we know what it is about), but also encourages us to believe that the artist has the meaning. This is sometimes plainly untrue, or a little too reductive, and more damagingly prevents us as listeners from creating our own lyrical meanings. It is also one of the reasons why I have never seen the meaning of a text as residing solely, or even chiefly, within the lyrical narrative.

The playing on this track particularly stands out, with the obvious elements – the sax break after each chorus – well balanced by more subtle touches such as the slide guitar and the three-beat feel of the rhythm section in the long run-out section overlaid with some cascading organ runs. As the two opening tracks are linked, the album effectively starts with a bold near seven-minute track.

'Strange Phenomena'

This track is probably a little too close in feel and structure to previous tracks to truly stand out. More interesting is the lyric, which broach one of the artist's recurring concerns – the supernatural, mystical or 'cosmic' qualities of existence. Such elements were resolutely unfashionable in the late 1970s, leading some critics to place the artist within 'hippie' stereotypes, aided by Bush's choice of hairstyle and dress at that time.

'Kite'

Here we are provided with the album's first break in feel. As well as utilising a 'reggae-lite' rhythm, the lyrics are noticeably less portentous, bordering on the whimsical ('my feet are heavy and I'm rooted in my wellios'). Similarly, Bush's vocals soar and swoop with child-like abandon between notes. This is particularly effective on the two-part chorus, where the single word 'diamond' becomes a luscious octave-jumping pirouette. In all, this track provides a welcome shift in affect, very much 'of its time' in the appropriation of reggae as a style, but charming none the less. David Paton referred to the freedom granted to individual musicians to 'compose' on many tracks on this album: 'I'm thinking of "Kite", where the chords were written but the bass part came out of my head' (Paton, in Jovanovic, 2005: 62).

'The Man with the Child in his Eyes'

In instrumental terms this is one of the sparsest of the artist's entire career, with just a heavily hall-echoed grand piano and an orchestral bed (mainly cellos initially, followed by violins, flutes, horns and violas) providing the backing. This is the second track to date from the 1975 sessions. After around 2: 40 it's all over, having given us just two verses and two choruses. It is a stately, classically English romantic ballad dealing with yearning and anxiety in an exquisite manner, and its simple beauty has been rarely equalled in the artist's subsequent career.

'Wuthering Heights'

To conclude the first side of the vinyl album comes the tour-de-force: an amazingly complex song, and a particularly bold choice for a debut single. After a simple piano motif, then repeated up an octave, we are straight into the narrative, delivered in a vocal key highly unusual outside of opera. The singularity of the artist's voice makes an immediate and provocative impact. Few were unmoved by her timbre and pitching – with many enchanted, and many repelled by this most un-rock'n'roll singer. For Jon Young, 'depending on your reaction it's either Minnie Mouse or the Heavenly Host' (Young, 1978). Writing in the 'serious' weekly *New Musical Express*, Steve Clarke described the song as being 'sung in a voice not unlike that of a newly-neutered cat letting the world know of his predicament' (Clarke, 1978). After a verse and pre-chorus the first chorus arrives (again around the standardised 50 seconds). The music has to perform time signature tricks to accommodate the unusual rhythm and line, even word lengths of this section. Particularly striking is the vocal section that is rendered as 'so co-ho-ho-hold let me in a' your windo-o-o-ow'. This looks pretty silly in print, partly because transcendent moments of musical beauty cannot really be translated or paraphrased. The music itself will always be the primary text.

The second verse, accompanied by strings, increases the power and resonance of the track. After the second chorus, at around 2: 18, comes the middle 8, or b-section. As within much of pop, this is accompanied by a key change, forcing the instrumentation and vocal melody upwards, and connoting greater energy and resolution. Particularly effective is the shift in lyrical register, with the close juxtaposition of an elevated term such as 'soul' with the more mundane 'grab'. This line, 'let me grab your soul away', thus throws us out of the romantic world of the bourgeois novel (obviously, to an appreciable extent this track is based on the novel of the same name, although the artist's reference point was a TV adaptation; she had not read the whole book according to Jovanovic, 2005: 51), with 'grab' being substituted for a more fitting, 'poetical' terms such as 'steal'. It imbues the line with a more earthiness and desperation. After this b-section we are returned to the repeated chorus after a moment's repose, punctuated by a powerful tom-tom roll. As the vocals depart a sustained guitar tone takes us into a beautifully executed solo, modelled partly on the vocal melody, and Ian Bairnson's finest moment. The extended album version of the solo lasts some 1: 15, with the very slow fade still leaving us somehow cheated. Right up to the last few seconds, with the sounds disappearing into the aether, the guitarist is fashioning new inflections and tiny delays out of the notes. It is a wonderfully complimentary solo (to a degree improvised, 'seat-of-the-pants stuff', Bairnson, in Jovanovic, 2005: 64) that concludes a classic song and the first side of the album in a thrilling manner. The musicians involved were very aware of the singularity and potential of the track, which had 'a style which flew in the face of everything else which was around at the time. This is so different, but interesting – it will either do really well, or bomb' (Bairnson, in Jovanovic, 2005: 62).

The second side of *Kick* gives us the only real up-tempo track on the album in the form of 'James and the Cold Gun'.

'James and the Cold Gun'

An 'attack' piano sound, close to 'honky-tonk' style, introduces guitar power chords before the whole rhythm section implements a boogie-style track in the vein of certain Elton John songs. Apparently inspired by stories of American outlaws such as the James Gang (Jovanovic, 2005: 64), everything swings along most effectively, with Stuart Elliott's drum rolls again demonstrating his inventiveness. Bush's vocals squeal and squawk effectively, although rock backing was never going to be a totally comfortable setting for her high pitch and pure timbres. The coda of the track drops the tempo and makes the transition to the next track less jarring than would have otherwise been the case.

'Feel It'

This track is built upon a more insistent and direct piano backing than many of the other tracks on the album, perhaps echoing the more direct and straightforward nature of this sexual narrative, expressed in lines such as 'it could be love, or it could be just lust' and 'here comes one and one makes one'. 'Feel It' is a more eroticised cousin to 'The Man with the Child in his Eyes', built upon the same simple structure, and an even sparser musical backing. Many critics at the time remarked upon the young female writer's unusual candour concerning sexuality, and this topic was to prove a very fruitful one for the artist. Suffice it to say that within this track the rising and falling cadence of a line such as 'synchronise rhythm now' is a thrilling vocal moment, full of direct sexual promise. The minimal musical backing marks this track out as unusual in the artist's canon, and its subsequent rarity is a source of regret to me. Bush's voice is perfect in such sparse settings, providing a stark beauty to the narrative that some later and fuller productions fail to match.

'Oh To Be In Love'

This song features some interesting instrumental textures, from both synthesiser and brother Paddy's trademark collection of 'ethnic' or traditional musical devices (in this case, mandolin). However, the promise provided by the verse is not fulfilled by the chorus, built upon a rather comical bass vocal 'oh-oh-oh to be in love' refrain that only succeeds in making the overall mood of the song rather ambivalent. Relative to the standard of the overall album, the track is rather too whimsical to truly stand out.

'L'Amour Looks Something Like You'

'L'Amour' completes the trio of songs relating a real or imagined sexual encounter, featuring another verse melody that has the interest and rise-and-fall of a chorus, but one that still prepares us for the actual chorus without overwhelming it. Again, the chief source of interest here is the directness of the lyric in describing a sexual union. This ranges from the blatantly erotic reflection upon 'that feeling of sticky love inside' to the more active urge to 'feel all the energy rushing right up a' me'. The use of the artist's immense vocal range is particularly well judged on this track, with the swoops to both the top and the bottom of her scale – often within the same melody line – being skilfully executed. The economy of the structure is also reminiscent of classic artists such as the Beatles. Within a track of less than 2: 30 we are still given the space to change from the home key, and to drop the pace for the concluding section, giving the song a breadth of mood it would not have otherwise possessed.

'Them Heavy People'

We are now returned to the 'tribute' mode of 'Moving', and the rhythmic impetus of 'Kite'. Beginning with the infectious refrain of 'rolling the ball …' this track makes effective use of the 'reggae verse, pop chorus' style soon to be popularised by the Police. The dynamic space allows guitar and drums to punctuate this essentially joyous and light-hearted narrative with charm and incisiveness. Another winning chorus, repeated to fade leaves us, like so much classical pop, delighted but unsatisfied, yearning for more yet somehow glad we are left unfulfilled. 'Them Heavy People' is the most positive and sunny track on the album, and one of a fair number of songs (four, five?) that would surely have been successful as singles, in addition to the two released in the UK.

'Room For a Life'

Here we have a song that has gender politics at its core. The narrative constructs a sorrowful, lonely female character 'with no lover to free her desire', misunderstood by men and trying to prove her superiority. It is then suggested that women shouldn't, or don't need to compete because they are 'built tough', before encouraging an active role 'hey get up on your feet and go get it now'. Women's transcendent role comes about through their ability to give life, which hints at *The Kick Inside* of the album title. In a similar fashion to 'Strange Phenomena', this track could be said to have a clear, if non-polemical feminist (feminine?) stance, although the artist's essential humanism – often expressed in interviews in answer to 'are you a feminist?' type questions – shines out in all her tracks concerned with gender and the sexes. The musical feel of the song is interesting in that the standard distinction between verse and chorus structures is dispensed with – the whole band does not 'kick in' during the chorus, as on many of the other tracks. Instead, percussive elements of a Latin or Caribbean nature slowly build as the track concludes, allowing for multi-tracked vocals to move away from lyrics into the realm of 'scat sounds' that reinforce the mood of celebration ultimately suggested by the narrative.

'The Kick Inside'

The final song on the album is the title track. Skilfully sequenced to follow 'Room For a Life', 'The Kick Inside' provides us with a very different, and more disturbing take on gender relations and pregnancy, although an individual's reading of the lyric is likely to be more ambiguous than that engendered by many of the other tracks on this first album. It is based on a traditional song called 'Lucy Wan' (Jovanovic, 2005: 65). Many have read this narrative as a tale of brother and sister incest and we also have the artist herself confirming this interpretation. In an interview with Jon Young in the US publication *Trouser Press* in July 1978, she admitted: 'She becomes pregnant by her brother … she doesn't want her family to be ashamed or disgusted, so she kills herself. The song is a suicide note. She says to her brother, "Don't worry. I'm doing it for you"' (Young, 1978). This being the case, it is a remarkably brave and challenging text, but probably only capable of being read sympathetically when delivered by a woman. Having said that, my own reading is a more confused, and less unified one, coloured by the fact that I had never considered the incest angle until undertaking research for this book. There are available readings that are less 'closed', preferring to see a kick as an urge for freedom, bolstered by lines such as 'you must loose me like an arrow'. And yet, now that the weight of anecdotal and biographical evidence is considered, it is possible to be of two minds.

What is less confusing than the notion of what the piece 'means' is the musical components of the song, which are simple, sympathetic and incredibly poignant. In particular, the final phrase of the song, and thus the album, is cut short, to end with the line 'oh by the time you read this…' and left hanging, similarly unresolved by the final fading orchestral minor chord. And so, musically and lyrically, we are left with an essentially artistic enigma, with some questions answered, and some left open for possible resolution through future exploration.

The Kick Inside is a remarkable debut. If some of the instrumental tracks and song structures are rather standardised, this only has the effect of giving the album a unity of feel, aided by the accessibility of most of the tunes and melodies. This is a pop album, full of strong individual tracks, yet moving beyond simple pop moods and lyrical concerns into areas of profundity and complexity. In dealing with subjects largely absent from pop songs, particularly those penned by female composers, Kate Bush did indeed 'open the door for female musicians to pen more serious songs' (Jovanovic, 2005: 65). Jon Kelly commented on the fact that, unlike the painstaking, overdubbing style of later albums, on *Kick* 'the performance was the thing' (Kelly, in Jovanovic, 2005: 65), and this vitality is fundamental to the imbued mood expressed within the songs.

It is too easy with the benefit of hindsight to say that its success was assured, but the one thing that the commercial pop market is not is fair. Many artists and albums deserve great success and critical acclaim, but achieve none – and for a wide variety of reasons. In the case of Kate Bush, a combination of planned and unplanned factors worked in tandem to place a debut album within the commercial and critical mainstream. Had the same album been released a year earlier or a year later, had it not been released in the wake of a hit single, well who knows? Leaving such conjecture behind us, the album stands: of its time, yet by virtue of the strength of its songs, timeless, and prefacing a remarkable career.

Lionheart

After a brief, hectic period of promotion, interviews and television appearances prompted by the widespread success of *The Kick Inside*, the artist was put under some pressure by her record company to quickly record and release her follow-up album, as she bluntly stated to Harry Doherty in June 1978: 'and now I've got a two-to-three month period for this one. It's ridiculous' (Bush, in Doherty, 1978a). This was probably the only time that EMI attempted to place the artist on the relentless treadmill that has proven so damaging, in personal and artistic terms, to so many. For the artist 'this type of exposure…made me feel like I'd lost bits of myself, that I'd become a public person, and the private person, and that's who I really am, was actually getting very frightened and lost' (Bush, in Jovanovic, 2005: 74–5).

The gatefold album package for *Lionheart*, released late in 1978, was a sumptuous affair, with many of the accompanying photo images, taken by the renowned Gered Mankowitz, having the lustre of those taken by MGM photographers of the likes of Garbo, Crawford and Harlow in the Hollywood of the 1930s. They presented Kate Bush as a beautiful, yet rather exotic young woman, far removed from the typical pop promo shots of the time. The cover shot had her in a lion suit, prowling on the top of a crate in an attic – an intriguing image, and, as so often with the iconography of the artist, slightly bonkers.

In overall terms the songs do suffer in comparison with the sublime standards set by the first album. It has also become clear in subsequent interviews that the recording sessions were less carefree affairs than those of late 1977. Although producer and artist did not have a 'falling out', tensions arose over recording processes and production decisions. Kate Bush, even at this stage, had clear ideas about how all elements of the recording process should go, yet was constrained by having Andrew Powell still ultimately calling the shots. According to Phil Sutcliffe, interviewing the producer in 2003, Powell favoured a more spontaneous approach to recording and vocal takes, whereas the artist would slog away, sometimes for days on end before being satisfied (Sutcliffe, 2003: 111). The rush to release the album, the relative decline in compositional standards and the tensions indicated all contrive to make *Lionheart* something of a disappointment. I remember at the time feeling this disappointment very keenly, as fans do. You feel 'let down' by the artist – frustrated, and even resentful. Looking back at the album now, those feelings have been replaced by a more rational view. The work still has many high points, but as online reviewer David Owens concludes, 'This is very much a continuation of *The Kick Inside* and maybe made up of mostly weaker songs that were left on the "cutting room floor"'(Owens, 2004). Even if there is no concrete evidence to support this judgement, the feel of the album does lend weight to the conjecture.

'Symphony in Blue'

Unlike the moody atmospherics set by 'Moving' on the first album, *Lionheart* begins with 'Symphony in Blue', a cheery but insubstantial pop tune that veers into middle of the road territory. Jovanovic claims that the piano work was inspired by Erik Satie's sparse style (Jovanovic, 2005: 88). It should be stated that this is not a criticism of the style as a whole, but that the promise of the first album was that Kate Bush would steer a quirkier path far removed from tracks encouraging a relatively passive response. As well as being disappointing in its lack of musical ambition – the performances are those of 'hired hands' – some lyrical phrases, such as 'the more I think about sex, the better it gets' border on the trite, far removed from the erotic edge of many earlier couplets. Pleasant is a pretty damning term in popular music appreciation, but it is the most suitable term for this track.

'In Search of Peter Pan'

Far more substantial is 'In Search of Peter Pan'. As with 'Wuthering Heights', this uses a much-loved literary text as a source, which, on this track, also provides the song with its beautiful melodic evocation of childhood flight in the intimate chorus beginning 'second star on the right …'. As well as being imbued with three effective, contrasting sections, 'In Search of Peter Pan' also concludes via a skilful transposition of the melody and lyric from the Disney classic 'When You Wish Upon a Star'. This altogether more complex and moody track would have provided a much better opening to the album; it would have sent out different signals as a statement of intent in the days before CD programming made such issues far less relevant.

'Wow'

'Wow' continues the sombre mood established at the end of the previous track. The lyric is an ambiguous narrative that is based upon a real or imagined ageing actor's fading career. The track builds nicely up to the chorus, which does, however, feel rather disconnected in mood and content from the preceding section, a little too 'triumphant'. In addition, I have always personally had problems with choruses that consist mainly of one word! It also incorporates some synth textures that have not aged as well as others, and the vocal gymnastics are less well conceived than on other tracks. Some might also consider the line 'he's too busy hitting the Vaseline' bordering on homophobic, especially when reinforced in the video by Bush patting her rear at that point. As so often on Kate Bush songs, the concluding section is intriguing and effective, returning us to the mood at the outset of the narrative. This song's structure and imbued affect confuses me, although it is mostly successfully realised, and it was a strong single and a deserved hit.

'Don't Push Your Foot on the Heartbrake'

'Don't Push Your Foot on the Heartbrake' is the album's 'rocker' and has a fine sense of dynamics in the interplay between slow and mid-paced sections and the sparseness and density of instrumentation. Despite employing the hardly original device of a gaggle of automobile metaphors standing for states of mind and heart, the song has a tension and an urgency that provide a lot of impetus to the narrative. The artist's vocal copes well with the widely contrasting sections, and her final 'oh COME ON!!' is a shrill scream of great penetration.

'Oh England, My Lionheart'

In complete contrast, the final track on the first side of the vinyl album is the pastoral and reflective 'Oh England, My Lionheart': an idealised fable focussing upon a wide variety of symbolic images, which cleverly reintroduces Peter Pan as an icon. This track obviously meant a great deal to the artist at the time, witnessed by its lyric being the only one reproduced in her own, rather child-like hand. However, this is one of the tracks that the ever-critical Ms Bush remembers less favourably. In 1993 she confessed to Stuart Maconie that there are 'absolutely loads … too many to mention' of old songs that make her wince, with this track as 'one of the ones I meant. It makes me just want to die' (Bush, in Maconie, 1993). I can understand why she (or anyone) might feel that way, as the song does pile on the bucolic air of Merrye Englande rather thickly, replete with harpsichords and recorders encouraging us to wassail down to the maypole. But for all its romanticism and tweeness, I find it an affecting fantasy of certain aspects of Englishness, with a strong emphasis on a child's best construction of the wonders of growing up amidst London's sights, sounds and factual and fictional representations. Very few artists could have carried such sentiments off, certainly not the myriad of British artists who have symbolically vocally ditched their ethnic identity via cod-Americanisms in terms of accent and musical style.

'Fullhouse'

Side two of the vinyl album commences with 'Fullhouse', for this writer one of the weakest tracks of the artist's entire career. For non-musicians, explaining why melodies are 'just wrong' is a difficult one, but the very first line immediately alienates me. As with 'Symphony in Blue', 'Fullhouse' provides another hesitant start to a side. The chorus melody in particular is angular and awkward, and the backing track tired and cluttered. As previously mentioned, the advent of CD programming and the potential for the construction of alternative compilations within contemporary software does allow us all to focus upon individual tracks and running orders in a more creative fashion. This is one of two tracks on *Lionheart* that I choose never to listen to.

'In the Warm Room'

This track returns us to familiarly sensual territory via an observing narrator addressing a male somewhat in the thrall of an active and possibly duplicitous female character. This lyric presents sexual desire in powerful, narcotic terms, comparing the effect of kissing to 'kicking a habit'. If some of the rhyme and word endings do seem a little too contrived – 'mellow/wallows' 'fingers/linger' and more particularly 'pillow/marshmallows/hollows' – the track, constituted by a single vocal track and a piano, does have a languid and woozy charm that oozes lust and more than a hint of danger.

'Kashka from Baghdad'

'Kashka from Baghdad' is the second track consigned to the digital dustbin on my personal compilation. Melodically, the verses provide a firm foundation for the memorable chorus that this track, unfortunately, does not possess. Compared to the strength of the verse/chorus relationships on the first album, 'Kashka' is unimaginative and falls short. It really feels like a 'filler', which, for an artist who claims to have 'had a couple of hundred. I was writing a song, maybe two songs a day' by the age of 17 (Bush, in Doyle, 2005: 88), makes its inclusion a strange choice.

'Coffee Homeground'

The mood lifts with the sublime pastiche of 'Coffee Homeground', sung in approximation of the younger sister of Marlene Dietrich, and telling the tale of a female poisoner. The backing track, all parping brass, shrill wind and crash cymbals, is wonderfully evocative of bygone days in the Weimar Republic, or the angular compositions of Weil and Brecht. The bass counterpoints of the vocal melody ('pictures of Crippen, lipstick-smeared') are more contemporary in feel, but work brilliantly. Multi-tracked vocals duck and dive across the stereoscape, and the artist's remarkable vocal range (and German-speaking abilities) are well exploited. The track is amusingly gothic and has precious little to do with almost anything in the popular music canon of the last 100 years, which greatly adds to its appeal.

'Hammer Horror'

Lionheart concludes with the first single released from the album, 'Hammer Horror'. Not the most obvious choice to storm the charts (it only reached 44 in the UK, with second single 'Wow' doing much better at 14), the track does have something of the ambition of 'Wuthering Heights', without possessing the latter's beautiful melody and soaring lead-out solo. In mood, it is a good companion piece to the previous track, and builds up to a stirring chorus, but it is much too fragmented in structure to be a successful commercial single. In short, it is an ambitious and effective album track, underpinned by probably the best musical arrangement on the album. Again, the artist turns to filmic narratives for inspiration, in this case the 'grand guignol' low-budget horror movies associated with the British Hammer film company particularly between the late 1950s and the 1970s. Her biographer claims that the specific inspiration comes from watching James Cagney's portrayal of the silent film actor Lon Chaney, in Joseph Pevney's 1957 biopic *Man of a Thousand Faces* (Jovanovic, 2005: 91).

In summary *Lionheart* reflects the conditions it was made under, which were hurried and laboured, the product of an artist coming under great pressure to 'sell units' and 'promote'. One of the main problems seems to be the lacklustre performances by the backing group – fundamentally the same musicians as appeared on the first album. The tensions relating to artistic control referenced between Bush and Powell may well have affected the performances. Phil Sutcliffe also claims that her own band, including bassist and subsequently long-term partner Del Palmer, had most of their work 'replaced' by the session players (Sutcliffe, 2003: 77). Significantly, the artist herself recognised these shortcomings, parting amicably with some of the established musicians before taking a much longer period to compose and record her third album. In addition, on this album the vocals often border on the self-parodic, with swoops, shrieks and growls sometimes a little overdone. A unique instrument, operating in an unusual tonal terrain needs to be a little more economic in its employment of its full arsenal of effects, or the extraordinary becomes the clichéd everyday. Lessons needed to be, and largely were learned in the wake of *Lionheart*'s qualified artistic success.

Never for Ever

Kate Bush's first two albums now feel like companion pieces, book-ending her emergent career phase. *Never for Ever* signals something of a new beginning, with important collaborators such as bassist David Paton and producer/arranger Andrew Powell moving on. The artist also renegotiated her contract with EMI, setting up her own company, Novercia, and obtaining ownership of her own publishing rights over the course of several months in 1980 (Jovanovic, 2005: 79). This new autonomy extended into areas of album cover design, with the artist credited as art director. Bearing in mind the somewhat bizarre front illustration, featuring a painting of the performer open-legged, with a 'Pandora's Box' of creatures billowing out from beneath her dress, it is tempting to guess that many within the record company would not have approved. Not only is the image downright zany, it is also, in common with so many other facets of the artist's career, sexually provocative in a disturbing, as opposed to a commercial, manner.

This album was co-produced by the artist (promoted from 'assisted by' on *Lionheart*) and Jon Kelly (promoted from engineer on the previous album). Even in the era of creative multi-tasking, for a woman barely out of her teens to co-produce only her third album constituted a brave move, but a logical one for an artist of her burgeoning (Sutcliffe referred to her as a classic 'overreacher' in 1989) musical ambition. This move towards a position of *auteur* is a key issue in the artist's career, and will be returned to within the next chapter. The key trigger to the new textures and compositional processes may well be indicated within the sleeve note where special thanks are given to Peter Gabriel 'for opening the windows'. The former lead vocalist with Genesis had been one of the true sonic trailblazers in popular music around the end of the 1970s. In particular, his third album (and the third to be entitled *Peter Gabriel!*), released on the cusp of the new decade, signalled a new way forward for pop, with its imaginative use of the Fairlight CMI sampler. Equally significant was the reliance on percussion (largely without the comforting treble metronome of the hi-hat cymbals) as the basis for the backing track. Kate Bush provided backing vocals on two Gabriel singles, 'No Self Control' and 'Games Without Frontiers' and seems to have been greatly influenced by the near-limitless sonic opportunities offered by new technologies. A final link between the two artists came with her later employment of John Giblin, the bassist who played on some of Gabriel's groundbreaking tracks.

'Babooshka'

Never for Ever was painstakingly recorded over six months in a variety of studios. It commences with 'Babooshka', which became the second single from the album (and should, logically, have been the first). The lyric was based on one of many cross-dressing or disguise narratives to be found in the genre of traditional folk, in this case 'Sovay, Sovay', re-popularised by Martin Carthy in 1965 (Jovanovic, 2005: 114). The ostensibly standard pop structure (an intro, two verses, two refrains, an instrumental break, a fade) masks the true textural innovations 'sneaked through' via a conventional song. Although uncredited, this track does utilise the sort of rudimentary, but effective sampling techniques pioneered by the likes of Peter Gabriel, Trevor Horn and later, the Art of Noise, consisting of bottles breaking, transposed and looped during the break and the segue into the following track. In addition, the narrative follows an intriguing path through disguise and incognito meetings. The way the lyric shifts from one character's view to the other is a master class in economy. Much of the most effective pop consists of familiar, almost clichéd elements often masking the underlying radicalism of true innovation. 'Babooshka' combines catchy melodic sensibilities and *musique concrète* in a seamless package. The song was a deserved hit, reaching number 5 in the UK, and the top 10 in several other countries.

'Delius (Song of Summer)'

'Delius', built upon the stiff rhythm track of a drum machine (whimsically credited to 'Roland') features skeletal lyrics relating to the English pastoral composer of the title and some delightful piano phrasing, underpinned by brother Paddy and Ian Bairnson's sometimes effective, sometimes annoying 'basso profundo' vocals. The album's two opening tracks signal the conceptual and compositional shifts already outlined. We are moving on from piano- and melody-led singer-songwriter ballads into a less stable terrain of multiple timbres, some programmed and some more traditionally played. The impression is that rhythm is starting to mould the track in the Kate Bush *oeuvre*, rather than fitting into the already existing song melody. In this crucial reversal the artist was helping pioneer the great shift in composition that took place during the early synth-and-sample era of the 1980s.

'Blow Away (for Bill)'

This track returns us to a more conventional musical terrain, featuring an intriguing narrative treatise on the nature of being, not being, and a life beyond. Another contributory factor was the accidental death of her lighting engineer, Bill Duffield, during the earlier tour. This real-life tragedy informs the directness of some of the lyrics ('One of the band told me last night' and 'Our engineer had a different idea'), but the song is far more than a mawkish tribute, instead using reality to spark a more metaphysical line of thought. The notion of 'rock'n'roll heaven' is cleverly evoked in a two-part chorus, the first section of which lists members of the regrettably large club for prematurely dead musicians. The writer's choices are typically eclectic, ranging from the iconic (Buddy Holly, Sid Vicious, Keith Moon) to the more esoteric (Minnie Riperton, Sandy Denny). The chorus then shifts into a more syncopated mode, accompanied by a lyric suggesting that the narrator is not ready to join this band of angels quite yet, but would rather just hear them play! The couplet 'Dust to dust, Blow to blow' punningly encapsulates the seductive mischief of this dream/ nightmare scenario. Such songs have the lightness of touch of Kate's best material, but have more substance than many of the tracks on *Lionheart*.

'All We Ever Look For'

'All We Ever Look For' is a fine companion piece to the previous track, again dealing with the sweet yearnings of desire and regret. As a lyricist, Kate Bush seems to possess the consummate skill to present barbed words expressing sentiments bordering on the cruel and vindictive, but with a sense of ambiguity that renders them complex and fully rounded. Thus, whilst it is suggested that our parents may envy their children's lives ('All they ever wanted, but they never did get'), and the children may often want nothing more than to return from whence they came ('All we ever look for – another womb … our own tomb') the overall impression of generational relationships is one of ambiguity and complexity, grounded in the reality that lives and personalities are never wholly good or bad, yet always worth working on – the cup of life is half full in this artist's world. This narrative is built upon a bed of instrumental textures and samples that are hugely varied in terms of pitch and timbre. Particularly delicious is the synth-whistle melodic counterpoint and also the stereo panning of 'found sounds' (running footsteps, doors opening and closing, birdsong, applause) that punctuates the latter part of the song and contributes to a consummate arrangement.

'Egypt'

'Egypt' is more of a lyrical vignette, giving us a few fragmental impressions rather than a fully realised account of its subject. More interesting is the space given to the backing band to play in an almost live, 'jamming' mode for the last two minutes of the track. The Moog work of Max Middleton is symbolically Arabic – feline and slinky in this section. The artist's brother's vocal contributions can vary in terms of effectiveness, with his bass often coming across as (knowingly?) comic; however, on 'Egypt' the vocal harmonies of brother and sister are richly octave-spanning, covering a range the equal of any four-part group.

'The Wedding List'

'The Wedding List', another of the artist's story lyrics, is reportedly based on the Truffaut film *The Bride Wore Black* (1968), although this connection is not made explicit in the lyric. Prior to researching this analysis I had assumed that the references to female revenge and the character of Rudi related to Rudolph Valentino, and the fans who apparently committed suicide after his premature death. But again, biography rears its sometimes unwelcome head. Musically, all is crisp syncopation, as the backing track weaves to match the melodic lurches in the verse. This is then completely countered by a chorus, which initially wallows in seductive strings before kicking back into the rhythmic intensity of the main body of the song. 'The Wedding List' is all about craft – set up a mood, replace it with its opposite, bring back the original mood, then do it all again without making the joins too obvious. The upward yelp of the final cry of 'Rudi!' has its mood of desperation continued by the opening power chords of the next track, 'Violin'.

'Violin'

This frenzied burst of neo-metal borders on hysteria, in the most positive sense of the term, with Bush extolling the diabolic virtues of the instrument and its players. Propelled by a whole series of 'over the top' instrumental performances, 'Violin' is an uncomplicated delight with, just for once, no hidden meanings or shades of interpretation to be drawn. According to Jovanovic, the violin was the artist's first instrument, but the experience of taking lessons was not greatly valued and she soon gave up and moved on to self-taught piano. Perhaps this track exacts a form of revenge?

    The artist drew upon the musical expertise of violinist Kevin Burke, well known in Irish musical circles as a member of the Bothy Band (Jovanovic, 2005: 118). This utilisation of traditional folk musicians was a facet of the artist's career that would become increasingly significant in the years to follow. 'Violin' would have made a great choice for a single, and one can only conjecture as to the nature of the accompanying video.

'The Infant Kiss/Night Scented Stock'

These segued tracks are easily thought of as one piece, with the second part being the vocal-as-instrumental coda of the first. 'The Infant Kiss' returns us to the mood and subject terrain of the first album, with the narrative focussing upon the potentially transgressive desire of an adult female for a young male. Part of the inspiration apparently comes from a British film called *The Innocents* (Jack Clayton, 1961), itself an adaptation of Henry James's *The Turn of the Screw* (originally published in 1898). It is suggested that this boy has powers beyond his years – the child with a man in his eyes – particularly resonant in the line 'You know how to work me'. This track focusses fascinatingly on roles and sexual politics, demonstrating that all songs are essentially 'gendered' in both composition and reading. If we reverse the roles we are really moving into the realms of paedophilia within the present climate of media-induced moral panic. Even within the scenario presented in this lyric, the male is still the potential, although impotent 'predator'.

Such issues are rarely ever broached in popular music, which, bearing in mind the essentially conservative and exploitative nature of the market, is probably a good idea when the sanity of the artist is considered. 'Night Scented Stock' is the artist at her most ambient, just 50 seconds of multi-tracked harmonies presenting a space into which we pour our own imaginations. Bearing in mind the minuscule gap before the next track, we are invited to treat the vocal interlude as either/both a conclusion and a preparation for the next.

'Army Dreamers'

'Army Dreamers' must count as one of the bravest choices for an album debut single by any major artist, and also as probably the gentlest protest song in the history of the top 40. Cleverly constructed in waltz time to counterpoint its military subject matter, 'Army Dreamers' makes great use of sampled sounds (rifle bolts, barked orders) to subtly punctuate the Celtic lilt of both the vocal delivery ('very vulnerable, very poetic', Bush, in Jovanovic, 2005: 120) and the lyric. Bearing in mind the artist's Anglo-Irish parentage and the 'troubles' between the two nations, it seems likely that the Ulster conflict was the particular reference point for this song. A beautifully simple four-note acoustic guitar chime threads through the narrative, which is both poignant and imaginative in its evocation of utter waste, a true 'Anthem for Doomed Youth'. Its understated power and haunting quality gave the artist a small and unlikely hit single, one that makes its point without recourse to the metaphorical 'wagging finger' of so much 'message' pop. Unlike previous albums, *Never for Ever* was partly composed in the studio itself. Jovanovic claims that this track 'was the first song that she'd written totally in the studio' (Jovanovic, 2005: 121).

'Breathing'

Never for Ever concludes with 'Breathing', another political song built around the prescience of an unborn child fearing a nuclear holocaust. 'Breathing' counters the subtlety of the previous track with an arrangement and delivery that aims for the epic and portentous, but in this desire it only partially succeeds. The verse and chorus section are well matched, and make great use of violent, yet poetic imagery ('Chips of Plutonium are twinkling in every lung') and some skilful punning phrases ('Breathing her nicotine … Breathing the fall out-in, out-in'). However, the concluding section, complete with 'What are we going to do' backing harmonies, does seem rather overblown and unnecessary, and only throws the triumph of the previous track into greater relief. Perhaps the intention to end the album on a rather bleak and disunified note was intended, but the album does end on a flat note whatever the reason.

Never for Ever can be seen as the transition album of Kate Bush's career, showing an artist moving towards creative control and, despite the success of both singles and album, away from the mainstream. The bright and winning melodies of the first album have largely been replaced by less immediate and often more challenging cadences on this album. Unlike the second album, which suffers in comparison to the first, this album can be viewed in its own terms as brave and largely successful. The imbued moods and tonal textures have leaped forward, aided by new players and new technologies, and the suspicion of previous 'session playing' by her musicians has been dispensed with by broadening the range of players. As well as being deeply affected by Peter Gabriel's way of writing and recording, the artist drew upon the experience of Richard Burgess, former member of Landscape, and producer of successful synth-pop act Visage. As Jovanovic is right to state, the synth-pop of this band, and others such as Ultravox and Duran Duran, had been 'democratising' the use of formerly avant-garde techniques in the same period (Jovanovic, 2005: 128). However, in retrospect it was the likes of Gabriel and Bush whose use of sampling was to carry the greater resonance for the new decade.

With her role in the music industry now secure (*Never for Ever* topped the UK album chart) Kate Bush could now plan her next album free from the pressures of touring and the album-a-year industry treadmill.

The Dreaming

Despite the numerous examples of experimentation on *Never for Ever*, the album was still packed with 'commercial' songs, conventional structures and actual and potential hit singles. It alienated few of the artist's core audience, and its commercial success suggests that new devotees were seduced by its varied charms. In direct contrast, her fourth album starkly refused to follow easy or expected paths. It was by far her most difficult album to assimilate up to that point, resulting in something of a polarisation between the relatively few who adored its eccentric textures and peculiar subject matter, and the many who found it too bizarre and wilful in its oppositional stance to polite pop and nice melodies. Close production collaborator Jon Kelly was politely, but decisively let go, with something of the artist's single-mindedness coming out in this statement from an interview with Phil Sutcliffe in 1989: 'Jon wanted to keep working with me, but we discussed it and he realised that it was for the best' (Bush, in Sutcliffe, 1989: 89). Engineering expertise arrived in the person of Hugh Padgham (XTC, the Police, Genesis) and later Nick Launay, producer of the highly experimental Public Image Limited (Jovanovic, 2005: 129–30).

The cover photo, heavily sepia-toned, features the artist in the process of kissing (devouring?) a male who is padlock-and-chained. Kate herself, mouth open, appears to have a small gold earring on her tongue, although the track 'Houdini' suggests that this may be a key enabling the padlock to be opened. According to Jovanovic, the cover is based on the depiction of Houdini and Rosabel (Jovanovic, 2005:

138). Ultimately, what we make of this image is for us each to decide, but again demonstrates the will and ease with which the artist can disturb us, and subvert the usually cosy world of pop iconography.

'Sat in Your Lap'

'Sat in Your Lap' is the leadoff track, and the choice for first single – a sound marketing device that the artist was always to employ on subsequent albums. The lyric consists of a kind of stream-of-consciousness muse about the nature of knowledge, and how to obtain wisdom, but is delivered in a real flurry of words, phrases and cadences that tumble over the music. The backing track complements the vocal perfectly, the mix being cluttered and manic. Particularly prominent are the tribal tom-toms, which launch the track and propel it with gusto. The vocals, heavily echoed in some sections, soar over the fractured funk of the rhythm, and the whole track exhibits a huge sense of urgency. Bearing in mind its radical sense of departure from previous singles, the artist's choice to release it was largely vindicated by its highest placing of number 11 in the UK. 'Sat in Your Lap' sent out the clear message that the artist had moved on in the (then) considerable period since the previous album, and, for listeners, the subsequent ride would not be smooth or comfortable.

'There Goes a Tenner'

'There Goes a Tenner' harks back to 'Coffee Homegound' in its evidently parodic construction and style. Unlike the 'Weimar gothic' of the earlier track, 'There Goes a Tenner', despite its references to US screen gangsters, is rooted within the minutiae of English identities, with the artist's wide-panned vocals marvellously confused about whether to adopt a Cockney or an upper-class accent. In its evocation of a safe-breaking crime that goes wrong one is reminded of filmic 'caper' narratives such as *Butch Cassidy and the Sundance Kid* (George Roy Hill, 1969), but more particularly of low-budget British gems such as *Two Way Stretch* (Robert Day, 1960) and *The* (original) *League of Gentlemen* (Basil Dearden, 1959). Musically, this evocation is strengthened by the backing track hybrid of music hall and ska, with the style of the quintessentially London band Madness being the closest reference point (Bush had previously expressed an affection for the band). Despite the long hiatus provided, fittingly, by the line 'We are waiting', this track's top-10 potential seems self-evident. The snare drum, all eighties-period compression and resonance, powers things along and the reggae 'skank' makes you want to move. However, it was a commercial failure and simply stands as an intriguing and satisfying album track.

'Pull out the Pin'

After the energy and immediacy of the opening two tracks, 'Pull out the Pin' is, in more than one sense of the word, low key. Danny Thompson's languid double bass and the absence of standard drumbeats both provide a mood reminiscent of Japan and David Sylvian's trademark avant-funk exoticism. The artist sings in a key positively subterranean by prior standards and her voice demonstrates a maturation and thickening brought on by both the passage of time and (probably) her heavy nicotine habit. This gives the line 'I love life' a gravelly edge that adds to her already impressive range of vocal timbres. The wide-panned backing vocals, courtesy of longstanding friend David Gilmour, are very effective, demonstrating what an underrated singer the Pink Floyd member is. The track doesn't possess the winning drive and melody of its predecessors, but suits the subject matter – another reflection upon the nature of (Vietnam?) warfare. As within several other narratives, the writing was inspired by a television documentary – in this case about a war cameraman disturbed by the imagery, but 'he'd just keep on filming' (Bush, in Jovanovic, 2005: 137). The artist's ability to transcend gender roles and place herself in alien situations is again most apparent.

'Suspended in Gaffa'

This track further demonstrates the breadth to which the Bush vocal cords can now be stretched. Unlike on the first album, where low vocals can sometimes sound too forced, by this period they sound confident and resonant. When counterpointed by a high refrain, as on this track's chorus, the effect is that of identical twins spaced an interval apart, so precisely are the lines dovetailed. The waltz-time backing track is so perky and celebratory as to provoke laughter. And yet, complete with the by now trademark skeletal drums and obscure lyrics, this was a very odd choice for a single, and one that didn't translate into high sales in most parts of the globe. In her homeland it was the first out-and-out flop of her career, but remains one of her most joyous tracks.

'Leave it Open'

'Leave it Open' is symbolic of the reasons why the album and the artist suffered a commercial setback at this time. Propelled by gated Phil Collins-style drums, and with vocals swamped in phasing, backward running and pre-echo, this track is very much in the mode wherein the mixing desk is the instrument and the effects unit is the producer. The connections with the 'archetypal' highly processed 1980s drum sounds are not incidental. As well as the aforementioned creative links with Gabriel and Collins, some of the album was recorded in the same 'stone room' that Collins utilised in creating some of his most memorable (and widely copied) drum sounds (Jovanovic, 2005: 131–2).

This track is pretty unsettling stuff – brave undoubtedly – but this alone should not be seen as a guarantor of quality. Other equally experimental tracks by the artist will work better in terms of overall albums, particularly when, as we shall see, they fit into a more conceptual framework, rather than having to stand alone as discrete songs.

'The Dreaming'

The title track of this album packs a subtle but considerable political punch, with its lyrical evocation of a magical Aboriginal people cruelly exploited by invaders that

'Erase the race that claim the place' and poison their communities as they 'dangle devils in a bottle'. This message is emphasised by the backing track, again built upon rhythmic gaps and tribal drums, which floats on the drone notes of the didgeridoo. Some might criticise it as an example of a rich western artist assuaging their conscience by dabbling in a little bit of 'world music tourism' but this writer sees it in more noble terms, as part of a more wide-ranging attempt to move away from the constraints of western musical hegemony that many fellow travellers (Gabriel, Simon, Bowie) took in the 1980s. The track has great latent energy that occasionally bursts out like a geyser (or 'takes flight' via samples) and succeeds in everything it sets out to do – but again, it was a downright unfathomable choice for a single, as its novelty value was submerged beneath far more laudable and weighty sentiments. A UK chart high of 48 suggests that only hardcore fans (and a few political 'right-ons') were seduced by its myriad charms.

'Night of the Swallow'

From one end of the ethnic spectrum to the other, 'The Dreaming' segues into the Celtic folk-flavoured 'Night of the Swallow' on a bed of penny whistles, uilleann pipes, fiddles and bouzoukis. The artist's musical heritage and acknowledged sense of ethnic identity should not be underestimated: in 2005 she commented 'Irish music is a big part of my ancestry … It's in my blood' (Bush, in Doyle, 2005: 89). This facet of the artist's career will be returned to in the next chapter. This track skilfully manages to accommodate both western electric instrumentation and traditional acoustic textures into one seamless whole without putting either element into subservience. Lyrically, this is another clear example of the singer's words becoming textures and timbres above and beyond direct meaning. The dilemma posed for me is not so much that I could not come up with a lyrical meaning, but that I don't want to. We move into the realms of tautology: the track is about the track, not what the words say. In a strange manner 'Night of the Swallow' can be seen as a 'dry run' for, in particular, tracks comprising the second side of her next album, and the sequence entitled *The Ninth Wave*. Again, removed from a longer sequence, this track loses some of its evocative breadth, but still serves as a strong and confident album track.

'All the Love'

'All the Love' cannot scale the heights of many of *The Dreaming*'s best tracks. Built upon fine melodic bass lines, the lyric returns to a familiar trope, a muse or lament for unrequited or unfulfilled existence and friendship. The chorus, using a choirboy treble vocal instead of the artist's own upper register, is an experiment that doesn't really work and the track seems to drag out its near four and a half minute length, with a run-out section incorporating a few piano patterns that, almost uniquely for the artist, seem misplaced and tentative.

'Houdini'

'Houdini' is another relatively weak track. The sections lack lyrical and narrative coherence and the low register of Bush's voice on certain lines does seem forced and gimmicky within this particular narrative. In terms of lyrical content, the lack of musical strength does encourage me to seek the comfort of a unifying message, but the narrative will not give one up. Programming the order of tracks was of crucial importance in the era of vinyl. Of course, the artist has an impossible job in trying to please individual tastes, but two substandard tracks in succession do constitute a major critical setback, particularly bearing in mind the numerous miraculous sequences that the artist's past albums have fashioned.

'Get Out of My House'

The potential redemption of a strong conclusion is cruelly dashed by the off-the-wall madness and downright ugliness of most of 'Get Out of My House'. This is one of the rare tracks in Kate Bush's career to which I have to hold up my hands and admit critical and interpretive failure. Indeed, had it not been for the purposes of this review I would have had nothing at all to say about it, having only been able to listen to it on two or three previous, distant occasions. Such tracks mark out our relationships to artists, indicating that I am a fan, and not a fanatic without the ability to discriminate – but all the more guilty as a result.

And so, *The Dreaming* poses us/me a dilemma, which is probably what the artist intended. As previously indicated, it is brave and experimental, which forces listeners to work hard and make hard choices. If you admire an artist part of you would like to love every piece of music they make, but this is impossible if we take a relativist approach to tracks and albums (better than … not as good as …). The album sold only a fraction of what previous albums had achieved, and garnered a very polarised public response, although the press were generally favourable. Phil Sutcliffe claimed sales of 60,000 up to 1989, as compared to the million-plus for the debut album, over 300,000 for *Lionheart* and over 100,000 for *Never For Ever* (Sutcliffe, 1989: 89).

Paradoxically, it actually secured her reputation for many, in the process severing any lingering ties to 'stoking the star-making machinery', in Joni Mitchell's words from 'Help Me' (Mitchell, 1972). Experiments fail: they must, by definition. Many of the experiments on *The Dreaming* work supremely well – particularly the trio of great, if unlikely singles – but from my own viewpoint, few albums end with as much feeling of anti-climax. A compromised 43-minute album becomes a superb 29-minute album on my CD version, which marks the album as another qualified success, what we might term her 'great folly'. For Simon Reynolds the album is 'extravagantly uncompromising' (Reynolds, 1993). The artist herself refers to *The Dreaming* as her 'she's gone mad album' (Bush, in Sutcliffe, 1989: 89). However, many positives come out of the whole recording and composing process. In writing from rhythms and samples rather than piano chords, and using acoustic instrumentation as the 'add-on' to synthetic elements, the artist was helping to pioneer what drummer Stuart Elliott claimed would 'soon became standard practice'. He goes on to add that this exhaustive non-linear process 'didn't do much for the connection between musicians', which may explain some of the disjointedness that runs through many tracks, but Kate 'needed that control' (all quotations from Elliott in Sutcliffe, 2003: 83). In addition, *The Dreaming* was the artist's first sole production. Some artists never can, or never want to take this step – it has taken Elton John, a man not noted for timidity or lack of self-belief, nearly 40 years to make the same decision. Looking back on the album, engineer Nick Launay claimed 'I thought it was amazing, and still do', before stating 'the mixes sounded a bit odd … Later I came to realise that this was because it had been mixed to a then new format called "digital"'(Launay, in Jovanovic, 2005: 139–40). This gives us another clue as to its downright peculiar nature, as doubtless many at the time were still listening with 'analogue' ears.

Kate Bush was now ready to embark upon the biggest challenge of her career – to oversee the construction of an independent studio and take even fuller creative responsibility for the production of her next project. She thus had the welcome licence to now be working at her own pace, in her own place. The boundless ambition and dedication to the craft of creating and recording music was about to be unqualifyingly fulfilled for the first time.

Part Two

Hounds of Love

Commercial Context and Critical Reception of *Hounds of Love*

In the period between the release of *The Dreaming* in 1982 and what became *Hounds of Love* in 1985 Kate Bush first retreated from promotional duties – as usual, 'exhausted' by the rigours of writing and recording – and then began working to obtain complete independence and autonomy over the production process by overseeing the construction of a recording studio. Even for an artist who had achieved great wealth, the cost of recording in state-of-the-art recording studios was considerable. By the 1980s, EMI's Abbey Road was charging £90 per hour for the use of its facilities, in some cases to effectively its own artists! The cost of *The Dreaming*, spread over six months and several studios, would have run into at least many tens of thousands. More significantly, many artists feel constrained by the process of working in hired studios, almost watching the clock tick, and for a painstaking and slow worker, this must add to the already considerable pressure placed upon the artist/producer; in Bush's own words 'it just zaps creativity' (Bush, in Sutcliffe, 2003: 79).

According to Phil Sutcliffe, work began on a 48-track studio in an old barn close to Bush's home, and that of her parents, in June 1983 (Sutcliffe, 1989: 89). After some work in Abbey Road, she began recording the album proper the moment her own studio was ready, in January 1984. As was by now customary, work proceeded very slowly, with the artist commenting 'you have to break your back before you even start to speak emotion' (Bush, in Sutcliffe, 2003: 78). The process was very similar to that begun on *Never for Ever* and perfected on *The Dreaming*, with a potent blend of programming and playing, with multiple overdubbing of elements onto existing rhythm tracks, and a judicious balance between the synthetic, the electronic and the acoustic. Holly Kruse observed that 'Bush frames her visions in arrangements that combine ancient folk instruments with the latest in synthesiser technology' (Kruse, 1990: 450). However, more provocative are her comments on the connections between recording styles and the album's subject matter: 'While the idiosyncratic piano proved the ideal accompaniment for *The Dreaming*'s introspection, *Hounds* requires an instrument that mirrors its focus on interpersonal relationships and the interrelatedness of life' (Kruse, 1990: 458). It is, perhaps, too prescriptive to so closely assign technological capabilities to states of mind, but certainly, the breadth of capabilities opened up by the Fairlight sampler, in particular, were to prove central to the textural colours and moods of *Hounds*.

Her group of musical collaborators consisted of a loose collective of players connecting back to all her prior work, with Stuart Elliott, Morris Pert and brother Paddy providing a link back to the first album, and newer musicians such as Youth and classical guitarist John Williams making their debuts with the artist. However, trusted long-standing players – those already mentioned and others such as Del Palmer on bass and programming – carried out the bulk of the work on *Hounds*. Important contributions were also made by string arrangers Michael Kamen and Bill Whelan, guitarists Brian Bath and Alan Murphy, bassists Eberhard Weber and Danny Thompson, drummer Charlie Morgan and the collective of Irish musicians who had first come together on the previous album's 'Night of the Swallow'.

By this point EMI knew enough about the artist's methods not to interfere or place too much additional pressure upon her. She did have to fight over the choice of first single, with 'Running up that Hill' winning out over 'Cloudbusting', but she backed down by amending the title of the single, placing the controversial 'A Deal With God' (its original title) in parentheses in order to assist potential radio airplay in certain countries. Clearly annoyed, but pragmatic, she commented that this was 'Ridiculous … still … I decided I couldn't be bloody-minded' (Bush, in Sutcliffe, 1989: 90). 'Running up that Hill (A Deal With God)' was released in August and made a great impact, reaching number 3 in the UK charts, her biggest hit for five years. The 12-inch mix also assisted her worldwide promotion, particularly in the US, where it reached the top 30 and was an unlikely, but deserved dance floor hit. In the wake of this momentum, with Bush and Del Palmer appearing at the album's launch as an 'item' for the first time, and bolstered by almost universal critical praise, the album rose to the top of the charts in several countries, also just breaking into the US top 30. All the major British music journals barring *Melody Maker* gave the album positive reviews. *NME* called it 'the best album of the year'. *Sounds* gave it a maximum five stars. Heavy Metal's *Kerrang!* magazine, in the guise of Mick Wall, was particularly gushing: 'Young Kate's a fucking genius' (Wall, 1985). Even Pam Lambert, in the august *Wall Street Journal* felt moved to state that the album 'compellingly states her claim as a major voice in pop music' (Lambert, 1985). At the other end of the market, teen magazine *Smash Hits* gave it 9 out of 10 and made it their 'pick of the month'. By June 1986 it had sold 600,000 in the UK alone – her biggest commercial success since the debut album in 1978. It was also the fourth biggest selling CD in Britain up to that point (Jones, 1986), but was the only work that transcended the essential conservatism of the other albums (Dire Straits, Phil Collins) and the demographic expectations placed upon the format by the then typical audience for CD.

Hounds of Love was released into a pop world that had changed radically during the early 1980s. Dedicated video channels were now a reality in many parts of the globe, and the pop promo film was superseding touring as the most cost-effective way to promote new releases. For an artist such as Kate Bush, possessing a strong visual dimension but unwilling or unable to tour, this proved to be a real advantage. The CD was becoming the format of choice throughout the developed world, although more copies of *Hounds* would have still been purchased on vinyl and cassette than the then comparatively new form. Thus, the album was still effectively split into sides – particularly relevant as each side had its own title (*Hounds of Love* and *The Ninth Wave*) and was conceptually differentiated (separate songs on one side, a linked suite of tracks on the second).

The market for pop, in terms of demographics, also underwent huge changes in the period leading up to *Hounds*. So-called 'adult-orientated rock', serving the needs of vast numbers of 'baby boomers' and fed by a new series of glossy, monthly publications (*The Face*, first published in 1980 and particularly *Q*, in the UK, which launched in 1985), exerted a conservative force upon the album markets of the west. The likes of Sting, Dire Straits, Fleetwood Mac, Sade and Eric Clapton all sold, or continued to sell in vast quantities, aided by the attraction of the new playing format, which favoured 'polished' sounds. The singles or more youth-orientated market had been growing increasingly fragmented since the late 1960s, accompanied by a huge proliferation of musical styles, genres and sub-genres. In the mid-1980s, popular music no longer had a core set of values. Indeed, perhaps it is a myth to suggest that such a concept had ever really existed. But certainly, the wide perception was of a leisure industry that had finally cast off most of the idealistic or 'hippified' shackles of the 'Woodstock generation' and was blatantly gearing most of its efforts towards shifting units and breaking artists on an ever more globalised scale.

An artist of Kate Bush's lineage and stature was well placed to exploit many of these market shifts. Her previous two albums had successfully repositioned her as a slightly wayward experimentalist, but one with the priceless gift of still producing unique, yet often commercial singles, so she avoided much of the negativity that other album-orientated artists got, and maintained her 'cred'. By 1985 she was accepted as a critically acclaimed, 'mature artist' lucky enough to still command the loyalty of a sizeable and devoted number of fans. This meant that anything that Kate Bush produced would sell at least moderately, but units were not really an issue for anyone except the record company and the chart compilers. More significantly, the industry also accepted her as one totally unprepared to compromise her work and her privacy through carrying out more than a bare minimum of promotion. Having said that, the number of radio, television and press interviews she undertook was still considerable, particularly in relation to the previous couple of years. In short, her position was secure, beholden to no one except the creative muse. Her initial, very loyal fan base had been augmented by others becoming more familiar with her work over the course of several albums and even the world's biggest market for popular music, the US, had slowly awoken to her talents, but in an organic and 'underground' fashion – it was on her terms.

Unlike today, when a ruthless celebrity-and-scandal based popular press will go to almost any lengths to intrude upon the lives of the rich and famous, the mid-1980s was relatively benign in terms of press coverage, allowing a very private celebrity a comparatively easy ride. The press, both popular and music-based, had always been intrigued by Kate Bush, this ostensibly un-rock star-like English eccentric, all 'goshes' and 'wows' in (rare) interviews, and one who gave very little away whilst being a stunning beauty, musically and visually provocative, and probably her country's most critically acclaimed and commercially successful female solo music artist. In the lead up to the release of *Hounds*, some rumours did circulate that claimed that the artist had 'ballooned' in size to some incredible weight, but these were discredited by both her infrequent promotional appearances and her video work. She had put on a little weight during the long months spent in the studio, sustained by chocolate and endless pots of tea, but the paparazzi were to be disappointed. In actual fact, the slightly more rounded Kate was at the peak of her beauty in 1985, her formerly tiny, balletic frame now having lost some of the gawkiness of her underweight emergent period. From the mid-1980s onwards, she has actually ceased to present herself visually as a pop star, instead resembling a film actress from a bygone age. Her iconic evocation (wittingly or unwittingly) of British stars of the 1950s and 1960s, such as Jean Simmons and Fenella Fielding, has been particularly noticeable in certain videos and photographs. This perhaps connotes her detached 'otherness' from the pop world, or signals an iconic attachment to the genre of film that her songs have frequently made manifest.

The album cover for *Hounds* reined in the zaniness apparent on previous releases, instead giving us a stylish and sensual portrait of the artist caressing two hounds whilst lying and staring at the viewer with a provocative pout. The colours are muted, with the facial make-up offering a pale imitation of her gown/sheet and the violet background. Her hair, fanned into flared tresses, does resemble hair floating in water, but the background is more reminiscent of a night sky. The overall effect is seductive and tastefully teasing. The back cover photograph is similarly stylish and 'composed', in muted near-monochrome tones that demonstrate her elfin beauty, yet give us little concrete clues as to any deeper symbolic value. Kruse reads this image as showing the artist 'wet, seaweed-strewn' (Kruse, 1990: 461). The overall impression given by the package, as with almost all images associated with the artist, is one of resolutely anti-pop values and connotations, clearly suggesting serious art and sophistication.

And so, happy, healthy, secure in a long-term relationship with a trusted musical ally, the signs all pointed to a successful continuation of her, by now, extensive career.

In terms of my own relationship to the artist in the run-up to *Hounds of Love*, it is fair to say that the intensity with which I responded to the debut album had a detrimental effect upon the favour afforded subsequent releases. After the disappointment of *Lionheart*, which had too much to live up to, I effectively 'punished' both myself and the artist by becoming a more detached and casual fan in the period book-ended by the release of her third and fourth albums. Both of these albums were borrowed from a record library in Wood Green, north London, rather than purchased – indeed, I only bought these two albums comparatively recently, as part of the research for this book. The release of the single 'Running up that Hill (A Deal With God)' did rekindle my interest, and after purchasing the 12-inch version, I spent many a blissful period wearing headphones, and rekindling my aesthetic interest in the artist during the summer of 1985.

At the risk of appearing self-indulgent, I feel it is important to briefly contextualise *Hounds of Love* in terms of my own biography. My life at that time was undergoing huge changes, which, in retrospect, do partially account for the renewed intensity with which I approached all music, and particularly Kate Bush's career. After 12 years of failing to become a pop star, and drifting from one unfulfilling job to the next, punctuated by periods of unemployment and boredom, I had attended an evening class at an adult education centre to study film in 1984. My intention, as I stated to my tutor at the time, was to prepare for a degree course – in the process finding out if I 'still had a brain'.

In the summer of 1985 I was accepted on to a degree course, studying English and History at the then Polytechnic of North London. Whilst being hugely excited at the prospect of quitting that office job and becoming a full-time student, I was also highly fearful, feeling that, at 29, it was effectively my big chance, but also my last chance of escaping the drudgery of the everyday workplace. At the same time, and doubtless influenced by these developments, my long-term partner and I decided to split up. This happened at the end of August. All these life changes had a profound effect on my state of mind – I lived on the brink of tears, became hypertense and also extremely sensitive to all forms of emotional and artistic stimuli. The release of *Hounds of Love*, on 16 September 1985, thus entered and directly contributed to the most intensely emotional period of my entire life. I have never subsequently undergone such huge shifts in mood – from euphoric, to depressed, to angry, to tearful and back to euphoric – as during the period of the autumn and winter of 1985–86. This album, along with such unlikely bedfellows as Tears For Fears, Marillion, June Tabor, Katrina and the Waves and Prince, helped sustain me through the schizophrenic world of excessive drinking, insomnia and sexual promiscuity that I now belatedly, and briefly inhabited. Looking back on the period, I subsequently realised that I was closer to a 'crack-up' than at any other time of my life. Much like the first album, *Hounds of Love* produces multiple epiphanies of memories that more accurately return me to specific physical spaces and emotional places than probably any other single album.

Such is the critical praise afforded *Hounds of Love* – both at the time of release and retrospectively – that a great deal more interpretation and analysis exists than about any other Kate Bush album. It is significantly the only one of her albums to date to have undergone an extensive reworking by EMI, complete with remastering, new sleeve notes and extra tracks as part of their anniversary reissues of 'classic albums'. The album thus stands in stark contrast to the pretty shoddy treatment afforded her earlier albums. The CD reissue of her first album can't make up its mind whether the album is called *The Kick Inside*, or simply *Kick Inside*! This oversight is symptomatic of the lack of attention paid to this woman's work, both by her record company and, to a lesser extent, by the music world in general.

As a tribute to the power of the album, many of the artist's most fervent online devotees now refer to themselves as 'Lovehounds'. Despite inevitable dissenting voices, the album has maintained a remarkably consistent and positive critical capital over two decades, and many of these other critical opinions will form an important part of this chapter. My intention is to express an individual interpretation filtered through many others' observations, giving a broad but not definitive or objective reading of what was, and is, a 'seminal text' in popular music.

The Conceptual Work

Hounds was the artist's first album to stake a claim to being a 'concept work'. Unlike within many other branches of art, this term possesses mixed connotations within popular music, in part due to some of the admittedly pompous and overblown albums released during the progressive rock era. Albums by the likes of Yes, Emerson, Lake and Palmer and Rush, to name but a few, purported to offer an elevated and philosophical treatise on weighty topics such as belief, mythology and existence. In some cases (The Who's *Tommy*, 1969; Genesis's *The Lamb Lies Down on Broadway*, 1974; Pink Floyd's *Dark Side of the Moon*, 1973) ambition and daring were vindicated by the concept album form, but equally often the form proved a critical stumbling block, with much approbation the result (see Stump, 1997). More broadly, the concept album did indirectly contribute to a creative climate that encouraged the rise of 'back to basics' forms such as pub rock and punk rock in the UK in the mid- to late 1970s. In the mid-1980s the concept album was still resolutely unfashionable, although acts such as Kraftwerk had cunningly attached the form to dance-based technologies and pop melodies with earlier works such as *Trans Europe Express* (1977) and *Radioactivity* (1975). Concept albums, and devices such as naming each side of an album differently and quoting stanzas from poetry (in *Hounds*' case Tennyson's *The Coming of Arthur*, 1870), do encourage a more 'lit crit' attitude to interpretation, with both reviewers and artists being tempted to make critical connections between influences, works and weighty matters of epistemological analysis. All such critical baggage can have a considerable impact upon the individual's critical terrain – how we approach an album, and what we bring with us.

More than two decades after the release, it is difficult not to bemoan the impossibility of a 'pure' or 'unconstrained' reading of *Hounds*, but the passing of time forces us to either confront the critical context as well as the artistic text, or run the risk of forming an interpretation based on inadequate or insufficient data, if that doesn't sound too clinical a description. As previously stated, we all have the right to come up with our own readings – ones that may run as oppositional to empirical or prevailing evidence. Equally, and inevitably, we will all adopt what critical methodology refers to as 'aberrant decoding' – interpretations based on the aforementioned insufficient or even unknown data. All anyone has to do, in my opinion, is to account for their own reading strategies, whilst avoiding the seductive appeal offered by notions of critical objectivity or biographical and historical 'proof'.

In terms of analysis, it is perhaps true that the more one knows about background, context and the critical climate surrounding a work, the less one is actually sure of individual interpretations and definitive meanings – background research tends to offer a wider range of readings, rather than solving any kind of interpretive puzzle. But we all bring something unique to bear when we interpret, because in our interpretations we actually reveal ourselves, filtered through the medium of the work under scrutiny.

Ideas and Influences

Unlike many other creative musicians, Kate Bush's inspirations for songs and albums often seem to come from other creative texts. Books and television programmes have provided many starting points for her own songs, with the artist referencing herself as 'one of the television generation' (Bush, in Pringle, 1980); but perhaps the most significant creative influence comes from the world of film, with the artist an avid and eclectic consumer of the form. Alfred Hitchcock seems to have been particularly influential (Bush, in Alexander, 1990). In addition, the artist herself has confessed to the importance of dreams and the many real-life characters that have visited her in her sleep. These influences contrast to the more usual pop narratives, which draw, in the main, upon stock phrases and stereotypical situations, or the omnipresent subjects of romantic relationships (or their absence), sex, altered states and dancing.

The songs comprising the first side of *Hounds of Love* demonstrate the artist's varied and unique range of creative influences. The most comprehensive interview with her on the subject of influences and meanings took place in 1991, when BBC radio DJ Richard Skinner interviewed Bush as part of Radio 1's *Classic Albums* series (originally broadcast 25 January 1992). The following brief and lyric-based interpretations give us a good clue as to where the artist herself gleaned her inspiration.

The opening track, 'Running up that Hill (A Deal With God)', deals with the relatively straightforward issue of the lack of understanding between the sexes, which the artist muses could be resolved best by the relatively unstraightforward issue of asking God to swap our places.

The album's title track is partly inspired by a film called *Night of the Demon* (Jacques Tourneur, 1957), with the artist making the connection between being hunted by hounds and chased by a form of love so strong that 'when it gets you it's just going to rip you to pieces' (Bush, in Skinner, 1992).

'The Big Sky' takes us back into the childhood reveries of the artist (although, as so often, the title is also that of a film, in this case a Hollywood western), seeing shapes in clouds and letting the imagination similarly change form and take flight. Another influence came from the artist simply observing 'this great cat I used to have who'd sit on this wall in the garden, looking up at the sky' (Bush, in Doyle, 2005: 89).

'Mother Stands for Comfort' is another of the many narratives in which the writer assumes the character of a male – in this case a murderer – and his use and abuse of the blind love of his mother. This maternal love will go as far as to shield the murderer from the forces of justice, punningly expressed in the final line 'Mother will stay Mum'.

'Cloudbusting' concludes the first side, and the *Hounds of Love* section of the album. This text was very directly inspired by *A Book of Dreams* (1973), in which Peter Reich reflects upon his childhood. One of his most powerful memories relates to the times spent with his father, the controversial psychoanalyst Wilhelm Reich, who designed a machine that, he claimed, could harness the power of clouds. The links between literary and musical narratives can be extended beyond this one track. For Kruse:

> Anyone familiar with Peter Reich's book ... will be struck by the similarity in structure between side 2 ... and *A Book of Dreams*. In the book Peter is hospitalised and wavers between consciousness and dreaming ... It is undoubtedly significant that side 1 ends with Bush making rain...an act in which waters are at her mercy. In contrast, Bush is at the whim of the drowning pool on side 2, as if her rainmaking got out of hand. (Kruse, 1990: 460, 461).

Despite containing common threads and themes, the songs on the first side do not possess the links or coherence of a unifying concept. Bush states that after she wrote 'And Dream of Sheep', 'that was it, that was the beginning of what then became the concept. And really, for me, from the beginning, *The Ninth Wave* was a film, that's how I thought of it' (Bush, in Skinner, 1992).

This conceptual suite of tracks, consisting of seven titles and running over 26 minutes really does allow the interpretive imagination full rein, with as many readings as there are reviewers (and probably listeners). Kruse closely links the musical concept suite to its literary influence: 'The cycle of birth, death and messianic rebirth central to Arthurian legend is also vital to "The Ninth Wave"' (Kruse, 1990: 461). For the artist, the narrative concerns a fictional character washed overboard, trying to keep their self alive and awake by letting their own imagination loose. As is so often the case with Kate Bush, much of the evocation and 'horrific imagery' is intended to be 'terrifying', 'quite nightmarish', 'terribly lonely' before the last track 'that's really meant to be the rescue of the whole situation, where suddenly out of all this darkness and weight comes light' (Bush, in Skinner, 1992).

A totally different set of critical readings comes within an interview conducted by an unknown journalist writing from the Irish journal, *Hot Press*. As might be expected, the artist's own Irish roots are investigated, but in terms of textual readings; the interviewer is clearly trying to establish, or expose, more controversial artistic influences. As well as drawing the artist's attention to the supposed drug connotations of 'poppies' in 'And Dream of Sheep', the reference to 'cutting little lines' within 'Under Ice' is forwarded as being about cocaine. The artist accepts the 'available readings' but rejects any intended connections. More controversially, it is later suggested that 'Hounds of Love' has clear connotations of bestiality, which, again, the composer rejects as unintended, and most others would never have even considered, I am sure (Bush, 1985). The far-fetched, even sensationalist tone of this interview, whilst inappropriate, does at least indicate the range of readings available within the text of *Hounds*, proving yet again that you will find what you are looking for within a work if you dig deep enough.

What all these brief readings provide us with is a key, or a starting point on which to base our far more complex and idiosyncratic interpretations. In addition, the lyrical narratives are only one component of the overall text, and not where 'meaning resides'. With these thoughts in mind it is time to embark upon the imaginative journey engendered by *Hounds of Love*.

Hounds of Love

'Running up that Hill (A Deal With God)'

As previously indicated, the opening few bars of the first song on an album can assume a huge symbolic importance as both a musical and artistic statement of intent.

Much like the opening atmospherics of 'Moving' from the debut album, 'Running up that Hill' immediately places us in an experimental and unstable terrain. The synthetic drone effect, resembling an air raid siren, is joined by what will become the hallmark drum sound for the album, the basic four-to-the-floor disco rhythm being augmented by an occasional syncopated tom-tom, panned wide to one channel.

By the time of the album's release, technology had advanced sufficiently to blur the line between 'played' drums, 'programmed' drums and drum machines. In interview, Bush stated that 'Del ... wrote this great pattern on the drum machine' (Bush, in Skinner, 1992) but the track credit also lists Stuart Elliott as playing drums, which suggests that we are dealing with a combination of techniques. Certainly, some of the rolls later in the song sound 'human', although it is hard to be sure. What this track's percussive elements do possess, along with much of the subsequent tracks, is a dated, but very effective drum sound – flat and bassy, and lacking in echo or reverb. The basic kick and snare sound is very reminiscent of producers such as Giorgio Moroder, who from around 1976 fashioned an innovative blend of 'cold' drum and synth textures which were then used as dance floor-based backing tracks by the likes of Donna Summer, vocalising in the archetypically warm and soulful style associated with r'n'b divas. Of course, using adjectives such as 'cold' and 'warm' is deeply ideological, as they trigger connotations. Historically, most popular music has aspired towards 'warmness', with its associated connotations of energy, feeling, emotion and authenticity. However, by the late 1970s, new instrumentation and studio techniques, allied to the generic shift from soul to disco, increased the sound palette and altered what people 'expected' from music. Thus, adjectives such as 'cold', 'robotic' and 'synthetic' came to be viewed in a more positive light. 'Running up that Hill' is a classic melange of cold and warm elements both competing for our attention. Another series of oppositions centres on 'retro' versus 'innovative'. The basic drum rhythms are knowingly old-fashioned, even monotonous, on many of this album's tracks, but they are often contrasted with 'cutting edge' synthesisers and sampling techniques to thrilling effect.

The rhythm track builds with the addition of melodic synthetic stabs before the vocals enter at 28 seconds. As with so many other vocal tracks on this album, main melody lines are augmented by non-lyrical lines, often in another register and sometimes fed through the Fairlight to pitch-shift them. On this track the backing 'yeah yeah yo's' are panned across the stereo picture as we are led into the chorus, which arrives at 53 seconds – around standardised pop time. A wonderfully effective shimmering bed of balalaikas, courtesy of brother Paddy, shifts the sound palette back towards a more traditional terrain. After an instrumental interlude, the second verse arrives at 1: 28. The vocals and lyrics become more insistent during this section, within lines such as 'Is there so much hate for the ones we love', and more plaintively 'Tell me we both matter don't we?', which never fails to provoke a personal moment of *jouissance*. After another chorus and musical interlude we come to what is effectively the 'change' section of the track, although the mood or key is not shifted in the accepted matter for a pop middle eight.

From 2: 52, and beginning with 'C'mon baby, c'mon darlin'', the main vocal line is harmonised before a hugely effective reverberant drum roll is complemented by a long and choral harmonic moan which abruptly ceases to leave us in a more sparse sonic terrain. This aftermath is painful in its sense of anti-climax. Popular music is all about the dialectic between tension and resolution. As listeners we need to be teased with the thrill of anticipation before being given brief climaxes. These, however, cannot last too long in the standard pop length song, before they must be snatched away from us. We are given nibbles on the biscuit, not the whole slice of cake; this is musical foreplay. So moments like the drum roll and choral section, which only last a few brief seconds, assume their effectiveness because they are basically unsatisfactory, akin to Oscar Wilde's description of smoking as an activity always leaving us wanting more.

The remainder of the track, still underpinned by the cavernous drone that runs throughout its duration, teeters on the brink of ecstatic cacophony at times, with several more explosions from both drums and the occasional guitar power chord being interspersed with vocal wails and whoops. Just before the track returns us cyclically to the opening drone, the final 'If I only could' refrain meshes Bush's natural voices with a pitch-shifted sample in the operatic bass range. The effect is both disturbing and sonically lush in its unrealistic timbres. Had a genuinely deep male voice been employed, the result would not have been the same; we instead get production examples of the 'Man Machine' syndrome, to quote a Kraftwerk album (1979) that is similarly on the creative border in expressing the marriage between flesh and technology. The artist herself reflected upon the nature of synthetic and acoustic instrumentation, and their associated feels, at some length during the Skinner interview, claiming that both cold and warm sounds: 'are very usable, depending on what you want to say ... really sounds now, are pieces of gold for people' (Bush, in Skinner, 1992).

The overwhelmingly brooding nature of the track – echoing the relentless activity suggested by the song's title – is partially countered by the sheer comforting insistency of the 'bog standard' disco drum pattern. Parts of the track, swathed in reverberant echo, give the impression of sonic hugeness, again contrasting with the flatness of the kit sound. These facets, topped with the sheer uniqueness and singularity of the vocal style, in the wake of her market place absence, signalled a powerful return into public consciousness. Aided by an even more radical 12-inch mix, the single was a big success, reaching number 3 in the charts, and an unprecedented (for the artist) 21 in the US 12-inch charts – people were clearly dancing to this chilling sonic experimentation.

'Hounds of Love'

Rather than being the title track of the album, this is simply the title track of side one. It begins with a powerful tom-tom drum rhythm, into which the sample of dialogue from *Night of the Demon* (1957) ('It's in the trees ... it's coming!') is woven. The drum pattern is fundamental to this track, with a highly mixed and resonant sound similar to the classic Phil Collins 'In the Air Tonight' timbres being employed. Almost devoid of conventional bass elements, the gaps provided by the syncopated drum rhythm are filled with only a chordal wash of keyboard and a lowly mixed chugging staccato cello. All the instrumental elements contribute towards a mood that perfectly complements the lyrical narrative, with all its evocations of hunter and chase, the hounds surging towards their quarry, and the transgressive power of obsessive love.

During the chorus section, a second, more prominent instrument, giving the track much of its edgy drive, joins the cello. The vocals are reverberant, the melody giving full scope to the artist's range. Her diction is precise and wonderfully 'home counties' in its enunciation of the stretched vowel in the lines 'it beats so faast' and 'I just caant deal with this'. But at other times she is powerfully growling, with the word 'throw' snarled and also anglicised by Kate's very English inability to pronounce the r-sound correctly. In this she joins other classically English vocalists such as Steve Harley and the Kinks's Ray Davies (as well as seemingly dozens of aristocrats, and MPs, in particular!). The passing chords under the 'do-do' vocal backing are almost ecclesiastical in their demureness, but the track has real bite.

As within some of the work of other wilful experimentalists, such as Prince or Van der Graaf Generator, the lack of a bass guitar removes the frequencies that are comforting and familiar, as well as rhythmic. This lack of frequencies somehow makes the backing track more fragile, like a building without foundations threatening to topple. Popular music is built upon familiarity and cliché, which is one reason why it is actually very easy to subvert the form, given the artistic wherewithal. Because the track has a staccato, insistent drive, it still carries us along, but the timbral manner in which this occurs is often far from apparent. Deconstruction, a particularly complex school of literary criticism, has as one of its main tenets the notion that it is within the gaps and contradictions that the true meaning of a text is revealed. Absence is a vital dimension in musical structure, but one that is often, and increasingly ignored within a system that seeks to saturate the listener with musical 'data' (the notion within so many contemporary recordings that 'we've got all this capacity and capability, let's make sure we use it'). This proliferation of elements can have the effect of 'completing' the text, giving us no way in as interpreters in much the same manner as many audio-visual texts seek to batter us with information to the point of excess. It takes courage to make choices to *not* do things within any form of creativity. In a sense, the artist and her close ally Del Palmer are making editorial decisions, in the process helping to convert the process from one of mere recording to one of musical *mise-en-scène*.

Despite being the third album track released as a single, some six months after the album's release date, 'Hounds of Love' was surprisingly successful, reaching a creditable number 18 in the UK charts.

'The Big Sky'

The artist admitted to having some difficulty with both the writing and achieving what she wanted to on this track. The statement 'eventually it just kind of turned into what it did, thank goodness' (Bush, in Skinner, 1992) suggests a certain dissatisfaction with the end result. For a perfectionist, its inclusion is therefore something of a surprise. Certainly, 'The Big Sky' does suffer in comparison to the force and bravery of the opening two tracks.

Underpinned by the disco-plus-percussion format employed on the opening track, the melody is again strong and complex, with Bush restricting her delivery for the half-strangled execution of the line 'You never understood me', and adding to her main melody with a mass choir of backing vocals. At points she warbles in mock-operatic style before whispering seductively within the same line. This is an artist totally confident with her own instrument, and still pushing the boundaries of how to employ it. One of the limitations resides in the backing track, which is too similar to 'Running up that Hill', but is less distinct in terms of mix and instrumental separation. Thus Youth's elastic bass is under-mixed, as are the acoustic guitars and tambourine that punctuate parts of the structure. Better employed are the flamenco-style rapid handclaps, which do go some way to pull the track out of the low- to middle-frequency muddle of the production.

At getting on for five minutes, the track overstays its welcome, particularly during the largely redundant 'tribal cacophony' that leads out the track sonically, the sounds to parallel the confusion and bafflement suggested by the lyric, but in overall terms 'The Big Sky' is one of very few weak points on the album. It was released as the 'milking it' fourth single from the album, and rightfully only just grazed the charts.

The artist suggested that she was writing a lot of the material for this album in the country, particularly Ireland, where she would 'watch the clouds rolling up the hill towards me', and that 'there is a lot of weather on this album' (Bush, in Skinner, 1992). After the gusts of energy provided by the opening track, it is fitting to symbolise 'The Big Sky' as a damp overcast squall ready to be shunted aside by the return to clarity represented by the final tracks on the side.

'Mother Stands for Comfort'

This track exemplifies the most common working practice adopted on this album. A skeletal and flat drum pattern, just kick and snare, provides the metronomic basis upon which a whole battery of percussive samples interjects from the scattered outskirts of each channel. On top of these elements come the acoustic warmth offered by some standard piano chording and a sinuous upright bass melody provided by Eberhard Weber. All other 'acoustic' sounds are presumably provided by the Fairlight, particularly prominent being the calliope-style whistle lines, which skilfully counterpoint the vocal harmony. Texturally diverse, this track's sparseness and sombre qualities provide a welcome hiatus after the relatively busy and up-tempo nature of the previous three tracks. Just the two musicians, Weber plus drummer Stuart Elliott, are credited, indicating that the lion's share of the conceptual and compositional work must come from the artist herself. Having said that, the support and technical presence of Del Palmer (responsible for all Linn drum programming, in addition to the other five engineers credited!) must have been hugely significant, particularly on tracks such as this.

Leaving aside the technology and tonal innovations, the melody, whilst resolutely 'low key' in both senses of the word, is intriguing, especially as a result of its *pas de deux* with the bass. The chorus melody is simplicity itself, a point of calmness amidst the background wails and synthetic breakages and beats. The lyrical evocations of 'mad love' – a perennial concern for the artist – are particularly well served by the rest of the track, which is a classic example of the 'album track' rather than the 'stand-out tune' that it prefaces. But all classic albums need to include both – another example of the tension/resolution dialectic.

'Cloudbusting'

The second single from the album, this would have been the safer, more commercial choice than 'Running up that Hill', but the artist had long since ceased to make choices based on such criteria. From the first confident and ringing melodic phrase, 'I still dream …', 'Cloudbusting' joins the list of classic Kate Bush 'stand out tunes', richly melodic, lyrically intriguing and instrumentally assured. It harks back to the days of the first album in its accessibility and exemplification of commercial pop values.

'Cloudbusting' is a clear example of 'played', rather than 'programmed' music that sets the track apart from the others on this side of the album. The strings of the Medici Sextet, arranged by Dave Lawson, are central to both the baroque drive and the melodic counterpointing of this track. They are strongly reminiscent of George Martin or Mike Leander's arrangements for the Beatles on tracks such as 'Eleanor Rigby' (1965) or 'She's Leaving Home' (1967). Particularly beautiful is the shift from staccato rhythm chords to the ecstatic descending counter-melody that takes place under the line 'On top of the world' at 1: 16. Backing vocals are cleverly employed to ape the string effects, but have an endearingly amateurish edge. Equally, the standard skeletal drumbeat is complemented by a loose-skinned deep tom-tom roll which is low in the mix, barely noticeable but much needed to provide a 'human' texture.

At 2: 28 the track begins a gradual lift in terms of playing intensity and with the addition of a high, slightly phased cello line, we are led on to the final chorus before the massed vocals of the 'yay-yo' run-out section are introduced, accompanied by the marching snares, giving the track a militaristic feel. This provides a stirring coda to a perfectly structured song that retains its interest for the full five-minute length. Not that it is apparent, but there is no real ending to the song, skilfully covered up by 'decoy tactics … we covered the whole thing over with the sound of a steam engine slowing down' (Bush, in Skinner, 1992). Thus this track, as well as having 'played' qualities, is also ultimately about human frailty – strangely appropriate considering the subject matter of the lyric. It also provides a 'visual' dimension to the track, and one well exploited by one of the artist's more successful pop videos, which, it is fair to guess, did contribute to the success of the single that, however, only reached a lowly number 20 in the UK.

Of course, as the second single from the album, its sales would have been diminished by this factor, and the already huge sales for the album on which it was placed. Had its release been reversed with 'Running up that Hill', hindsight suggests that it would have repeated, or even bettered the success of the debut single. It remains probably her best-known track next to 'Wuthering Heights'.

'And Dream of Sheep'

The linked suite of tracks that comprise side two's *The Ninth Wave* commences with another track that harks back to the piano-based compositions of the artist's early recordings. Apart from some spoken word and gull-call interludes, and some minimal inclusion of bouzouki and whistles, the track is based on just one piano and one vocal track. For this early part of the suite's narrative, the author has to lyrically symbolise a complex set of emotions. Despite the 'horrific imagery' of a person washed overboard, the lyric also has to convey a paradoxical calmness and reverie as the character floats, almost mesmerised by the flashing light within the lifejacket. Bush admitted to being influenced by many maritime war films where sailors are swept overboard, awaiting rescue (Jovanovic, 2005: 158). The knowledge that the character cannot fall asleep for fear of turning over and drowning is countered by the optimism of some of the narrative, but subverted by the almost narcotic urge to 'be weak … sleep … and dream of sheep'. However, the real fear lies not within the reality of the situation, but with the power of the imagination – so there is terror, but a calm and frozen form of terror. As this part of the suite concludes, the character is slipping under, again with the drugged connotations suggested by mention of poppies and of being taken deeper.

The melody and vocal style do little to represent the darker side of this narrative. In actual fact, the sung elements are elegiac and seductive, only presenting the pleasurable dimensions of loss of consciousness and 'drifting off'.

The song is quite beautiful, although I do wonder if this personal reading is a little too one-dimensional, almost if, like the drowning character, I am being seduced only by the dream-like dimensions, rather than recognising the true horror of the situation. Perhaps the song is really the symbolic 'calm before the storm' and functions to lull us all into a false state by virtue of its simple, melodic charms. The track is separated from the following episode by a brief moment of silence and repose before this mood is shattered.

'Under Ice'

The artist somewhat disingenuously claimed that after the composition process she 'didn't have much to do with this' (Bush, in Skinner, 1992). Bearing in mind that she admitted to composing the cello tune on the Fairlight and that the lyrics and vocals are almost all her, we must conclude that she is referring to the overwhelmingly programmed nature of the track.

In its reliance upon sampled sounds and voices, 'Under Ice' is one of the most minimal and austere tracks on the album – chilling in both imbued atmospherics and subject matter. We have been transported from open water to a river that is frozen over within this narrative, with a narrator 'looking down' upon their drowning self. This reflects upon all the empirical evidence of people who have 'died' whilst observing themselves from an elevated, out of body position. The descending, staccato string sounds closely mirror multi-tracked vocal lines, with Bush again strongly enunciating her southern English accent on 'fast' and 'past'. Other interesting textures are provided by samples of running water effects, thunder (or ice cracking?), the submarine radar 'pong' associated with maritime war narratives and some snatches of incoherent dialogue and voices calling.

The Ninth Wave will disappoint the pedantic listener who attempts to construct a coherent and consistent narrative. Not only have we somehow moved from an open expanse of water to a frozen river (the writer described it as 'this frozen lake', although the song lyric does not), but also the narrator appears to have obtained a pair of ice skates in the process. But all thoughts of narrative consistency should be disregarded in favour of artistic licence. This unfolding narrative is one of linked impressions and emotions with the fear of death by drowning being the leitmotif, or recurring thread. Using the image of skating is as much about providing the lyric with a set of harsh and abrupt sibilants and fricatives ('skating', 'cutting', 'splitting', 'spitting'), which chop up the phrases into little shards of sound, as it is about pushing the narrative.

The artist admitted that this track 'was really simple to record' (Bush, in Skinner, 1992) and that the process only took about a day, and something of this simplicity and freshness does come across within its economic mix and duration of just 2: 21 – one of the shortest tracks of her entire career. 'Under Ice' really demonstrates the huge possibilities offered by the Fairlight, allowing for a conceptual artist to bring into the studio close to a mastered backing track. This track could then be added to and remixed. Unlike today's cheap and hugely sophisticated computer-based virtual studios, an acoustic space was still needed in the 1980s, but in a sense this combination of different settings and processes does allow for a richness and diversity of timbres that many contemporary recordings lack. In particular, the muffled samples of dialogue and ambience do 'humanise' the feel of this album – much needed in view of the essentially human dilemma central to *The Ninth Wave*, which at the end of this track is represented by the fading cry of 'It's me', as the narrator struggles, trapped under the ice.

The track achieves everything it sets out to do – the sense of loneliness and impending doom is perfectly realised, yet achieved by using minimal instrumentation. The temptation to emphasise the melodramatic nature of the narrative is resisted, in favour of a starkness that unnerves the listener.

'Waking the Witch'

This track falls into two linked parts. The first section, lasting around 1: 18, is built upon plangent open-ended piano chords, sometimes echoed and occasionally abruptly curtailed. The early part of 'Waking the Witch' bears evidence to Bush's often overlooked skill as a keyboardist. Whilst not in the league of a classically trained pianist such as Tori Amos – to whom she has been compared – Bush's playing is invariably 'fit for purpose'. In 1993 she stated: 'I don't think of myself as a musician ... [but] as a writer, I suppose. I only ever play the piano to accompany myself singing' (Bush, in Maconie, 1993: 104). Despite these self-deprecating comments, she is a most capable accompanist – as this sequence demonstrates.

Her backing provides a multi-faceted bed on which numerous samples of voices and phrases are placed. Many of these voices are encouragements to awake, in a sense calling back the soul into consciousness. Other elements include a whale effect that could be a distant echo of the opening sounds of Bush's first album and a vocal phrase harking back to 'And Dream of Sheep'. There also appears to be some kind of religious intonation at one point. A lot of these samples are tremendously evocative, particularly of childhood years – who has not been greeted by a favourite aunt or cousin with the introduction 'Look who's here to see you'? The communal values engendered by this section are further emphasised by the use of friends and family as the vocal samples. Included are all of her immediate family, plus Del Palmer and Brian Tench from the mixing team, and actor Robbie Coltrane – who she would go on to work with on a later common project with the Comic Strip.

Without warning, this reflective reverie is crudely shattered by the second part of the track. By using the metaphor of the witch and the ordeal of the ducking stool, the artist can introduce the issue of gender politics into the suite. This track sequence is far more musically collaborative, with much of the aggression provided by a relentless drum pattern, played by Charlie Morgan, heavily 'gated' to trim the natural decay of the beats. Also hugely effective is Alan Murphy's nagging, damped rhythm guitar, chipping away at our confidence. The incorporation of a helicopter blade sample, sequenced to chop its rhythm in time with the backing track, is also well executed. Not only does it connect us to other nightmare narratives such as *Apocalypse Now* (Francis Ford Coppola, 1979), but it also returns us to the artist's crucial early mentor, David Gilmour. The helicopter sequence was taken from Pink Floyd's *The Wall* album (1982) – another conceptual work full of dark moods and horrific imagery.

The vocals take the form of an exchange between the accused and her interrogator, whose pitch-altered voice was also provided by Bush. However, this track does suffer from incomplete crediting, with many lyrics missing from the transcription, so some interpretation is nothing but conjecture. The paradox inherent in this ordeal – if you drown, you're innocent! – is not lost within this lyric. The artist described the track as being symbolic of wider issues such as 'the fear of women's power…female intuition and instincts are very strong, and are still put down' (Bush, in Skinner, 1992). The addition of a baying crowd renders this scenario as a mob trial, with the imbued hysteria and collective cries of 'Guilty, Guilty, Guilty' returning us to similar narratives such as Arthur Miller's *The Crucible* (1953).

Highly theatrical in its construction and exposition, yet needing a huge amount of close attention to musical nuances before its true complexity is revealed, 'Waking the Witch' is the most successfully realised part of the whole suite of tracks. Its symbolism broadens the narrative, connecting it with one of the artist's favourite subjects – gender power politics. In close conjunction with 'Under Ice', this sequence is one of the scariest in the whole popular music canon, doubly effective in that it works more by stealth and nuance than by employing the bludgeoning tactics of gothic rock or heavy metal. Interestingly, when returning to this album years after its recording, the artist confessed to being unsatisfied with the results: 'I was a bit disappointed with that. I think if I'd had more energy I would've pursued that with an actor doing the speaking part rather than myself through a digital delay' (Bush, in Doyle, 2005: 89).

'Watching You Without Me'

The next track in the song suite both radically shifts the affective mood and returns us to the liminal status of a character drifting between death/life and dream/consciousness already explored on *The Ninth Wave*. As with 'And Dream of Sheep' the overall imbued affect is one of woozy, narcotic torpor. The descending chime-like synth lines and the fretless slap-and-twang of Danny Thompson's double bass are reminiscent of many other examples of classic ambience – whether Thomson's own work with John Martyn on several of the latter's unclassifiable albums such as *Solid Air* (1973) (the title says it all), or the exotic orientalism of Japan. Stuart Elliott's drums are precise and unobtrusive, with much use of rim shots and tuned percussion to leave the sonic spaces open for other elements.

There are several vocal devices utilised on this track – some of which, deliberately I think, are there to deny us meaning and narrative closure. As the lyric is fixated by the failure of communication between the narrator and someone still in the real world of consciousness and existence, these denials are very appropriate. Some of what is sung lacks any enunciative clarity. Early on in the track we need printed lyrics to make out the line 'You can't hear me', which is delivered open-mouthed and with little distinction between syllables or words. Again, the example of Roy Harper or John Martyn's style springs to mind, with our assumptions as to his supposed perpetually drugged/drunk persona adding to the supra-linguistic qualities of his voice and lyrical obscurity.

Towards the end of the track we have a harmonic vocal sequence that may be sung in a foreign tongue – again the lyrical transcription is inadequate. The microtonal slides between intervals are very non-western at this point, prefacing the artist's later interest in the styles of singers such as the Trio Bulgarka. Perhaps the most challenging vocal effect comes at the climax of the track, where her voice is both heavily echoed and syllabically 'clipped', leaving only shards of sound and making comprehension almost impossible. However, am I alone in constructing small elements of meaning in hearing phrases such as 'Listen to me' and 'Talk to me'? Again, we cannot be sure. There are transcriptions available that seek to clarify these tracts, but that seems to miss the symbolic point of the masking processes. This track is particularly enigmatic and unwilling to provide us with any concrete satisfaction, but is yet another success in every sense. The contributions of the artist herself are immense, but still improved by the differing collaborative groups of musicians that most of the tracks on this album employ.

'Jig of Life'

After the trials and tribulations to which her character, expressed in her classically understated phrase 'this poor sod' had been exposed, the author explained 'it's about time they have a bit of help' (Bush, in Skinner, 1992). Given the complexities explored by *The Ninth Wave*, it comes as no surprise that this takes the form of a temporal leap in an exchange between present and future manifestations of the narrator. These take the style of a remonstrance, with the future character admonishing their younger self to stay alive, not least in order that others unborn might live. This dialogue carries strong echoes of the three ages of Christmas in Dickens's *A Christmas Carol* (1843), but the warnings are generally couched in a positive and colloquial manner far removed from those of Marley's ghost, with repetitive phrases and use of the vernacular widely employed, as in 'C'mon let me live girl' and 'Never, never, never, never let me go'.

The musical accompaniment to this spirit of hope is mainly provided by an experienced troupe of Irish traditional musicians, whose parts are arranged by Bill

Whelan. Much of the listeners' estimation of the success of this enterprise depends upon an appreciation of the charms of the high-paced, flurries-of-notes, modal progressions provided by fiddles, whistles, bouzouki, uilleann pipes and bodhrán. Whilst not an avid listener of acoustic Celtic folk, I do appreciate its charms, and in the context of both the narrative and the musical suite, the delving into an alternative musical ethnicity works very well. Particularly powerful is the atonality provided by a flattened tone 44 seconds and again at 1: 34 into the track. Shortly after this second clash of tones – a great rarity in the artist's work up to this point – the track breaks down before being gradually reconstituted. The marriage between traditional textures and the instrumentation of electric bass and two rock drummers is seamless.

The only false note is provided by the assumption of an artificial 'Oirish' accent by the artist (echoes of 'Army Dreamers'), and more noticeably her brother John during his 'Celtic rap'. Leaving aside the genre of rap itself, spoken word interludes are notoriously unsuccessful in popular music, although the rhythmic intensity and lyrically incendiary nature of even mundane raps does at least give them a visceral vitality. John's more bardic attempt at recitation falls some way short of matching the best examples of spoken word on record. Despite the Bush family being Anglo-Celtic, there is no hint of an Irish brogue in the artist's 'estuary English' speech in interviews, and one would assume that John's accent is similar. Bush admitted to writing this track in Ireland and to the countryside having a great impact upon her, but the reason for this accentual affectation still escapes me. To be fair, had the poetic interlude been mixed lower, the jarring nature would have been lessened. Despite my bafflement and criticism, these are minor issues: both within the track itself and certainly taking the suite as a whole into account, these false notes matter little.

'Jig of Life' is brilliantly arranged and has a tempo and timbral mix that aptly measure up to the air of positivity suggested by its title. The promise of 'Night of the Swallow' on the previous album is fulfilled by this track, and further emphasised by its positioning within a suite of tracks, rather than standing apart as a separate, if seductive 'curiosity'.

'Hello Earth'

At 6: 13 this is the longest track in the sequence, and another example of human indecision resulting in a successful artistic outcome. Bush admitted to having 'great holes in the choruses' (Bush, in Skinner, 1992) which were eventually filled by the rewriting of a traditional melody that she heard in the film *Nosferatu: Phantom der Nacht* (Herzog, 1979). Words were composed on the basis of sounding something like those heard in the original, giving the track a real flavour of Germanic or Slavic choral works at points.

The main body of the song is a rarity on this album, being a full-blown romantic ballad, but again focussing on the narrator attempting to imagine a reversal of the scenario of floating in the water looking up at the sky, instead looking down upon the planet and seeing reflections of the stars upon the waves. Bush describes it as 'a lullaby for the earth' (Bush, in Skinner, 1992). This is certainly an apt description of the opening verse, with a simple vocal and piano track only assisted by some minimal sampling of astronauts' speech. However, at 58 seconds the rest of the backing track, built on reverberant and highly mixed drums, soars in to give the piece a huge spacial presence far removed from the intimacy suggested by the term lullaby. The second part of the chorus, with the Richard Hickox singers intoning in German over a bed of synthetic strings, moves the track into another affective terrain, one with sombre and rather sinister undertones. In addition, mention of 'the Tempest' and lines such as 'Murderer. Murderer of calm' do add a Shakespearian flavour to the text.

The second verse-to-chorus build-up adds chanted warnings to those groups of people (fishermen, sailors, lifesavers) still in the water. This has the effect of giving a global dimension to the unfolding narrative, which is being opened out beyond the struggles of one individual during the course of the song cycle. Some of the fan-based discussion relating to this track suggests that the composition may have been influenced by an actual loss at sea covered in a news story. The Celtic instrumentation of the previous track is reintroduced in a more stripped-down manner, with Liam O'Flynn's uilleann pipes adding important colour. The second sequence of choral singing is more extensive than the first, and deepens the tension, accompanied by a skilled slide up, and contrasting slide down the 'virtual fret board' by two string sounds, while the submarine echo device dolefully seeks its quarry low in the mix. As the track concludes the artist presents a brief Germanic litany, again quite disturbing in its textures and intonation (although Kruse suggests '"tiefe, tiefe" is synonymous with "deep" in the sense of "profound"' in its original tongue, Kruse, 1990: 463), before concluding back in lullaby terrain with the phrase 'Go to sleep little earth'.

Lyrically, 'Hello Earth' is fragmentary and impressionistic, rather than providing us with a clear progression in the narrative. However, for Kruse it is 'the most dramatic track ... a climactic moment' (redolent of) 'Christian connotations' (Kruse, 1990: 464) which I am probably unable or unwilling to ascribe. The track is a triumph in terms of arrangement and structure, but leaves the listener a little confused and ambivalent about how to feel, and where we are being placed in the unfolding narrative. Far better, from my viewpoint, to merely luxuriate in the particularly assured and varied singing, and the dynamics between the understated and almost overblown elements, which meld wonderfully.

'The Morning Fog'

The sequence, and the whole album, is concluded with what I personally have always experienced as one of the most intensely emotional and uplifting pieces of music produced by any musician. 'The Morning Fog' never fails to move me deeply, even to tears on certain particularly sensitive occasions, and is a marvellously executed example of the power of music, voices and lyrics to be life affirming.

The previous six tracks have had the effect of leaving us emotionally battered – tossed by the artistic waves. The sequence has skilfully juxtaposed widely differing timbres, tempi, structures and scenarios – in the process taking us on a journey through a huge number of imbued moods. The final track is written as a deliberate attempt at 'rescue' in more than one sense, to pull us out of the mire and back into the light of redemptive love and familial warmth. Bush stated that this is where 'they get pulled out of the water' (Bush, in Skinner, 1992), thus suggesting that broadening the narrative in the previous track has indeed moved us away from individual concerns back into those of humanity as a whole. It is also about 'being so grateful for everything you have' (ibid.). These powerful feelings of positivity are expressed by a very simple instrumental mix and structure in a track of only 2: 35 that always seems to finish much too soon.

The dynamic of the track gives a wonderful sense of lightness and space, expressed particularly well, in different points along the tone range, by both Del Palmer's bass lines and John Williams's ringing Spanish guitar flourishes. 'The Morning Fog' is undoubtedly Del Palmer's finest work on record. Not only does one melodic bass line seem to express real human personality (yet again, whale-like cries, or am I just getting obsessed?) in its swoops and counterpointing of his partner's vocals, but he dubs a second, more low-key and tonally grounded line into the mix at points, giving a fantastic double-tracked mesh of warm bass elements. John Williams, as might be expected from a classical virtuoso, brings clarity of texture to his simple double-tracked guitar lines seldom equalled by any rock guitarist.

Backed by her own unique combinations of harmonies and wordless chants, the lyrical narrative is direct and filled with emotion, although with the classically Bushian paradox of not allowing the narrator to emerge from the ordeal into bright sunshine, but rather 'into the sweet morning fog' (Bush, in Skinner, 1992). Perhaps, as Kruse suggests, the descent mirrors the 'falling from the spirit world back into the material realm' (Kruse, 1990: 464). During the second part of the lyric the character of the narrator and that of the writer herself fuse into one. In the last verse it is clear that we are listening to Kate herself saying 'thank you and goodnight'. Her expressions of love for her family are packed with sincerity, leaving me with the bittersweet feeling of envy that she can talk of such things in a manner that most of us are unable or unwilling to do.

Summary

How are we to summarise this album, broadly perceived as her finest work? The first point to make is that the author was in a very good and positive state of mind throughout the recording process. Her creative partnership with Del Palmer was at its peak, and their collective use of the Fairlight sampler (and its limitations) was varied and assured. In addition, as previously indicated, the period in which the album emerged was the bridging era between the largely acoustic and musicianly methods common earlier, and the era of digital programming and hard disc recording about to be embarked upon. Timothy Warner quotes Zak's historicisation of this period, who stated:

> British recordings of the early 1980s marked a turning point in terms of both sound and public awareness. With an abundance of sound processing, new electronic instruments, and resurgent experimental attitudes, the distance between the natural sound world and the sound of records increased markedly. (Zak, in Warner, 2003: 140).

This allowed for a unique blend of methods and sounds to be fruitfully brought into creative contact on *Hounds of Love*.

The artist's use of collaborators was never more successfully demonstrated than on this album. By this period she had the confidence to know how much freedom fellow musicians needed, and no reports of the tensions that arose earlier in her studio career have come to light. She referred to the writing and recording process as being 'the happiest I've been ... everyone that worked on the album was wonderful' before concluding, 'in some ways this is the most complete work that I've done, in some ways it is the best' (Bush, in Skinner, 1992).

One reason for this was the new challenge posed by the conceptual nature of the work – not only the sequence of tracks that comprised *The Ninth Wave*, but also the separate songs making up *Hounds of Love*. It was the clichéd 'game of two halves', each section of which needed the other to provide breadth and creative scope. As I have stated, the song sequence does lack a certain narrative consistency, and 'The Big Sky' doesn't make it onto my edited version of the album, but otherwise it is a near flawless work – brave, a little crazy, experimental, yet resolutely accessible to anyone prepared to meet it halfway. The artist's voice had an assurance and mature 'thickness' in its deeper registers that gave her an increased expressive range. This did go most of the way towards assuaging the loss of the extraordinary helium-based purity of her earliest vocal performances – vanished in the mists of time and possibly to the ravages of the dreaded nicotine habit.

A Daughter of Albion?: Kate Bush and Mythologies of Englishness

At this point it is important to break free from the linear analysis of tracks and albums that have informed much of the previous narrative. As I suggested in this book's introduction, Kate Bush symbolically reflects upon several different socio-musical dimensions that beg further exploration. By the time of the release of *Hounds of Love* many of these dimensions had already been engaged with. However, in some respects they had been broached, rather than fully exploited. As a result, the final sections in this chapter will reflect back upon these dimensions, as well as indicating how they would go on to inform her subsequent work. Nevertheless, it can be argued that each of the three areas to be explored – *auteur* theory, national identity and video creativity – were all greatly influenced by the experience of planning, writing and working on *Hounds of Love*; and in the wake of the critical and commercial success that the album represents, this seems an appropriate moment to make these three 'critical interventions'.

The 'Englishness debate' ('Oh, England', indeed!) or 'the national question' has assumed a huge significance in cultural studies, particularly in the post-1945 era of global decline and the faltering moves towards multiculturalism. Robert Colls summarises this situation in these terms:

> Anyone born on England between 1945–55 was brought up with the myths of the Anglo-British imperial state embedded in their lives ... by the 1990s the British knew they weren't what they were anymore. National identity was unravelling with astonishing speed ... In the light of these changes, from about twenty years ago historians and critics started asking the national question again. (Colls, 2002: 4, 5).

Some of the dilemmas surrounding English identity were well expressed by the musician and political activist Billy Bragg:

> I am an Englishman ... I was born in Essex; my father was born in Essex ... and so on, for 10 generations. But my mother's father was born in Italy, and my wife's father was born in Spain. I sing Woody Guthrie songs and 'The Internationale.' So what does it mean when I say, 'I am an Englishman.' (Bragg, in Himes, 2002).

Bragg was referring to some of the issues raised by his album *England, Half-English*, (2002), which itself explicitly references a collection of essays by Colin MacInnes. Many of Bragg's lyrics exemplify the multicultural issues in a society that now counts chicken tikka masala as its national dish, American hip-hop culture as its linguistic and style referent, and the French and Spanish coastal domicile as its eventual aspiration.

Concepts of Englishness in popular music are always problematic. An American reviewer begins his analysis of a Faces album with the declaration that the act are 'one of the few English bands left willing (nay, all too happy) to flaunt their Englishness' (Mendelssohn, 1971). Whereas their appearance, lifestyle and some aspects of their lyrics certainly do tap into cores of English mythology, it would take an experienced musicologist to extricate much Englishness from either their vocal or playing styles. The Faces stand as yet another example of the paradoxical 'coals to Newcastle' syndrome established by the likes of the Beatles and the Rolling Stones in the early 1960s – an English/Scottish act selling aspects of idiomatic American music back to its originators. This reversal went as far as to encourage Americans to discover their own musical heritage – particularly regarding the blues – after the reworkings of foreign musicians had brought such idiomatic genres to wider attention. Bragg's early musical career saw him playing in a band called the Flying Tigers, covering songs by the Faces and Jackson Browne, whilst also performing 'self-written distillations of the transatlantic rock'n'roll dream with such titles as "Little Miss Julie" and "The Rain Came Down on Main Street". (Bragg stated) "It all seemed to be about living in America ... wearing a cheese-cloth shirt in an open-topped car"' (Bragg, in Harris, 2006: 60). Later, after being galvanised by seeing the Clash (performing an anglicised take on the largely American generic form – punk), Bragg renamed his band Riff Raff, whose repertoire drew upon a more home-based set of mythologies, with titles such as 'Romford Girls' and 'Comprehensive'.

It is interesting to note that questions of English identity are often tinged with defensiveness – even the use of the term is deeply problematic for some; much of the agonising doubtless stems from a sense of national guilt imbued by the dark shadows thrown by imperialism. One of the few positive legacies of the dismantling of the imperial yoke has been the positivity with which the so-called 'Celtic nations' have reappropriated their musical traditions in recent times, following the dismantling of the physical and hegemonic 'empire'. Unfortunately, unlike in, say, Ireland or Jamaica, an ethnic English musical tradition as in 'folk' has, for the most part, existed in the exotic, often derided periphery of mainstream popular music. English folk traditions are more a source of embarrassment, rather than a source of pride or ethnic affirmation for the great majority of the English. Within more 'mainstream pop' there is, of course, a long lineage of mythically English bands and performers, to name some salient examples: the Kinks, Ian Dury, the Jam, many of Britpop's acts and near-contemporary acts such as the Libertines, Kaiser Chiefs, Arctic Monkeys and Babyshambles, whose 2005 album was fittingly entitled *Down in Albion*. To an extent, however, all these quintessentially English acts do achieve success and notoriety for 'going against the grain' – literally – within hegemonic globalised pop styles.

The success of British, and in particular English musicians in aping, popularising or transforming North American idiomatic styles has resulted in a situation where it is the norm to sing in an American accent (anyone from Cliff Richard and Dusty Springfield through Rod Stewart and Elton John to Robbie Williams and Rachel Stevens in the present day), or to operate within an American genre (from jazz, blues and country through r'n'b and soul to urban and hip-hop today). This phenomenon is echoed in many other aspects of culture. It is significant, and to my mind annoying, that English writers have to 'ask' their computers to spell in Standard English, rather than its American-English derivative: the 'default setting' – within language, as in accent – is determined by the economic and cultural forces of hegemony.

It is a sad indictment of the marginalised nature of English identity in popular music that certain artists are actually lauded for doing nothing more than embodying their own ethnic roots and traditions. Thus Kaiser Chief's 'I Predict a Riot' gains critical currency for its use of everyday, idiomatic and regional expressions such as 'lairy' and 'I tell thee'. These traditions are often 'mythical constructs' that essentialise or stereotype Englishness, but should not be condemned as a result. Roland Barthes's groundbreaking work on myth (1972), which he regards as a culture's attempts to disguise historical and ideological processes behind a mask of what is 'given' or 'natural', encourages us to not simply condemn the process, but rather to reflect upon it as a signifying, deconstructive practice. Mythical constructions of Englishness do have resonance, and can become self-fulfilling in a positive as well as a negative fashion.

Within the partial global hegemony of North American pop and culture, myths of England actually function as much-needed counter-hegemonies. However, critical shortcomings can result. Michael Bracewell's wide-ranging account of what he subtitles 'Pop Life in Albion from Wilde to Goldie' encapsulates the problems faced by the mythologising project when he refers to 'that tic in England's hymning of itself that believes the past to be a somehow better place, with its Englishness less diluted by progress' (Bracewell, 1997: 7). Within this scenario, the wider connotations of 'hymning' – myth making – do little more than serve the needs of a neo-conservative cabal. Kate Bush has herself suffered myriad examples of journalistic mythologising. In relation to this section, Stephen Troussé's reportage of her 'in the role of Grand Recluse – the mad woman in the attic of British pop, a last spectral link to that Old Weird England' (Troussé, 2005: 98) neatly summarises this widely adopted critical conceit.

In addition, the overt anti-Americanism that resulted as part of the myth-making process (see Colls, 2002: 189–90) was at its best chauvinistic, and at its worst blatantly racist. Bearing in mind these shortcomings, myths of Englishness within popular music have to be rescued from narrow self-interests and placed in a wider context of shifting and fluid ethnicities. English ethnicity may be a construct; it may be more of a construct than other national ethnicities, for complex reasons, but it is a much overlooked area of study within popular music. Kate Bush is one of the most resonant exemplars of Englishness in popular music, but we must break down this statement into its constitutive factors.

Genealogy

Fred Vermorel's 1983 exploration into both the art and genealogy of Kate Bush is a quixotic, often annoying, sometimes illuminating account of 'the fragile chances and distillation which produced her' (Vermorel, 1983: 12). His exhaustive delving into the Bush family ancestral vaults, whilst often fanciful and florid, does provide us with useful historical data relating to geography and class in particular.

The paternal Bush line can be traced back a long way, especially considering the family's humble roots in agrarian Essex, to John Bush, born 1769 (ibid.: 18). The family line continues through his descendents and the associated evidence of poverty, disease and premature death familiar to all in their class until the Bushes move, in both physical and class terms, when Kate's father, after winning a scholarship to a grammar school and graduating as a doctor in 1943, marries Hannah Daly, a staff nurse and Irish daughter of a farmer. The couple settle in the comfortable suburbia of Bexley, in Kent and move into the 350-year-old East Wickham farmhouse that becomes the family home for them and their three children (ibid.: 52).

Despite Vermorel's attempts to at least partially account for the artist's subsequent career through the significance of genealogy, his mythologising attempts remain incomplete and partial. Almost all the research explores (and much of the time unnecessarily) the paternal line, and at the absent expense of the maternal line. This is a major oversight, not least for considerations of ethnicity and other more specific dimensions that result. Whilst the paternal Bush ancestors are evidenced to be Protestant, and non-conformist (Wesleyan Chapel), the maternal ancestors are, we assume, Catholic. Indeed, the young Catherine Bush was educated at St Joseph's Convent Grammar School and refers to its importance: 'school was obviously quite religious ... A lot of Catholicism is still in me, deeper than I can see' (Bush, in Vermorel, 1983: 85). For more insight into her genealogy and the impact of her Anglo-Irish identity upon her life, work and sense of ethnicity, we have to look to other sources.

Jovanovic's account of the Bush family primarily focusses upon the years since the birth of Kate Bush in 1958, although we do learn that both her parents have differing musical talents. Mother Hannah was the winner of several folk dance competitions in Ireland, and father Robert reportedly sold the publishing rights to one of his compositions in order to purchase an engagement ring (Jovanovic, 2005: 12). However, this author's account of the artist's relationship to Catholicism differs slightly from Vermorel. He quotes Kate Bush as claiming a more ambivalent connection to her faith: 'It never touched my heart ... I would never say I was a strict follower of Roman Catholic belief, but a lot of the images are in there; they have to be, they're so strong. Such powerful, beautiful, passionate images!' (Bush, in Jovanovic, 2005: 13). This essentially emotive, symbolic dimension is echoed in her sense of ethnicity:

> I feel that strongly, being torn between the Irish and the English blood in me … my mother was always playing Irish music … when you are really young, things get in and get deeper because you haven't got as many walls up … It's really heavy, emotionally. The pipes really tear it out of your heart. (ibid.: 13–14).

This Irish/folk dimension is also doubtless inculcated from the passions of her brothers, particularly Paddy, who stated 'our uncles played on accordions and fiddles and stuff … we were always hearing Irish dance music … I happened to go to school, here in England, with a guy called Kevin Burke, who's considered the best fiddler in Ireland!' (Bush, P., in Swales, 1985). Paddy Bush subsequently devoted much of his life to a wide variety of traditional music, becoming a musical instrument technologist specialising in mediaeval devices.

These accounts all add up to a coherent construction of ethnicity based upon a hybrid English/Irish genealogy, both of which are linked through a love of folk sounds, styles and instruments in particular. Kate Bush has gone on record as extolling the Irish take on music as a joyful and vital aspect of everyday life. This is then brought into contact with English reserve: 'It's hard for us to learn to enjoy ourselves' (Bush, in Reynolds, 1993). All these root influences are then complemented by the artist's own choices of sounds and styles as she begins to actively construct her own sense of ethnicity.

Creative Influences

Kate Bush's referenced musical influences stand as quite consistent with the ethnic picture being painted, although still highly informative in what they tell us about the creative process. By far the most insightful account of the artist's influences comes within Peter Swales's interview that took place just after the recording of *Hounds of Love* was completed. The notoriously guarded Ms Bush seems very eloquent within this interview, aided perhaps by both the presence of trusted ally Paddy, and also the 'musicianly' nature of the questions, which steer clear of the more biographical journalistic probing that the artist finds uncomfortable. When questioned on the relationship of her music to American sources, the artist replies:

> I think probably most of the stuff I've liked, though, has actually been English, and possibly that's why my roots aren't American. Whereas perhaps with the majority of other people … most of their heroes would have been American. (Bush, in Swales, 1985).

This is actually understating the extent and breadth of the American influence upon both British pop musicians and audiences. Not only is the ethnically American influence huge, but in addition many British musicians in genres as diverse as soul, blues, jazz, rap and disco are measured by their ability to adequately 'ape' American idioms.

The artist proceeds to list her musical and vocal influences, the list includes: David Bowie, Bryan Ferry and Roxy Music (also Brian Eno's groundbreaking sampling techniques), Elton John, Billie Holiday, more generally folk (especially Irish) and classical music and, rather surprisingly, Captain Beefheart, Frank Zappa, Steely Dan and Rolf Harris (Jovanovic, 2005: 124). Possibly the brave experimentation and left-field feel of such artists are the points of inspiration here – very little direct connection can be made between such music and Kate Bush's own work. It should be noted that Zappa and Beefheart, whilst both American, are influenced as much by the European modernism of Stravinski and Varèse as by indigenous models. The Bowie link is further deepened as both Bowie and Bush studied mime and dance under Lindsay Kemp at different periods. Indeed, Kate Bush may have danced to David Bowie tracks during her classes, as Kemp used them in this context (Buckley, 2000: 51). She was also to attend Bowie's final performance as Ziggy Stardust, on 3 July 1973, Doyle quoting her as she recollects her adolescent self crying with emotion, a few feet from the stage (Doyle, 2005: 84), and his use of different personae featuring costume changes may have influenced her own subsequent stage performances. Despite the transatlantic inflections of Elton John (and the artist seems to value his playing and songs specifically, rather than his voice), Bowie and Ferry are two of the classic exemplars of what is possible when making the active (self-conscious) choice to sing popular music vocals in an English accent, or variations on such. Ferry, in particular, is offered as being deeply influential: 'I thought he was the most exciting singer that I'd heard. His voice had limitations, but what he managed to do with it was beautiful, I mean, b-e-a-u-t-i-f-u-l. For me it covered the whole emotional spectrum' (ibid.). Her choice of Ferry as possessing a voice to be loved is highly unusual when we consider his mannered use of singing styles.

On the Roxy Music debut album (1972) Ferry can sound cod-American ('If There is Something'), but he can also sound very English ('2HB'). On 'Bitters End' this is pushed to the point of parody when the singer seems to pastiche the clipped, exaggeratingly English tones of Noël Coward. On other albums, Ferry develops a European 'croon', as on the aptly named 'A Song For Europe' (1973), which climaxes with echoes of Charles Aznavour and Edith Piaf in his cry 'jamais, jamais, jamais, jamais'. Much later Bush was to fall in love with the Slavic harmonies of the Trio Bulgarka, who, even more than Bowie and Ferry, are operating far from the hegemonic terrain of transatlantic American vocal styling. Amongst the few artists whose work Kate Bush has contributed to, special mention should be made of Peter Gabriel and Roy Harper. Although Gabriel's work did move into a transatlantic generic style during the mid-1980s, for the most part his music and vocal style are very English in terms of accent and subject matter. Roy Harper is even more maverick in his explicit Englishness, and Kate Bush, an admirer, contributed vocals to several Harper albums. He returned the favour by singing on 'Breathing'. As a final comment on influences, it should be noted that the artist has referenced the overwhelmingly male nature of her creative influences (see Jovanovic, 2005: 24–6). Kate Bush has spent much of her career as often the only woman in a male world of musicians, engineers and creative collaborators, but by 1985 she was the titular and artistic 'queen' of this domain. I will return to this phenomenon below.

Less explicitly referenced, but also important to considerations of Bush's ethnicity, are the classical composers that have come to be associated with the construction of an overtly English, pastoral tradition: Elgar, Delius, Butterworth, Grainger and Vaughan Williams. I do not have the space within this book to adequately explore this whole separate ethno-musicological terrain, but certain dimensions of the English pastoral have both timbral and ideological resonance within the Kate Bush *oeuvre*, particularly as her career progresses.

The English pastoral project, allied to the development of other areas such as William Morris's Arts and Crafts Movement and the English Folk Dance & Song Society, comes into being as, to an extent, a reaction to changing social conditions and the rise of political and cultural rivals such as the United States and Germany in the decades preceding World War I. Composers in other European countries, such as Debussy and Bartók, were undertaking similar experiments based on diverse ethnic influences. In 1934, Vaughan Williams published the text *National Music and Other Essays*, in which he stated: 'what is the classical style? It is nothing more than the Teutonic style. It so happened that for nearly a hundred years, in the eighteenth and early nineteenth centuries, the great composers ... were all German or Austrian' (Vaughan Williams, in Brocken, 2003a: 6).

The English challenge to this baroque and classical world of Bach, Mozart, Haydn and Beethoven, with its tendencies towards an almost mathematical structure and the clear resolution and recapitulation of themes, came through pieces that connoted a less grounded, diffused, more 'impressionistic' terrain often expressed through 'washes' of sound. In sonic terms, despite a wide variety of imbued moods, the broad adoption of strings and wind as dominant elements over brass sections is a unifying characteristic in the pastoral tradition. Such softer, or more diffused timbres are echoed in Kate Bush's use of string synths, drone samples of cello-like sounds resting on a keynote, or the Celtic pipes of *The Ninth Wave*.

It is no accident that landscape and seascape are frequently employed as inspirations or accompanying texts. George Butterworth's adaptations of A.E. Housman's bucolic narrative poem cycle *A Shropshire Lad* (1911, 1912) conjure up many mythically English settings which diverge from the pomp and stridency associated with the Teutonic tradition. One particular vocal cadence on 'The Lads in Their Hundreds' is almost precisely echoed within the triple-time ascending melody on the later album *Aerial*'s 'Bertie' – accident, coincidence or homage? Equally, both in mood and naming, the undulating restlessness of Elgar's 'Where Corals Lie' from *Sea Pictures* (1899) finds echoes in both Kate Bush's song cycles *The Ninth Wave* and *A Sky of Honey*, as well as the track 'A Coral Room'. The importance of topography and the symbolism of dreams are both shared by Elgar and Bush. Vaughan Williams's *The Lark Ascending* (1914) has its title referenced within the lyric of *Aerial*'s 'Prologue'. The fragment 'Delius: Song of Summer' on *Never for Ever* is another example of a concrete, if nebulous connection to the traditions of the English pastoral.

Stephen Banfield, when situating the work of Arnold Bax, claims that both the history of Irish political struggle and the Irish landscape had a huge impact upon his pastoral works (Banfield, 1995: 186). This mixed Anglo-Irish inspirational lineage is made manifest throughout Kate Bush's career, but registers particularly strongly on *Hounds of Love*. Equally, the figure of the wanderer, or 'spiritual pilgrim' (ibid.: 187–8), which Banfield associates with Vaughan Williams and Elgar, can be equally applied to the narrator of *The Ninth Wave*, or later the principal narrative voice in *A Sky of Honey*.

Because of the lack of corroborative biographical evidence, we must be careful not to make the connections too concrete. When Swales tries to establish the artist's literary influences he refers to her as 'a sort of Doris Lessing of rock', to which Kate Bush replies: 'I'm sorry, Doris who?' (Swales; Bush, 1985). My point here is not to criticise the artist's lack of knowledge, but to make the point that, for the most part, both musically and creatively, Kate Bush is an autodidact, often fashioning (wonderful) material from anecdotal, impressionistic or fragmental knowledge – 'Wuthering Heights' being a classic example. But in this diffuse process, heavily influenced by Irish inflections of blood, music and terrain (many of *Hounds of Love*'s lyrics were written staring out on an Irish 'big sky'), the artist manages to construct a musical terrain that is strikingly British, and more specifically southern English. The relationship of Kate Bush's music to American pop does carry notable echoes of Elgar and others' challenge to the Teutonic tradition, as both are essentially counter-hegemonic.

I have already touched upon the artist's extra-musical influences, and will return to this subject when studying later albums. At this juncture it is worth reiterating that literary influences include Brontë and, particularly relevant for *Hounds*, Tennyson – a classically English late-Romantic poet. Amongst the many films and directors to influence the artist, the figure of Michael Powell looms largest. This influence will be explored during the research into *The Red Shoes*, but at this point it should be noted that Powell's work is seen, for the most part, as inhabiting an archetypically English terrain. Ethnically English genres such as gothic 'Hammer Horror' and militaristic 'heist' narratives (*The League of Gentlemen*) are also directly referenced in the artist's *oeuvre*.

Kate Bush has been drawn to particularly English forms of comedy, specifically the surreal, postmodern parodies produced by the collective 'The Comic Strip'. This group of writers and performers (including Rowan Atkinson, Ade Edmondson, Dawn French, Rik Mayall, Peter Richardson, Jennifer Saunders and Alexei Sayle) can be viewed as carrying the torch of 'Pythonesque' comedy forward into the 1980s. Not only do songs such as 'Coffee Homeground' inhabit a similarly parodic terrain, but also Kate Bush was to contribute the song 'Ken' to The Comic Strip's TV docu-comedy *GLC* in 1990. In addition, one of the artist's very rare later stage performances came within a charity performance featuring many of those already mentioned. Peter Richardson was to appear in the film *The Line, The Cross and The Curve* (costumes designed by Hazel Pethig, from the Monty Python team) in 1993 (as well as co-directing the video for 'The Sensual World' track), and comic Lenny Henry contributed backing vocals to *The Red Shoes* album.

What all these extra-musical influences and collaborations do is to further emphasise the fundamentally English world that the artist inhabits. In this global era of North American hegemony it can be considered as nothing short of deliberate, and possibly even blatantly ideological in its re-presentations of ethnicity.

Accent and 'The Grain of the Voice'

Almost every English singer in popular music sounds, if not actually North American, then at least 'transatlantic'. The reasons for this are varied: they are something to do with hegemony; something to do with style and genre indicators; something to do with mythologies of 'coolness', and something to do with linguistic factors such as poetics, metre and accent. All of these factors impact upon what Barthes refers to as 'grain' (Barthes, 1977: 179–89). In his short but wide-ranging essay 'The Grain of the Voice', the theorist tries to justify his comparative like and dislike for two operatic voices, and to deal with 'the impossible account of an individual thrill that I constantly experience in listening to singing' (ibid.: 181).

To simplify his sometimes convoluted theories, Barthes draws upon the work of the theorists Jacques Lacan and Julia Kristeva in constructing a pair of binary oppositions – the first pair to describe two singing voices, and the second to describe the individual affective response. Barthes uses *pheno-song* and *geno-song* to differentiate the voices. The former term refers to those aspects that allow us to comprehend through clear expression and representation (similar to another term familiar to semioticians – *langue*). The latter term refers to the materiality of the voice, 'not at what it says, but the voluptuousness of its sounds-signifiers' (ibid.: 182). This is similar to the concept of *parole*. *Pheno-song* and *geno-song* each carry clear echoes of two associated terms – *plaisir* and *jouissance*. *Plaisir* can be termed a rational, detached, unemotional response to stimuli, as opposed to *jouissance*, a term with no precise translation that connotes feelings such as ecstasy, loss and chaos, even orgasm.

We must be careful not to stretch Barthes's theories too far – the binary aesthetics of post-structuralist critical theory can be too reductive and quasi-scientific for wide application in popular music. But certainly, some critical dimensions relating to grain are of great use in analysing both singing voices and their wider relationship to concepts of ethnicity and national identity.

The principal counter-argument to Barthes's theories is the postulation that all individual voices have grain – materiality, physicality and, to a varying extent, individuality. No singing voice is ever just about *plaisir* or *pheno-song*, regardless of our individual likes or dislikes. What we are in fact dealing with is the degree of grain, rather than the binary opposition of presence or absence. However, there is some intrinsic link between the degree of grain and the affective response imbued in that voice. In the case of popular music we can extend Barthes's theories to include the importance of accent upon *jouissance*. It can be argued that an overtly English, particularly southern English accent is very unusual within the entire body of popular music, and as such assumes a greater degree of individuality and uniqueness. This accounted for much of the exaggerated criticism of her voice when she first emerged, with a reviewer in *Melody Maker* 'offering that she sounded like "a cross between Linda Lewis and Macbeth's three witches"' (Jovanovic, 2005: 73). When we hear Kate Bush pronounce the long vowel sounds in words such as 'dance', or the r-less pronunciation of 'far', or the unflapped t-sounds in 'water' we are experiencing both a hegemonic challenge to the norm and also a personal and ethnically related physicality to sounds. There is thus a degree of both *plaisir* and *jouissance* present in this critical reading, but a greater degree than that made possible in a more standardised, transatlantic delivery. In addition, the artist's wide and varied adoption of non-literary sounds, which go far beyond the standard 'do-dos' and 'la-las' of popular music, does encourage a response that focusses upon grain rather than explicit meaning.

We can substantiate this conclusion by focussing on physical, linguistic distinctions between Standard and American English. Many in this field (see Bryson, 1990; Elmes, 2001 and Freeborn, 1998) have researched some of the crucial differences, such as the American 'flapped' t (as in 'budder', for the southern English 'butter') and the greater degree of 'enjoinment' or 'slurring' between American syllables, as opposed to the more clipped and divided English style. Another distinction, less noted, is that Americans open their mouths wider. This empirical observation is corroborated when we observe original American adverts that have been dubbed by English voices. We notice the disparity not because the lip-synching is bad, but because the American mouths are opening too wide for the linguistically 'alien' sounds appearing to emanate from within.

What all these linguistic distinctions suggest is that it is actually easier, or perhaps even more 'natural' (a dangerous term!), to sing global pop in a modified, or American style. Not only does American diction and metre give a smoother, more melismatic flow, but also the wider mouthings add scope for a greater degree of physical, oral dexterity. It is surely no accident that many lead vocalists possess very large or wide mouths – Kate Bush being one clear example. We might conclude with the final observation that pronouncing t-sounds in the unflapped mode requires more care and more breath than its transatlantic variant; and breath is the vocalist's 'finite energy resource'. Yet again, as the result of a variety of factors, to sing global pop in southern English is to disorientate the listener, to remove their aesthetic experience from the 'default setting' that hegemonic forces establish as mythologies. But of course, to counter the rigid distinctions of Barthes, we are experiencing (or, more fittingly, 're-presenting') the *jouissance* of southern English grain and materiality through the *plaisir* of detached rationality. We need the structure of language in order to critically engage with concepts of this mythical pre-linguistic state.

It is a cliché that certain singers use their voices like a musical instrument – all do; but again, the real issue is the extent and ambition involved in this process. By the time of *Hounds of Love*, the artist's voice had matured, gaining physical thickness (actual, not just symbolic grain) in the process. Her adoption of a deeper, 'choral' voice for harmony sections, often abetted by technological pitch shifting, allowed for a huge tonal range to be employed, with clear aesthetic implications the result. In addition, unlike on earlier albums such as *Lionheart*, the battery of vocal devices – squeals, growls and whispers – was being employed more sparingly, but more effectively as a result. At various points the artist has drawn upon foreign tongues – another clear victory for *jouissance* over *plaisir* if this device denies the reader narrative comprehension. On *Hounds* the use of German is a very effective demonstration of *geno-song*, as is the employment of backward-taped words at the end of 'Hello Earth'.

The issue of grain and gender must also be considered. Jeremy Gilbert and Ewan Pearson (1999) note that many appropriations of Barthes's theories relating to grain seem to intrinsically connect the concept to 'gravelly' voices. Within this paradigm:

> the 'dirty', untrained sounding voice has come to signify sincerity, authenticity, truthful *meaning* of a kind which a trained singer (supposedly) might not be able to produce … *in the service* of a phonological ideal of the voice as the site of unmediated truth … It is important to note here that the 'grainy' rock voice is almost always *male* (Gilbert and Pearson, 1999: 68, 69; authors' italics).

These authors are attempting to problematise a partial adoption of the term grain as symbolic of maleness and 'rockist values'. As they rightly say, grain is an important aspect of timbre, and is central to instrumental dance music, as much as it is to vocal rock. My own take on grain is to dismantle its role as guarantor of gender-based and timbre-based authenticity. A 'pure' or trained female voice is as capable of conveying grain as any other in its more holistic application. Furthermore, Kate Bush's voice has the flexibility to sometimes growl and have 'grit', whereas the voices with inherent 'dirt' often do not have the ability to be 'pure'.

The folk musicologist A.L. (Bert) Lloyd makes an important critical intervention into vocal styles when he divides Europe into two main geographical and singing traditions. In brief he sets up an opposition between centre and fringe that is echoed in what he terms the 'plain syllabic tradition' and the 'elaborative tradition' (Lloyd, 1971). For Lloyd the plain syllabic tradition dominated in areas such as Germany, northern France, the Netherlands and southern Britain; for the most part these countries have strong links with either the Reformation or an organised nation state, which results in a vocal style that is orderly, structured and has precise pitching and clear intervals. At its most pronounced this results in the 'one note per syllable' approach of some English folk, pastoral orchestral music and many nursery rhymes. This can be contrasted with the elaborative traditions of areas on the geographical fringes of Europe: 'Celtic' Britain, the Balkans, Spain and so on. In these areas drone notes rather than chord progressions can dominate, along with vocal styles that meander melismatically and chromatically (even microtonally) in stretching one syllable over several notes. This can be heard demonstrated in the work of the Trio Bulgarka. Indeed, some might argue that some of this tradition filters via emigration and slavery into the construction of the gospel, blues and soul tradition of North America (and thence into the vocal inflections of a young English singer such as Joss Stone, herself heavily influenced by African-American styles).

As with all binary oppositions we must be wary to temper the rigidity that the process can imply. Most singers employ elements of both these traditions, but the degree varies. In the case of Kate Bush, it is fair to judge her vocal work to fall, in the main, within the plain syllabic tradition – phrasing is precise, sounds and tones are rendered in a clipped and accurate fashion, and there is relatively little recourse to excessive melisma or 'blue' notes that are found in African-American or modal folk to a greater extent than within typically English pop. In fittingly, mythologically English fashion, melisma and slurring of notes is used sparingly, for effect, in much the same way that strong outbursts of emotion are broadly 'contained' within the

English psyche. It is interesting to note that one of her most prominent uses of melisma comes within a rare cover version, in this case the Irish traditional tune 'My Lagan Love', which was included as a bonus track as part of the remastered *Hounds of Love* album. On the original album elaborative melisma assumes greater significance as a direct result of its sparse and infrequent incorporation. On 'And Dream of Sheep' the line 'My face is all lit up' is repeated, the first time in plain syllabic mode and the second time the melody arches up and then down into a brief melismatic cadence that adds both emphasis to the lyric and dynamism to the melody. Were the device to be employed more regularly it would not have the same impact – mythological English restraint and economy remains the watchword.

All of these aspects contribute to the degree of uniqueness and individual grain of Kate Bush's voice. Her independence and relative 'isolation' from the wider pop world may well have helped her maintain or even strengthen this important dimension in both her career and her physical expression of Englishness. Particularly in the period around *Hounds* her vocal style was assuredly, rather than exaggeratingly southern English. Some earlier tracks such as 'Oh England, My Lionheart' do overemphasise the diction to the point of parody. This does perhaps reinforce the lyrical message, but still comes across as contrived. On the other hand, certain tracks on the albums after *Hounds* do see a noticeably transatlantic inflection emerge. In common with some ill-advised attempts to 'get on down' in a funk mood ('Constellation of the Heart', for example) these vocal modifications do not ring true. Perhaps more tellingly, even within material as un-American as 'Bertie' on *Aerial*, the vocals in the verses demonstrate a rootless, geographically vague phrasing that can be found throughout mainstream pop, regardless of ethnicity. The reasons for these accentual shifts can only be guessed at, but the reality of the resulting compromised timbres cannot be read as anything but a 'retreat'.

Language and Register

In common with the hegemonies of accent, the idiomatic use of language in popular music discourse is hugely indebted to North American models. This factor is as much influenced by the demands of a market-led structural model built around standardised three-minute pop songs as it is around American hegemony, but this aspect will be explored below.

In her book that seeks to function as some kind of composer's guide to lyric composition, Pamela Phillips-Oland (2001) sets up certain 'rules of thumb' that must commonly be adhered to in order to write a commercial song lyric. These include advice to always make the title prominent in the lyric, to always include hooks or refrains, not to twist word order out of the 'conversational', not to use archaic phrases and not to be too personal (Phillips-Oland, 2001: 3–4). The overall intention seems to be to set up a sharp delineation between the lyric and the poem. The important issue is not that many of the rules are prescriptive, contradictory and frequently broken – even within the standardised field that the author inhabits – but rather that many of them either implicitly or explicitly express North American values or idioms as the generic norm for the popular song form.

Kate Bush's lyrics do, as a body of work, often inhabit a relatively standardised terrain, in structural terms. However, never has any British artist more stridently placed issues of poetic and ethnic register before a pop audience than within the first few stanzas of Bush's debut single, 'Wuthering Heights'. Not only is the word 'wiley' archaic, but also the following phrase 'we'd roll and fall in green' is so redolent of the English poetic and pastoral tradition that its challenge to dominant values cannot fail to be explicit.

In a more conventional manner, as well as broadly fulfilling Phillips-Oland's criterion that no more than two sections in a row should have the same structure, most of her songs do concur with the 'rules of thumb' outlined above. The first two albums, in particular, consist largely of three-minute songs conventionally structured around verses, choruses and b-sections. The lyrics, although unusually explicit, (particularly in terms of what 'the market' expected from a young woman), did also deal with many standard pop tropes such as romance, love, desire and feelings. However, as her career developed, her song structures, production processes and her lyrical concerns broadened out beyond the stereotypes moulded, to an extent, by the commercial pop industry dominated by 'tin pan alley' and North American models. Examples would include the complete eschewing of chord progressions and the extensive use of drone notes on 'The Dreaming', or the lyric-less choral modality of 'Night Scented Stock'.

With *Hounds of Love* Kate Bush moved beyond the accepted pop album structure – separate songs – into what can best be described as song suites. Particularly in the case of *The Ninth Wave* the models for this process come from outside the pop world, as will be referenced in the section on influences below. With regard to both language and lyrical structures, by this point in her career Kate Bush as a lyricist is skilfully combining 'low' and 'high' registers in a way that stretches and challenges the conventions of pop, yet without dispensing with them. The very opening track demonstrates this process. In the second verse of 'Running up that Hill (A Deal With God)' the lyric runs thus:

> You don't want to hurt me
> But see how deep the bullet lies
> Unaware I'm tearing you asunder
> Ooh there is thunder in our hearts

The first line is standard pop in every respect, and has doubtless been employed in many songs. The second line is more unusual, but her use of a powerful, emotive metaphor, whilst more 'poetic', is still a well-employed device within pop. However, to reflect back upon one of Phillips-Oland's rules, the word order is changed from the more everyday and prosaic 'the bullet is lying deep'. The third line employs a term – 'asunder' – which whilst not archaic, is not a feature of conversational, contemporary English. The fourth line is standard pop discourse and is almost a cliché (As I write this section a record entitled 'Thunder in My Heart' is number 1 in the UK singles chart). Lyrics assume coherence from both their selection and combination, and it is true that this fragment is being taken out of context of both the song and the whole album. Nevertheless, this example (picked, to an extent, 'at random') does demonstrate the distinctiveness of Kate Bush's very English approach to lyrical construction. Two of the lines have a noticeably colloquial 'global' register, but they are juxtaposed with two other lines that do not. We must also be aware that one of the reasons for using the word 'asunder' may be to offer the rhyme for 'thunder' in the middle of the next line. Again, rhymes coming within the couplet rather than at its end are unusual by pop standards, but far from unknown. What is more unusual is that none of the line endings rhyme. This is less important for verses than for choruses, but the chorus within this song is similarly unconventional, with the line endings being 'road', 'hill', 'building' and 'oh'.

Examples of this clash of rules, conventions and registers abound in the work of the artist. Within 'Waking the Witch' we have the archaic phrase 'What say you, good people?' I have previously commented on the thrilling friction engendered by the line 'Let me grab your soul away' on 'Wuthering Heights'. Part of the power of this line comes from the insertion of the everyday term 'grab' into a narrative that in other respects demands the term 'steal'. On 'Running up that Hill' the b-pattern includes the idiomatically American line 'C'mon baby, c'mon darlin'' (printed with apostrophes and deliberate 'slang spelling') before the couplet is completed with 'Let me steal this moment from you now'. As with the previous example, the choice of 'steal', 'expected' in 'Wuthering Heights', comes as a surprise here and gains gravity as a consequence. Examples of slang, American-English terms or spellings are unusual in Kate Bush's lyrical world, but their occasional insertion gives them added power, as well as encouraging the focussing upon ethnicity that her lyrics make manifest.

Within *The Ninth Wave* the lyrics function as part of an unfolding narrative. This allows the writer even more licence to challenge the conventions of the popular song. The lyric shifts in time, tense and space, between dreams, consciousness and unconsciousness, out of body experiences, omniscient narratives, dialogues and internal soliloquies. On occasions logic and linear structure are dispensed with, or possibly just 'misplaced'. But the sheer extent of the ambition wins through. As with the song suite *A Sky of Honey*, within such structures *The Ninth Wave* inhabits a terrain far removed from that normally adopted by Anglo-American popular music.

Of course 'eccentricity' or 'experimentation' should not be taken as automatic guarantors of worth or value. And it is true that aspects such as regular scansion and standardised metre in song lyrics are even more important than in a less 'fettered' literary form such as poetry as a result of being physically performed and commercially mediated. Phil Collins assumed the role of lead vocalist in Genesis after Peter Gabriel left. When talking about the importance of lyrics, he made these interesting, although slightly contradictory observations:

> I've always been a firm believer in the sound of the word, rather than what that word means … It's very hard to sing someone else's words. We were listening to some of our old live tapes, and 'bread bin' was in one of the lyrics; now, how do you sing, 'bread bin?' Or how do you sing 'undinal', which is in 'Firth of Fifth'? (Collins, in Fielder, 1984: 125).

We do not have privy to the workings of the lyricist's mind behind those two highlighted lyrical snatches. But what we can state is that both 'bread bin' and 'undinal', as with many of Kate Bush's lyrical devices, transgress the pop norm, each in a different fashion. In addition, as with all lyrics they serve simultaneously as signifiers and signifieds – as the sound in itself, and what it symbolises as a unit of meaning. As well as being transgressive in normative terms, they are also symbolic of two styles of 'un-pop' English – the one form low culture and idiomatic, and the other elevated and literary. Whether such lyrical examples work is for the individual to judge within the context of both the song and the setting, but what has to be challenged is any preconceived notion that certain words or styles should be somehow proscribed. Kate Bush's lyrics provide us with countless examples of similarly idiosyncratic language that, as with her use of accent, root her within a particularly English tradition. This tradition will always assume oppositional or counter-hegemonic status in the global marketplace for popular music.

Style Indicators

Certain genres or styles come to stand as symbolic of a particular race or ethnicity through pop's internal mythologising process. To an extent, this is part of the authenticity paradigm that functioned as the bedrock upon which much pop criticism and analysis of the past 40 years has operated. As previously argued, the important aspect of mythology does not lie within its essentialising imperative, but in its resonance as a self-conscious critical device that enables us to focus upon stereotypes, assumptions and self-fulfilling prophesies.

In terms of Kate Bush's music, there are certain style indicators that all contribute to the construction of English mythologies relating to genre, 'feel' and imbued affect.

The first point to make is that the vast majority of the artist's musical collaborators are from the British Isles. This is particularly true of *Hounds of Love*. With the exception of American Michael Kamen, the orchestral arranger, Australian guitarist John Williams (guitar, on one track) and Eberhard Weber (bass, on two tracks), the musicians are, in the main, English or Irish. This, of course, reflects upon the artist's own genealogy. It can only be critical conjecture – and may be an example of my own mythologising – but this broadly British group of musicians do partly account for the unified and focussed feel present throughout the album. Later in her career the artist was to draw upon Slavic influences in the guise of the Trio Bulgarka. As shall be referenced below, this contribution from a very different vocal tradition did often add to the timbral palette in an effective manner. However, it could also detract from the unity of the albums, and imbalance the overall feel of the works. In addition, the incorporation of 'guest artistes' such as Prince cannot be counted an unalloyed triumph, because it compromised the authorial and ethnic integrity of Kate Bush, on occasions rendering her the guest artiste within somebody else's track.

On *Hounds of Love* the strongest non-English flavour comes from the Irish players Donal Lunny, Liam O'Flynn and John Sheahan, along with the arranger Bill Whelan. Kate Bush had 'experimented' with Irish traditional elements on the previous album's 'Night of the Swallow', but on *The Ninth Wave*, ethnic instruments such as whistles, fiddles, uilleann pipes and the 'honorary' Greek/Irish bouzouki fundamentally augment the sound palette on 'And Dream of Sheep', 'Jig of Life' and 'Hello Earth'. The acoustic textures do make important narrative connections with the suite's exploration of weather, elements and space. In particular the chromatic and microtonal slides on pipes and whistles do echo the undulating, unstable environment of sea and wave, and do much to add to the often eerie, 'rootless' mood imbued by the tracks. One of the triumphs of the album is its contrasting use of old and new musical timbres, which is typically symbolised by Irish traditions rubbing up against global technologies in the main utilised by English musicians. The importance of orchestral flavours, particularly violins and cellos, should also be noted.

In terms of genre, positioning *Hounds of Love* is problematic. As previously argued, many of the regular 'four-to-the-floor' beats and rhythms on side one place the work within a rock/dance hybrid terrain. In addition, the 'commercialism' (memorable melodies, refrains and hooks) throughout the tracks released as singles, which skilfully popularises and makes accessible the more experimental timbres, effects and lyrics, does place them within that most unspecific of meta-genres – pop. However, side two's song suite, taken as an entity, does encourage the listener to makes connections with that most English of genres – progressive rock.

'Prog' can lay claim to being the most misunderstood, and certainly the most derided, of musical genres. For a variety of reasons that I do not have the space to adequately explore, it is also one of the few genres never to be critically or commercially recuperated since its commercial decline (its 'glory years' roughly spanning 1968–76). Although some of its leading exponents continued (continue) to enjoy success long after its peak, it is significant that they did so playing an amended form of the genre (for instance, the later work of Genesis, or Jethro Tull). Prog has suffered a very negative critical press since the late 1970s, particularly in the UK, the country that provided most of its significant acts. Since the 1990s, interest in the form has been reactivated, although it is significant that much of this activity has originated from North American, often academic, sources. It is almost as if the American appreciation of this most British of genres carries clear echoes of the British critical devotion to indigenous American genres such as blues, soul and country.

For an adequate overview of prog, many accounts exist (see Borthwick and Moy, 2004: 61–76 or Holm-Hudson, 2002). My focus here lies within the many ways that *Hounds of Love* incorporates prog style indicators, yet avoids the critical opprobrium that the genre typically garners. One of prog's principal structural models was the classical song suite or tone poem. It was particularly interested in representations of an English sense of the pastoral, as well as weighty lyrical concerns with metaphysics, fantasy narratives or histories and mythologies (in the pre-Barthesian sense). Despite the often important incorporation of elements of psychedelic, jazz, avant-garde and folk styles, the central element consisted of keyboard-based English rock/pop instrumentation played in a deliberately un-American manner. As argued with my co-author in a previous book, this was a deliberate procedure involving 'breaking the blues lineage' (Borthwick and Moy, 2004: 61). This manifested itself in a variety of ways, many of which are echoed, particularly in *The Ninth Wave*.

Foremost is the sequencing of tracks into a near seamless suite of differing textures, rhythms and tempi. The track segues on *The Ninth Wave* are relatively sympathetic, lacking the jarring juxtaposition of loud and quiet or fast and slow sections found within much classical or 1970s prog sequencing. Indeed, the most jarring jump probably lies within a track – 'Waking the Witch' – but this is not unusual within the prog genre.

Another classic prog device is the juxtaposition of different time signatures, often ones highly unusual within pop (for example, Genesis's self-explanatory 'Apocalypse in 9/8' towards the climax of the suite *Supper's Ready*, 1972). Whilst Kate Bush's music does jump in tempo and time signature, it typically gravitates between the more standardised pop signatures of 4/4, 3/4 and 6/8, giving her music the feel of contemporary jigs or reels. Whilst this is far more ambitious and 'progressive' than standard pop, the deliberately 'un-groovy', overly complex self-consciousness of classic prog is moderated in favour of 'flow' or even standardised common time.

Instrumentally, *Hounds of Love* employs the updated arsenal of acoustic, electronic and computerised timbres available by the mid-1980s. The artist's use of the album's catalogue of timbres is classically prog in its willing experimentation and eclecticism, and also in its deliberate denial of classically American timbres and styles. This is made manifest by the total absence of instruments such as slide or pedal steel guitar, slap bass or jazz brass. There is little doubt that had samplers, sequencers and digital composition been available during the prog era then they would have been enthusiastically adopted. Prog acts made great use of the newly available synthesisers and the mellotron, which as well as functioning as a rudimentary sampler also allowed for orchestral washes of sound and choral voices to place the resulting music in a European (and affordable orchestral) setting. By the mid-1980s, the mellotron's descendants – Fairlights and polyphonic synthesisers – were central to Kate Bush's compositional and playing processes. Indeed, it could be argued that the limitations of these new techniques actually allowed for a more experimental form of creativity to result, as opposed to the 'everything is possible' world of contemporary Pro-Tools, hard-disk production sequencing and limitless amounts of sampling. Timothy Warner states that the Fairlight available in the period of the recording of *Hounds* produced samples that were 'veiled, indistinct ... "grainy": a quality, which at the time was regarded as, a deficiency but which nevertheless had a particular charm and character' (Warner, 2003: 98). These qualities clearly provoke connotations of 'warmth', thus exposing the artificiality of the binary oppositions of 'human' and 'machine' technology.

Kate Bush's lyrical scope and ambition have already been referenced – another clear link to prog's intention to break with the constraints of most Anglo-American pop. Unlike many prog narratives, *Hounds of Love* is more grounded in 'realistic' feelings and states of mind, or more ambitious narratives that still retain 'credibility' in spite of their elevated language and subject matter. As a result, Kate Bush escaped the many accusations of 'whimsy', 'hippiness' or 'public schoolboy mythology' often directed at the likes of Yes and Genesis by members of the rock press (see Macan, 1997: 167–78).

In conclusion, *Hounds of Love* is, on balance, classically prog in broad conceptual and often musical terms. However, it reined in many of the excesses of the genre, thus rendering its ambition and experimentation more accessible and palatable to a mainstream audience as a consequence. It thus managed to function almost as an interloper within a genre that dares not speak its name. In addition, her status as a solo female performer within the overwhelmingly male band world of prog, and the fact that by 1985 she was a studio composer rather than live performer, may have helped differentiate Kate Bush from the genre. It has certainly helped her escape the negative connotations of the genre that it belongs to in an important, yet somewhat marginal and unacknowledged fashion.

Kate Bush and *Auteur* Theory

One of the most important contributions of 'screen theory' has been the research done into creativity, centring on our understanding of the constructed role of the *auteur*. As this term suggests, much early work was carried out by French screen theorists associated with the journal *Cahiers du Cinema*. *Auteur* analysis was investigated by many prominent screen theorists, (see Sarris, 1968; Wexman, 2003; Wollen, 1998). Their co-option of 'mainstream cinema' into the fine art canon was, in part, predicated on the need to elevate hitherto 'journeyman' directors such as Alfred Hitchcock, John Ford and Howard Hawks to the status of *auteurs*, whose artistic imprint was considered to render their films personal, artistic and 'authored' in the same fashion as the works of canonic authors in other creative fields.

Much good was achieved by *auteur* theory, including its boost to film as a valid field of critical and academic research. However, in overall terms, it went too far is assigning creative responsibility to one man (almost inevitably a man) – the director. *Auteur* theory mutated into various 'schools', including 'structural auteurism', which studied oppositions within an *auteur*'s *oeuvre*, and 'poststructuralist auteurism', which 'present their makers not as originary artists but as transmitters of cultural knowledge' (Wexman, 2003: 12). Some theorists drew upon Barthes's influential notion of 'The Death of the Author' (Barthes, 1977: 142–8), which places authorial agency upon the 'reader', whilst others challenged the more extreme manifestations of this position in arguing for the political validity of the authoring process, particularly for feminist or 'marginal' criticism (see Silverman, in Wexman, 2003: 50–75). Sarris, as one of its most prominent exponents, argued that it was a fundamentally disunified stance that was 'enabling' rather than a discrete theory (Sarris, in Wexman, 2003: 21–9). However, its legacy can be felt everywhere today when we talk of 'a film by Martin Scorsese' or see the screen credits beginning or ending with the director's name. Wexman argues that Hollywood in particular likes 'marketing directors as saleable commodities.' (Wexman, 2003: 1). Of course, on one level, the iconic profile of the popular music *auteur* tends to be higher than that of the film world. However, it is true to say that George Martin has little iconic status, whereas Prince has a great deal.

Areas such as television and popular music production share with film a similarly collaborative *modus operandi* that combines the contributions of technicians, artists, writers and producers (the music equivalent of the film director). We might consider the process of producing a television programme or a motion picture to be akin to producing a music album. Tim Gardam states that:

> Programmes are never one person's inspiration but the collective will of passionate, stubborn individual intelligences somehow bonding for a moment to create something more than any one of them alone could have imagined. (Gardam, 2006).

This summary effectively dispels the notion of the solitary genius whose will shapes the complete collaborative text. Theories of authorship in popular music are rightly ambivalent in assigning the ultimate authority to one individual, or role. On some occasions it is assigned to the artist or star, on others to the writer(s), on others to the producer, on others to the DJ or mixer and on others to the label (a Motown record, a Studio One production). However, when one individual combines more than one of these roles the assumptions relating to authorship are, quite logically, made more manifest.

Typically, almost all popular music *auteurs* are considered to be male. In this, such a discourse draws upon prior models (for instance, 'romanticism') relating to concepts such as creativity and 'genius'. As Emma Mayhew suggests, 'Women have often been devalued through a construction of femininity as an unskilled, and/or "natural" musical position' (Mayhew, 2004: 150). Christine Battersby has established the prevalence of the assigning of the secondary roles of 'muse' or 'foil' to women connected to male genius (Battersby, 1989: 3). Popular music allows us to problematise such assumptions, although it must be added that much popular music discourse actually perpetuates these conservative, sexist assumptions: 'authorship is normally defined with little reference to the problematic and contested nature of the role' (Mayhew, 2004: 152). Popular music discourse is still fundamentally, and overwhelmingly, romantic and 'masculinised'.

In this section I will be applying *auteur* theory to the music of Kate Bush, but with a particular added emphasis paid to her gender. Comparisons will be drawn with other prominent female *auteurs*, such as Madonna and Björk, to more broadly situate the concept, and to explore differences in the degree and nature of authorial input.

In the creative world of popular music, the 'glass ceiling' preventing women from escaping stereotypical roles is still rigidly applied (see Mayhew, 2004: 149–62; McClary, 1991; O'Brien; 2002; Whiteley, 2000). Keith Negus's research into A & R and record companies was very informative in the way it exposed the explicit sexism of the industry:

> From their earliest contact with record companies acts will be prioritised and accorded different levels of treatment. This tends to result in a self-fulfilling reproduction and extension of the live, white, male, naturalistic rock tradition. (Negus, 1990).

Thus, the female record producer is as rare as the female film director. However, as Mayhew rightly acknowledges, 'commercial longevity' (Mayhew, 2004: 149) can grant female musicians the power to move into production. In classically Marxist terms, the economic base can still determine the superstructure – on this occasion, to the benefit of women. Sometime Bush collaborator Richard Burgess has claimed to not know the reasons for the rarity of the female producer, and falls back on sexist fallacies attached to unsociable hours and uncivilised working conditions (Burgess, 1997: 185). I am sure that the vast numbers of female nurses would have something to say on this subject. The real answers are more complex and sociological and have to do with the mythologies of technology, 'embedded patriarchal roles' (Mayhew, 2004: 149), lack of female role models and outright discrimination from a 'boys' own' mentality. Kate Bush, as the exception that proves the general rule in popular music, is thus a fitting example worthy of analysis. In particular, her long path to authorial control, which culminates by *Hounds of Love* in her fulfilling the roles of principal writer, player, performer and producer, needs to be traced. It sheds light not only upon her as an individual character, but also upon gender and the world of popular music as a whole.

From *Ingénue* to *Auteur*

In investigating the path of Kate Bush from *ingénue* to *auteur*, what is immediately striking is her lack of referenced recourse to explicitly ideological feminism. At points she has gone as far as to be downright derogatory to the ideology (see Bush, 1985). Whenever the subject of gender in relation to creativity or musical 'politics' is raised in interviews, the artist adopts an essentially humanist, if mythically 'feminine' tone. This often takes the form of praising 'masculine values' or eulogising about the beauty of the male form. It is hard to imagine a strident feminist stating 'It's not such an open thing for women to fantasise about the male body ... A lot of women, if they see a male pin-up, they think it's funny. I can't understand that. I think the male body is absolutely beautiful' (Bush, in Jovanovic, 2005: 64). On another occasion, she tellingly commented: 'I'm always getting accused of being a feminist ... I think that I am probably female-oriented with my songs because I'm a female and have very female emotions' (ibid.: 90). However, on other occasions the artist seems to more closely relate to masculinity: 'when I'm at the piano I like to think I'm a man, not physically, but in the areas that they explore ... most male music ... really lays it on you ... it really puts you against the wall ... I'd like my music to intrude. It's got to' (Bush, in Doherty, 1978a). The fact that she uses the term 'accused' strongly intimates an antipathy to feminism, with the less ideological term 'female' being preferred. In addition, one can only guess at the feminist connotation placed upon the phrase 'puts you against the wall'.

Femininity is stated to be an important dimension in the artist's life and work, but any kind of separatist, or oppositional feminism is conspicuously absent. Paradoxically, within the terms of the popular music industry, Kate Bush stands as one of the most prominent examples of the independent, empowered woman who engages with all aspects of the profession on her own terms. On her only tour in 1979, as well as her performing and compositional roles she had a significant input into stage choreography, set and costume design, and even hiring dancers and crew (Whiteley, 2005: 75).

Kate Bush is best defined as an implicit feminist who chooses not to be referenced as such, which is her prerogative. As stated in the introductory section to this book, this observation does perhaps account for her relative absence from popular music analysis that is concerned with issues surrounding gender – Kate Bush is not one of the 'angry wimmin'. But if we explore her career it is hard not to conclude that, in her understated, feminine way she has actually achieved more goals than almost all males in the industry, let alone females, when we consider dimensions of autonomy and creative choice.

As already referenced, the young and inexperienced artist did need to draw heavily upon the experience of older (almost exclusively) male arrangers, producers and musicians when she entered a professional recording studio and emerged with her debut album. Despite her inexperience, David Paton claimed that 'she could talk to any one of us as easily as we could talk to one another' (Paton, in Jovanovic, 2005: 60). As well as possessing a rare self-confidence for a young female in a male domain, engineer Jon Kelly references her emotional importance to the process: 'Kate was there the whole time, encouraging us. She was the shining light of the entire sessions. You couldn't deny her anything' (Kelly, in Jovanovic, 2005: 61). David Gilmour, her most important early mentor, claims to have advised her against her choice of the first single. But this young woman rejected the advice of a mature member of a multi-million selling global rock act in favour of her own instinct. Gilmour went on:

> She was a deceptive little thing because she was just a young girl who you wouldn't have thought would've been quite as definite about what she wanted, but she knew exactly what she wanted. She can see and hear exactly what she wants to get, and then she has to struggle to try and achieve it. But she gets there in the end. I think she found that the Fairlight gave her much more control and helped her to achieve her vision. She is a true artist. An auteur one would call her if she was in the cinema. (Gilmour, in Doyle, 2005: 81).

This is a telling quote, not only in its use of the word control, which crops up continuously when collaborators talk about her creativity, but also in its referencing a piece of enabling technology. This challenges the received mythology relating technology to masculinity, and is an issue that will be returned to below.

Unusually, particularly for a young woman, the songs were all solo self-compositions. She has gone as far as referring to covering other people's songs as 'cheating' (Bush, in Jovanovic, 2005: 52). As Jovanovic rightly judges, in the historical context of her emergence, she stood opposed to contemporaneous women such as 'Donna Summer, Diana Ross, Olivia Newton-John and Elkie Brooks' (Jovanovic, 2005: 94), none of whom had (or were allowed to have, or fought to have) anywhere near Bush's breadth of input. This autonomous strategy has held for the rest of her career, with only a few cover versions sneaking onto b-sides or CD singles. However, even at this early point, with none of the influence that sales and success subsequently bestowed, the artist was prepared to stand up to management and the record company over the choice for the debut single: 'It felt like a mission. Even before I'd had a record out I had a tremendous sense of conviction that my instincts were right. *There could be no other way.*' (My italics, I find this polite insistency very telling – Bush, in Jovanovic, 2005: 66.) Reports of this meeting vary, although the artist has been firm in refuting accounts that she had to somehow resort to tears to get her way, as one EMI staff member claims (Mercer, ibid.). Whatever did transpire, it was an early victory for the individual female 'instinct' over the collective market-orientated male will of EMI.

Andrew Powell was a crucial musical and technical mentor during the making of *The Kick Inside* and *Lionheart*. However, one of the very few documented examples of 'creative differences' comes across in the recollections of Powell and Bush on their collaborative work. Not only was the artist rushed into recording the follow-up to the first, hugely successful album, but Powell's more spontaneous approach, particularly to recording vocals and not taking her seriously, seems to have genuinely upset Kate Bush:

> I feel I know what I'm talking about in the studio now. I know what I should hear. The reaction to me explaining what I want in the studio was amusement, to a certain extent. They were all taking the piss out of me a bit. (Bush, in Doherty, 1978b).

In addition, Powell wanted to retain the services of the session musicians who had played on the first album, whereas the artist wanted her own choice of musicians. On this occasion Powell and EMI won, with the backing tracks already recorded being jettisoned (Jovanovic, 2005: 83–4). Even at this early stage of her career she wanted to control almost all aspects of the composing and recording process. As Reynolds comments, 'she's one of the few female artists to go so deeply into studio mastery' (Reynolds, 1993). After releasing *Lionheart*, Powell's services were dispensed with – firmly, but without rancour.

From the third album onwards, produced by Kate Bush and Jon Kelly, Kate Bush has taken on board much of the overseeing of the technological recording process – a traditional male terrain. Tellingly, for a woman, she referred to this autonomy as 'so exciting for me, to actually have control of my baby for the first time' (Bush, in Jovanovic, 2005: 109). Being in Abbey Road studios also galvanised the artist. As a daughter of Albion she was inspired by the legacy of not only the Beatles, but also Edward Elgar (Doyle, 2005: 89). In this 'hands on' role she has been closely aided by perhaps her most important collaborator, Del Palmer. Palmer has subsequently been credited with performing various roles, from playing bass and programming the Fairlight sampler, to simply 'recording' (by which I assume a form of engineering, mixing or remixing is carried out). Despite the ending of their romantic relationship, their creative one endures. This strikes me as an unusual occurrence following what was effectively a 'marriage'. Yet again, this pays tribute to the respect that exists within the musical world over which Kate Bush presides.

In certain respects their creative relationship does mirror mythical gender roles, with the male as the technological 'boffin' dealing with beats and samples and the female artist using words and melodies. But the difference lies in the degree and extent of the female artist's critical agency, and also within the fact that, ultimately, the important decisions rest with Kate Bush – she is the boss, she exercises executive will. This extends to her relationship with her long-suffering record label, which has learned from bitter experience that no pressure can be placed upon the artist to tour, promote or even release material – the artist will decide. This balance of power is almost unheard of in the popular music environment, where, more typically, all the decisions that count rest within the industry rather than the artist (see Negus, 1993). It is even more unusual for a woman to exercise absolute authority. The battle to achieve autonomy was hard fought. The artist claimed that the record company questioned her decision to be the sole producer on her fourth album, *The Dreaming*. Although the album did well, it was by far her poorest selling to that point. When *Hounds of Love* was much more successful (albeit with a much more accessible sound), the artist sounded a note of hubris: 'Sorry, what's that you said? Sorry? Didn't want me to produce it? They left me alone from that point. It shut them up' (Bush, in Doyle, 2005: 90). Very few popular music artists are 'left alone' by their record companies, or manage to have fashioned the status and autonomy to 'shut them up'.

It seems evident that the strength and security engendered by the Bush family has been central to the artist. For the most part, the active creative support has come from the male members; although all those in her immediate family were listed as directors of her own management and publishing company, Novercia, set up in 1980. This process allowed the 22-year-old to gain the future ownership of all her recordings, as well as controlling the rights to aspects such as promotional materials and newsletters. Novercia licensed the artist's work back to the parent company, EMI (Jovanovic, 2005: 79). Not only was this degree of independence unusual for any artist, now or then, but also the added elements of youth and gender make the situation almost without precedent. The vital term here is, again, control, as opposed to the more negative term 'controlling'.

Most of Kate Bush's 'mentors' have been male. In technological terms, particular reference must be paid to both Peter Gabriel and Richard Burgess, who both encouraged the artist to rethink her composition processes after she was exposed to the possibilities of sampling. In addition, the sonic experimentation of the third Peter Gabriel album and Burgess's work with producer Trevor Horn can be felt on both *The Dreaming* and *Hounds of Love*, particularly within percussion. Burgess played drums on Horn's act, the Buggles's 'Video Killed the Radio Star' in 1979. Horn asked Burgess to play like a drum machine (see Warner, 2003: 48). At the time, acceptable programmable drum machines were not available, but such experiences as this recording – and later recording sessions with Burgess's group Landscape – informed his work within both the timbres and styles of drumming employed on Kate Bush's mid-1980s recordings. The 'dry', somewhat robotic drum tracks on *The Dreaming* and *Hounds of Love* bear witness to Burgess's influence, and the experimental technologies of the time.

Burgess was one of the true unsung innovators of music during the early 1980s. As a producer, mixer and musician, he was one of the first to programme music using a Roland MC-8 Microcomposer. This allowed complete rhythm tracks to be sequenced and stored. It was the principal device behind the Human League's groundbreaking *Dare* album (1981). In addition, he was also instrumental in direct inputting ('DIing') drums into mixing desks, and triggering drums from a computer 'to get a more alien sound' (Burgess, in Cunningham, 1998: 288). All these moves were helping to construct the new sonic zeitgeist that moved production away from mythologies of the organic, 'real time and space' and the acoustic. Kate Bush became instrumental in this process, with her recordings functioning as sonic exemplars.

Along with Peter Gabriel, Burgess was the earliest British-based musician to invest in the Fairlight CMI in 1980. He then conducted Fairlight programming on the *Never for Ever* album, teaching Bush and Palmer in the process. He reflected that:

> it was really exciting because Kate's one of these really open-mined people who when you walk in with a new device looks at it and immediately grasps its potential ... Kate and her brother bring in a load of ethnic instruments ... he played them all into the fairlight and Kate and I created whole orchestrations around these sampled sounds ... She wanted the sound of a rifle being cocked ... which we sampled ... as far as I know it was the first time anything like that had been done. (Burgess, in Cunningham, 1998: 289).

In chronological terms, Burgess is pretty accurate. Gabriel's own groundbreaking third album had been released earlier in the same year as *Never for Ever.* These production and timbral influences made a deep impression on Kate Bush's *modus operandi.* After the comparatively 'dry' and cymbal-less early and mid-1980s albums, she reverted to older methods of mixing drums. Her authorship of this shift is evidenced in this quotation, where Bush reflects upon her relationship with her principal drummer, Stuart Elliott: 'he's so easy to work with because he knows what I'm like. Occasionally I'll even ask him to use cymbals on a track now! He's been through that whole stage where I just couldn't handle cymbals or hi-hats' (Bush, in Jovanovic, 2005: 174). Bush's mentors may have been male, but her subsequent accomplishments transcend both actual and mythical gender constraints.

As a keyboardist, Kate Bush has brought a particularly 'musical' sensibility to the Fairlight, in a similar way to that of Anne Dudley, one of the members of the innovative Art of Noise collective. This has resulted in samples used as textures or as additions to more acoustic timbres, rather than as simply looped beats, which is more common within popular music. The sampler has also allowed her the freedom to compose and store whole rhythm tracks, which are then used as a reference point by collaborators such as Palmer or drummers such as Elliott. As well as encouraging a painstaking process, it also engenders a sense of control bordering on obsessive perfectionism, which suits the artist's mentality. But it is a collaborative perfectionism. Little on the specific mechanics of the working process exists in interviews (or, to be fair, in general popular music analysis). The most informative accounts come within 'musicianly' interviews for titles such as *Electronics & Music Maker*; Jovanovic's interviews with engineers such as Nick Launay, who worked on *The Dreaming*; Skinner's *Classic Albums* radio broadcast (already referenced within this section) and Palmer's article published by a fan newsletter that accompanied the release of *The Sensual World.* From what can be ascertained, the process was very similar to that undertaken on the previous album, *Hounds of Love*, and is thus also worthy of exploration. Fortunately, these sources relate to the period in Kate Bush's career during which full creative autonomy is established. And certainly, many would argue that her 1982 and 1985 releases include her most experimental material, drawing heavily upon the Fairlight in ways few have equalled. Interestingly, although easier and cheaper samplers superseded the Fairlight during the mid-1980s, Kate Bush continued to use the instrument long after this point, although the reasons for this are unclear.

Jovanovic claims that Kate Bush was exposed to Launay's work on the Public Image Limited album *Flowers of Romance*, and was impressed, particularly with the feel of the tracks and their 'big drum sounds' (Jovanovic, 2005: 129). Launay claimed that he and the artist were:

left to their own devices to make whatever crazy sounds they wanted ... She is very descriptive when explaining the mood and emotion she wants to get across with each instrument ... Some days I'd come in to great requests such as, 'Nick, can we make the drums sound like distant cannons on the other side of the valley?' ... On one song she wanted it to sound like she was floating down a river. (Launay, in Jovanovic, 2005: 130).

The engineer summed up his role in these terms: 'I felt it was my duty to catch all the wild ideas flying around Kate's head' (ibid.: 131). He looks back on her as 'still one of the most influential innovators even today ... Kate is still to this day one of the most gifted people I've ever met' (ibid.: 132). Despite the artist referencing her great satisfaction with the album at the time, it was to be Launay's only period of collaboration. In common with many autonomous creators, Kate Bush's restless quest for new sounds and experiences resulted in the 'promotion' of Del Palmer to a more prominent role on the next album, *Hounds of Love*, whose recording was to be realised in a new 48-track facility built, Jovanovic claims, to 'Kate's precise specifications' (Jovanovic, 2005: 148). Perhaps this statement needs tempering, as the specifications seem to have been more in the area of design than equipment, with the artist stipulating that the recording room should be windowless, with all communication to be via microphones. Another reason for the complete move to a home studio was to avoid unnecessary expense. By 1985 Kate Bush was undoubtedly a rich woman by any standards, but it is another indication of the breadth of her dominance over her complete *oeuvre* that economic narratives needed to be dealt with.

In terms of the specific division of labour between Bush and Palmer, the former can typically be viewed as the writer or 'ideas' person, whereas the latter's role is to act as an enabler, sounding board or executioner of wishes (choosing microphones, their placement, EQing and so on). On 'Running up that Hill' Palmer's role went as far as writing the drum pattern, which, combined with Bush's Fairlight drone, formed the basis for the whole of the track. A major departure on *Hounds* was that most of the material was written on synths and the Fairlight, as opposed to the piano of previous albums. This allowed for a wider range of timbres and their connotations ('cold' versus 'warm', 'synthetic' versus 'acoustic') to be brought into close contact. Equally, on 'Cloudbusting', decisions on how to end the track rested with the composer, but constructing the actual sampled sounds was more collaborative. Conceptually, the artist was by far the most important contributor, but the physical processes were often mutually realised.

By 1985, the artist had largely dispensed with synthesisers, preferring to compose on piano, or Fairlight, claiming that the sampler had an 'ability to create very human, animal, emotional sounds that don't actually sound like a machine' (Bush, 1982). She referred to this piece of technology as 'an old friend' (ibid.). What is interesting throughout this very technological interview is the ease with which the artist deals with the jargon-filled world of harmonisers, vocoders, compression, echo processes and harmonic structures. This is a mythically male terrain, both physically and linguistically, and although Bush adopts mythically feminine terms to describe the intended feel of the music, by 1985 she is successfully straddling typically male and female discourses across all aspects of her profession.

Palmer, her most long-standing collaborator, maps out the typical working arrangement as one wherein a Kate Bush recorded idea is passed on to him at an early stage. After the artist conveys the kind of 'feel' she is looking for Palmer spends time with the Fairlight trying to construct a pattern or rough arrangement. After the artist is happy with this mix the rhythm pattern is recorded and becomes the basis for a final mix. Many elements on this mix are subsequently replaced by played elements, drums in particular, although some other parts survive. Then rough keyboard and vocal tracks complete this phase. At that point the demo recording would be evaluated by the artist and the decision whether to continue or drop the track made. Eventually, elements of all phases of the process could well make it onto a final mix. Palmer will typically engineer all these recording phases and liase with the musicians. Palmer states that in many cases musicians are merely asked to reproduce the actual transcriptions or recordings that have already been written or played by the artist. Numerous 'takes' would be recorded until 'Kate is satisfied with what we have' (Palmer, 1989). Often, after a period of a couple of days the artist would decide which take or (more usually) composite series of takes would form the basis for the final track.

In some circumstances, backing musicians were given explicit instructions, Madonna-style orders in fact: 'I want that Pink Floyd guitar sound please Dave' (Bush, in Palmer, ibid.). Drummer Charlie Morgan claimed to be greeted in a session by a whole range of drums, including Irish instruments such as the lambeg and bodhrán, with Kate Bush informing him that 'I want this track to sound like an Irish army on the march' (Morgan, in Jovanovic, 2005: 150). During the recording session it was often the artist, rather than the engineer who was his point of contact at the other end of the microphone. Looking back on her time working with guitarist Alan Murphy, who was to die prematurely, Bush remembers asking him 'to be a racing car … a big panther creeping through the jungle' (Bush, in Jovanovic, 2005: 184, 185). This again references both her dominion and also her metaphorical, but jargon-free feminine mode of communication.

The *auteur*'s extreme perfectionism extends to minute details, often involving Bush telling her collaborator that one of the multi-tracked backing vocals is out of tune, despite nothing being apparent to anyone but the originator of the vocal lines herself. The artist's domain over vocal elements was almost absolute, indicated by this statement from 1982: 'For the male voice parts, I just sing to them what I want them to do, and I tell them the particular phraseology and timing. Then they go out and do it, while I oversee it in the mixing room' (Bush, 1982). For her own vocals they were often exhaustively recorded with just Bush and Palmer present. For *The Sensual World*, a fresh engineer would often be called in to oversee the final mixdown, as Bush and Palmer decided that after sometimes working off and on for two years on one track they needed a more objective input.

Not a huge amount of detail is vouchsafed us in technological printed sources, although the perfectionism and painstaking nature of the artist does again shine through. There is no evidence that Kate Bush songs have any outside input regarding lyrics, chord structures, melodies and vocal tracks or, in most cases, song arrangements. In overall terms, as concepts, compositions and recordings, the songs and albums are overwhelmingly the results of her talent and will, albeit with vital contributions from others, particularly Palmer and, more recently, Dan McIntosh. She has tellingly admitted to always regretting any compromises in achieving her vision (Jovanovic, 2005: 163). The extent of her dominion over her art is huge, and almost without parallel in popular music as a whole. This issue of agency and control possibly holds the key to her retirement from stage performance. In reflecting back over the process and her public perception she commented:

> it worries me, too, that people may think I'm totally manipulated by the dance teacher, the record producer, the record company. That I'm not intelligent and don't think for myself – the rubber doll. I consider myself very strong. I do control a lot of what happens around me and I try to control it all. (Bush, in Sutcliffe, 2003: 77).

By jettisoning the vagaries of live performance she was better placed to achieve her goal.

Despite the inherent tensions involved in any convoluted and complex creative process, numerous collaborators vouch for the warm and pleasurable atmosphere engendered by Kate Bush. No evidence of 'prima donna' behaviour existed; all collaborators were made to feel important and valued, with Elliott commenting 'If she's having a bad day you will be the last to know about it ... She comes into the studio and smiles and it's all bright, airy and sunshine. She really does care about people' (Elliott, in Jovanovic, 2005: 151).

Whilst the extent of this authoring process is rare, particularly for female musicians, it is not without comparative examples. At this point it is interesting to contrast the nature of Kate Bush's authorship with others, in this instance Madonna and Björk.

Shades and Degrees of Authorship

Despite the many contrasts and many similarities between the careers of Kate Bush and Madonna, in terms of *auteur* theory it is the disparity in the nature of the executive responsibilities that is most relevant to this investigation. Although Kate Bush relies, to an extent, upon collaborators she is still more musically autonomous than Madonna. This observation is documented by the credits assigned to both artists' work. Madonna's compositions and productions are invariably joint works whereas Bush's compositions are solo and, by *Hounds of Love* she is similarly the sole producer. This is not to set up a qualitative divide between the two, but rather to highlight the differing, but broad challenges such female musicians have posed to the patriarchal world they inhabit.

Madonna's authorship has been more focussed in areas such as performance, image changes and promotion and constructing star personae, although it is important to maintain that without her vital and significant musical input, these other aspects are rendered meaningless. At this point it is enlightening to contrast the two artists' self-perceptions of their roles. Georges-Claude Guilbert quotes Madonna as stating that 'even when I was a little girl I knew I wanted the whole world to know who I was, to love me and be affected by me' (Madonna, in Guilbert, 2002: 26). We can compare this to Bush's own career perception: I'm not a performer ... I'm someone who, from an early age, wrote songs, and then gradually learned to sing, and then gradually there I was in the studio ... really everything so far has stemmed from songwriting for me' (Bush, in Alexander, 1990). From these observations the comparative nature of their authorship can be extrapolated. Bush's identification of 'a chord' as 'the most exciting thing in my life' (ibid.) takes this aspect of her character to its most extreme. Although both artists became at least partially independent from record company dictates early in their careers, Madonna has made the greater move into the role that Stan Hawkins terms 'business entrepreneur' (Hawkins, 2002: 53). This has come about through the establishment of the aptly named Maverick company. Although still linked to the global company Time-Warner, Maverick has allowed the artist to effectively 'sign up' acts that she admires, or considers commercially viable. This has resulted in the US distribution of British act the Prodigy, and the worldwide success of Alanis Morissette. In addition, a documentary project such as *Truth or Dare: In Bed With Madonna* (Keshishian, 1991) was issued as a Maverick production. Madonna's control and promotion of her career can be seen as essentially authorial, but in a more market-orientated and expansionist mode than Bush's own business interests.

One of Madonna's great strengths lies in her ability to recognise and then obtain the services of 'hot' producers/writers who will effectively author a sound that Madonna's vocals and lyrics 'embellish'. This process has taken her across varied genres, and has achieved huge and prolonged crossover success. Early in her career Jellybean Benitez was an important mentor, before being superseded by Nile Rodgers. Patrick Leonard was a long-standing compositional partner throughout the period following 1986. In the 1990s, following a phase of relative underachievement, Madonna turned to writer/producer Willam Orbit, who (with additional contributions by Marius de Vries and Patrick Leonard) was the most important collaborator on what was to be her most critically acclaimed release, *Ray of Light* (1998). Orbit's role on the following release, *Music*, was partially superseded by that of Mirwais Armadzaï, another 'multi-tasker' before 2005's album *Confessions on a Dance Floor* found her collaborating with the individual (Stuart Price) known professionally as Les Rhythmes Digitales.

The important observation is that, regardless of the quality of the collaborations, the authorship rests, to an often significant extent, upon the shoulders of the collaborator rather than upon the artist. Some of the tracks on *Ray of Light*, such as 'Skin' and 'Sky Fits Heaven', bear the sonic imprint of her co-writers and producers to the extent that Madonna's role consists of 'guesting' on her own songs. Of course, it is dangerous to assign 'proprietorial' dimensions to any sound or timbre, but many of *Ray of Light*'s textures (neo-Baroque counterpoint, pure sine-wave synth sounds redolent of the 1970s Moog, extensive use of filters, compressors and vocoders) are typical of the work of the Orbit *oeuvre*, in particular. It is only a slight exaggeration to term *Ray of Light* an album on which the ostensible author in fact makes 'personal appearances', in authorial terms. In addition, as a relatively basic musician, she is reliant upon others for elements such as arrangements, chord structures and hands-on mixing and producing. Burgess quotes Shep Pettibone, one of her principal 'enablers' on the *Erotica* (1992) album. Whilst Madonna would be very involved in certain aspects of the process, in some cases her role was more creatively detached, yet managerial: 'Sometimes Madonna would call me in the middle of the night and say ... I hate this verse, fix the bass line ... I didn't like the idea of taking a Philly house song and putting "Isla Bonita" in the middle of it. But that's what she wanted so that's what she got' (Pettibone, in Burgess, 1997: 28–9). Again, this quotation speaks volumes, not only about the strength of the artist's will and her ability to impose her views on her 'employees', but also on the nature of her musical collaborations. It is not that Madonna does not possess the conceptual will to author tracks, but that she is far more reliant on others' abilities to execute this will and achieve concrete results than is Kate Bush.

A final observation to make regarding Madonna's (and indeed, all artists') relationship to *auteur* theory is that there is no intrinsic connection between the degree of authorship and the quality of the final product. Holding dominion over all aspects of the creative production process can actually mitigate against successful or groundbreaking work. Kate Bush herself substantiates this claim when stating that her combined duties on the film *The Line, The Cross and The Curve* adversely affected both her and the work itself – essentially she overreached herself (Bush, in Jovanovic, 2005: 193–4). Some of Madonna's most enduring tracks are not written by her, and have little creative input beyond the vocal performances. Equally, as a mature artist, Madonna's authorial decisions relating to collaborations can be flawed. On *Ray of Light* the sheer breadth of styles and expertise provided by her collaborators allowed for a series of musical settings that best exploited Madonna's limited vocal and lyrical attributes. On later albums such as *American Life* (2003) and *Confessions on a Dance Floor* (2005) the musical shortcomings of the artist were left exposed (and these can only be subjective judgements) by the mundane and generic compositions and arrangements. Similarly, Mayhew's research shows that whilst, in overall terms, Bush's authorship of *Hounds of Love* garnered much critical praise, later work such as *The Red Shoes* was criticised in terms of claims that the artist had 'over-reached' herself, and would have benefited from an outside, or objective pair of hands/ears (Mayhew, 2004: 156).

As part of the research for this section I undertook a critical comparison of Madonna's 2005 album and Rachel Stevens's *Come and Get It* (2005). Whilst aesthetic judgements can never be objective, I would still argue for the Stevens album's clear overall superiority on every level in terms of composition, production, vocals, melodies, lyrics and breadth and scope of tracks. The important point is that Rachel Stevens is not an *auteur*, whereas, in many respects, Madonna is. In addition, Madonna is over 20 years into her career whilst *Come and Get It* is only Stevens's second album. The sheer banality and standardisation of Madonna's lyrics and melodies suggests that taking a less authorial role would actually benefit the artist, in aesthetic if not necessarily commercial terms.

Björk shares many similarities with Madonna, particularly in being a performer and singer rather than as principally a traditional studio-based 'composer' in the Bush mould. In addition, she has drawn heavily upon 'hot' producer/writers (Nellee Hooper, Graham Massey, Marius de Vries, Goldie, Mark Bell) and has moved on to new collaborators as her career has progressed. However, varied sources substantiate the observation that the degree and extent of her authorship is closer to that of Kate Bush rather than Madonna. Firstly, even on her first adult solo album, *Debut* (1993), Björk was the solo composer on several tracks, as well as undertaking production, programming and playing duties. Whiteley claimed that:

> she had spent two years collecting material and ideas … All the songs had been mapped out, with an intro, bass line, chords, music, melody, lyrics, with the result that the process of recording took, on average, two days for each song. (Whiteley, 2005: 105).

How different to both Bush's endless recording sessions and Madonna's more limited authorial input over final tracks. It is true to judge her first two albums as heavily influenced by then current generic dance genres such as house, and to an extent reliant on collaborators to help achieve her musical goals, but by the time she released *Homogenic*, in 1997, research points to the extent to which this work is the product of a singular, authorial will.

A fascinating documentary (Walker, 1997) mapping out the recording of this album bears evidence to this conclusion. We see the artist clearly expressing her visions for tracks and playing styles to the string players who contribute much of the melodic and harmonic elements. Often these visions are expressed in mythically feminine terms, drawing upon metaphor, physical gesture and gendered historical influences in a manner that closely connects to the critical concept of the 'chora', or '*écriture feminine*' associated with the feminist theory of Julia Kristeva and Hélène Cixous (see Whiteley, 2005: 117). 'It needs more vibrato, more drama, just very Mata Hari. It's almost too [acts out extravagant gesture]. It can be a little bit [another gesture]' (Björk, in Walker, 1997). Her relationship with collaborators is essentially nurturing and emotional, although she is well capable of executive decisions. Arranger Eumir Deodato commented 'When she sends me something it's pretty much done' (Deodato, ibid.). Fellow musician Evelyn Glennie states 'she is able to hold onto her own identity, to her own style no matter who she collaborates with. And a lot of the musical combinations she has have never been done before' (Glennie, ibid.).

At another point in the film we see the artist walking alone on a beach, 'female' shopping bag hanging from her arm, programming beats and vocals into a portable sampler. Her competence over what she terms 'techno' is evidently considerable, but her vision is still expressed in mythically feminine, 'non-jargon' terms: 'Beats for this album, very simple, but explosive, still in the making, like Iceland. There's a lot of energy here, I wanted the beats to be like this' (Bjork, ibid.). The artist's connection to nature is closely allied to Kate Bush's references to cloud patterns, waves and landscape: 'Nature is perfect. God made the world in absolute perfection' (Bush, in Alexander, 1990). Both are 'earth mothers' in mythical terms that express their control and dominion utilising anti-masculine, or at least 'cross-gender' discourses.

One of the most remarkable aspects of Björk's career has been the progressive 'paring down' of albums, in terms of instrumentation, genre and mood. This has been accompanied by a concomitant increase in the extent to which we are invited into an individual and singular music world. The artist commented that by *Homogenic* the songs were 'all one flavour. I'd used up my back catalogue. It's just tunes from now, from a similar place. It's kind of like a 31-year old female – me' (Bjork, in Whiteley, 2005: 111). In sonic terms, *Homogenic* is principally constructed out of beats, strings and vocals. As well as encouraging and establishing the mood for the strings players, the artist's own musical, melodic, lyrical and vocal contributions were immense. With the release of *Medulla* (2001), the extent of the artist's authorial scope was the equal of Kate Bush's work on *Hounds of Love*. The album, an austere, uncommercial exercise in minimal arrangements centred on voices and programmed beats, was largely self-produced and Björk's musical contributions were wide-ranging in terms of playing, programming and arranging the tracks. Another reflection upon the authorial process lies in its wilful denial of 'user-friendly' elements. Without the comforting dance beats and melodies of the first two albums, *Medulla* was never going to appeal to a mainstream audience, but rather just the artist's 'hardcore' fans. Parallels could clearly be drawn here with Kate Bush's *The Dreaming* album, and in the pressures placed upon her by record company representatives to bring in outside producers to help 'temper' her authorial excesses and increase sales potential.

As Whiteley has rightly stated, both Björk and Kate Bush shared the initial status of 'child prodigy' (Whiteley, 1995: 118), although the former's talents lay in playing and recording in her very young days, whilst the latter concentrated more on composition in her early period. Madonna's lack of formal musical knowledge – her initial route into music came as a dancer – allied to her comparatively late commercial breakthrough (1983, already in her mid-20s), has doubtless had an impact upon the nature of her authorial status. In addition, her blatantly ambitious desire to be a global pop star and achieve huge sales contrasts with both Björk and Kate Bush's more studio-orientated, music-based goals.

How can we summarise the relationship of Kate Bush to that of the constructed *auteur*? Perhaps the key to her success has lain in the application of mythically masculine traits (control, technical perfectionism, executive single-mindedness) via a mythically feminine emotional atmosphere (nurturing, calm, limited use of jargon, metaphorical incorporation of 'the natural world', 'maternal'). In addition, her relatively low iconic status (again, 'authored' by the artist) has allowed her to largely escape a sexualised pigeonhole by the forces of patriarchy and hegemony. In 1990, she stated: 'I didn't want to be famous. I didn't want to make lots of money. I didn't want to be successful. But I desperately wanted to make an album ...' (Bush, in Alexander, 1990). The consequence of this 'manifesto' has doubtless been a compromise in terms of the amount of commercial success, but she has achieved all her intended and unintended goals to at least a significant degree. For Madonna, the situation has been very different. Indeed, she has been one of the few global pop stars to have actually over-exposed herself (both literally and metaphorically) to the point where partially retreating from view in the period up to the release of *Ray of Light* was probably the best marketing decision she has ever made.

Much has been made of Kate Bush providing musicians or interviewers with refreshments in a motherly role, and her collaborators being welcomed into the bosom of the extended Bush family. When we bear in mind the length of some of her relationships with musical collaborators – mostly male – the affection, admiration and even love in which she is held is very evident. Not only is it hard to find anyone with a bad word to say for her, but she reserves almost all criticism for herself, rather than others – again reinforcing the extent of her 'ownership' of the creative process.

In reflecting back upon the previous investigations of grain, it must be stated, somewhat tautologically, that all voices are unique and possess authorial status, but some voices are so startlingly original as to be particularly unique. When we compare the physical vocal grain of Madonna, Björk and Kate Bush, we are faced with, in Barthesian terms, one voice leaning further towards *plaisir* in both its execution and reception (the notion of 'average culture'), and two more closely linked to the concept of *jouissance*. Madonna's voice is a functional one (perhaps the reason she and her team use vocal effects so heavily?) that draws upon the hegemonic accent of global pop. Whilst this voice is recognisably hers, it is not particularly distinct from other archetypal or standardised examples of a female popular music voice (we might draw comparisons with Kylie Minogue, Debbie Gibson, Rachel Stevens and Holly Valance, for example). Similarly, for all their aspirations towards self-discovery and spirituality, Madonna's lyrics seldom escape from the tropes of romance, dancing, sexuality and emotional confession central to pop narratives.

The vocal grain of Björk and Kate Bush shares advantages – both inherent and constructed – over Madonna that grant them greater individuality and authorial status. Firstly, to an extent, both choose to sing in distinctive geographical accents that are marginal and distinct from 'transatlantic' norms. In addition, both have vocal ranges far superior to that of Madonna, who had to be 'varispeeded' on her early recordings to raise her pitch and sound more 'girly'. As Whiteley states, a large vocal range allows for a wider range of readings to be made available that relate to issues of sexuality, age and gender (Whiteley, 2005: 65–122). Furthermore, the additional effort required for a singer to pitch at the top and bottom limits of their vocal range does result in more bodily elements being emphasised. Their prodigious ranges are complemented by greater recourse to both supra-linguistic dimensions and also the physiological manipulations – growls, squeals and mouth and throat shapings – that emphasise their uniqueness and set them apart from all other singers. If a Madonna vocal is identifiable after a verse or a phrase, our other examples can be identified after a word, or even a phoneme. In my own experience, Tori Amos singing at close to the top of her range can sound quite like Kate Bush (on 'Winter' [1992], for instance), but this is a rare similarity. What I am suggesting is that the distinctive sonic imprint of artists such as Kate Bush is another contributory factor in the construction of an authorial dimension that moves us on from creativity, planning and production and into a performative (as opposed to performing) setting.

Does the comparative difference in emphasis between the authorship of Madonna and Kate Bush automatically indicate that the latter is the greater artist? This is not really the issue, although, to an extent, analysis does reflect qualitative judgements based upon personal critical values, desires and prejudices. What this section's research has again emphasised is that there is a little of Theodor Adorno in all of us when it comes to assigning aesthetic status. Stan Hawkins's account of the authorial role of Madonna within the track 'Music' (Hawkins, in Whiteley, Bennett and Hawkins, 2004: 180–90) states that her 'role in the studio has steadily evolved to a point where her input into the final product has been almost total' (Hawkins, ibid.: 181). Madonna's work is frequently referred to in proprietorial terms that suggest she is the only producer (which composition and production credits suggest is not the case). This argument results in statements as comprehensive as referring to 'Madonna's control over every milli-second of the mix' (ibid.: 188). This degree of authorial agency would be a first for any popular music artist, or producer or mixer, let alone a clearly referenced collaborative artist such as Madonna. My point here is not to 'disprove' Hawkins's thesis, but to show that out of a collaborative authorial process, intentionalist assumptions are made for a variety of reasons. At the very least, it could be argued that Hawkins's appropriation of terms such as 'authorship' is specific to his own personal and ideological agenda: there are as many interpretations of 'authorship' as there are shades and degrees of artistic authorship. He assumes a different degree of authorial creativity for Madonna than I do, despite going to some length to map out the precise input of co-producer Mirwais to specific tracks which, at the very least, problematises the complete extent of the artist's contribution (ibid: 186–7). The artist herself, not noted for her modesty, has perhaps been more accurate and even-handed when reflecting upon the authorial process – in this case, that of the collaboration with William Orbit on *Ray of Light*: 'I was the anchor, he was the waves, and the ship was our record' (Madonna, in Rule, 1999: 23).

What cannot be disputed or denied is that the authorial breadth and independence of Kate Bush has helped fashion a career that succeeds more completely *in its own terms* than one constructed or predicated by the demands of the commercially mediated, and compromised, market. Reynolds and Press have reflected upon the feminine challenge to male authorship that comes about through recourse to methods relating to the 'death of the author' common to post-structuralist theory. This is achieved through 'a conceptualisation that suggests "language speaks us"; that poetry occurs at the point of friction between the impersonal system of language and the individual's unconscious desires' (Reynolds and Press, 1995: 376). In this scenario, mapped out by '*écriture feminine*', mythologies of femininity, nature and emotional closeness, the 'artist as godlike, omnipotent' (ibid.) is challenged by a newer, less patriarchal model more in tune with changing times and changing gender roles. Bush spoke of communicating with the Trio Bulgarka:

> through cuddles rather than words. In fact, we could get on perfectly well without translators. At one point ... when the translator walked in (and) we all shut up because she'd made us all self-conscious about what we were doing. (Bush, in Sutcliffe, 1989: 91).

This seems to me a classic demonstration of feminist linguistic theory.

There is still a way to go. Whiteley quotes an online reviewer who terms Kate Bush 'A Studio wizard, and a master with synth-sequencing technology' (Whiteley, 2005: 78). Perhaps one day 'man-made language' will cede more ground: the term witch will replace wizard, and in the process be freed from the negative connotations placed upon it by patriarchal discourse.

Audio Texts, Video Texts: Extensions or Detractions?

Whilst the focus within this book is overwhelmingly sonic, an investigation of some of Kate Bush's music videos is necessary for several reasons: firstly, the artist herself has always had creative ambitions in this area:

> Music videos, it becomes an extension of the song … I've always been very interested in the visual side of things. I've always loved film. And it just seemed like a natural progression to get more involved in what I did musically and visually. (Bush, in Alexander, 1990).

Secondly, the artist's background and talent for mime and dance have allowed her to bring different disciplines to bear within the pop video form. John Mundy has commented on pop videos being 'essentially authorless texts' (Mundy, 1999: 242), arguing instead for the authorial role being subsumed within performance and star personae. In view of research already carried out into *auteur* theory, and the fact that the artist progressed to being her own video director, this is another fertile area for investigation. Finally, the often problematic relationship between the media of sound and audio-visuals can be fruitfully explored by focussing upon Kate Bush's work on film and video.

Ian Inglis claimed that an important dimension within film studies reflected 'a tradition which maintains that film is essentially a visual and spoken medium, to which music may be a useful but ultimately peripheral addition' (Inglis, 2003: 3). John Ellis's *Visible Fictions*, despite its title being an overview of the aesthetics of cinema, television and video, reflects upon the writer's (and the subject field's?) 'engagement with the subject … [which] comes from my enduring fascination with images' (Ellis, 1988: 4). In the chapter entitled 'Cinema as image and sound', Ellis devoted under a page to the specifics of cinema sound, and 22 to visual aspects such as fetishism, voyeurism and the gaze (ibid: 38–61). As Mundy has commented, 'cinema and television have always been as much about sound as vision, had we but analysed them properly' (Mundy, 1999: 229). Pop video is the ideal vehicle to challenge such a specular hierarchy through analysis.

Space will not allow me to comprehensively summarise Bush's complete video *oeuvre*, as dozens of examples exist dating back to 1978 and 'Wuthering Heights'. What I propose doing is to concentrate upon several 'promo' videos from phases of her career that explore different rationales and methodologies. In addition, the video album entitled *Hair of the Hound*, which followed the release of *Hounds of Love*, and the later album *The Line, The Cross and The Curve* (which followed *The Red Shoes* and was also released as a film, as well as in video form) will be investigated as complete entities.

I should also make my own critical position clear at the outset. As the result of aesthetical and (doubtless) generational factors I am more critical of the video promo form as a complete entity than I am of popular music, although evidently, great work has resulted from the fusion of songs and audio-visual accompaniments. Despite the pleasure that certain pop videos afford me, the sonic text is still the primary one in terms of my personal aesthetics, and the subsequent analysis is doubtless informed by this observation. Another factor worthy of attention is the artist's own stance regarding both performance and video. She has argued that 'the song lays down every key move, who you are, what you wear, what color [sic] the set is, you know. It's really the song dictates it all' (Bush, in Pringle, 1980).

Kate Bush has been particularly critical of her own work in this field – sometimes with admirable, and justifiable, honesty; but equally sometimes her own negativity can be judged excessive. In 1983 she commented: 'out of all the videos I've done, there're really only a couple that I'm pleased with. Unlike my songs … video has terrible limitations of time and money' (Bush, in Reimers, 1983). Years later, her criticism had hardened: 'They're so clichéd and narcissistic. Most of what I've done makes me cringe' (Bush, in Sutcliffe, 1989: 87). Sutcliffe's conclusion is one many would agree with: 'Perhaps it's only in the studio that she can truly encompass what she strives for' (Sutcliffe, 1989: 89). Such criticism has a bearing on both the overall efficacy of audio-visual forms of popular music, and also upon the nature of iconic re-presentation – are artists, and indeed audiences, more critical of music when it is mediated in this mode? An investigation of pop video has the capacity to encourage a profound questioning of how the senses function, and how they are structured into a hierarchy in contemporary society.

The Society of the Specular

In terms of the academic and critical terrain, the establishment of the pop video and the subsequent introduction of dedicated TV channels such as MTV have encouraged a large number of studies to be published. Several of these adopt an overly screen-based approach that, at the very least, partially overlooks the musical dimensions of the works (see Kaplan, 1987). However, in combination, many others do offer a holistic interpretive model that it is expedient to explore before individual examples are engaged with (see Banks, 1996, for an analysis based on political economy; Goodwin, 1993, for a critique of the video aesthetic; Mundy, 1999, for a screen-based historical overview and Frith et al., 1993, for a wide-ranging summary of critical positions). As I have previously argued (Moy, 2000: 112), the central dialectic within both pop video analysis and the videos themselves centres on the question of ratio. Is a pop promo an equal balance of musical and non-musical elements? Should, or does, one component 'drive' any other? Are pop videos there to merely promote an extant text – the song; or do they function to complement, broaden or even transform and transgress the song? In some cases does the song actually become little more than the sonic accompaniment to the primary audio-visual text?

Responses to such questions are varied. In one extreme example, Pete Fraser quotes Joe Saltzman, whose position is that:

They now provide pictures for the songs in our heads. Goodbye imagination … All kids have to do is watch and listen, stare straight ahead. No need to think, to embellish, to create, to imagine. The electronic fix is in. (Saltzman, in Fraser, 2005: 9).

Here, as is invariably the case, extreme positions usually contain a grain of truth. Adam Sweeting modifies this stance, whilst still maintaining the incompatibility of television and music by stating that 'music is already its own self-contained world of emotions, memories, urges and sensations, and it only needs television as a promotional tool' (Sweeting, 1994: 5). Again, this position is contentious, but is one I would personally be sympathetic to. Will Straw argued that pop video is important in demonstrating 'the relationship between rock music as a culture of presumed resistance and television as the embodiment of mainstream show business' (Straw, 1993: 4). The use of 'presumed' is an important caveat. Rock often operates under the guise of revolution, whilst being essentially a conservative form. Equally, for all the compromises imposed upon pop video by the market, challenging and subversive work can still result.

Some early music video theory did foreground fears about the potential for image to 'vanquish' sound through encouraging 'theatricality' and 'diminishing the interpretive liberty of the individual' (ibid.: 3). Lawrence Grossberg spoke of the shifting ratio between sound and vision in youth culture (Grossberg, 1993: 186). Whilst not arguing for any shift in the importance or quality of music within this scenario, he did argue that the primacy of sound as a mythical guarantor of authenticity had been challenged by what he termed the 'ironic' dimension within pop video.

A commonplace use of pop video in social settings now dispenses with sound altogether. Locations such as shopping malls sometimes broadcast merely the images. This does not mean that the text is worthless, or 'silent', as we can never shut off our ears from environmental ambience; but it does, by necessity, function to the detriment of the musical component. However, the automatic granting of superior status to visuals has been rightly challenged; particularly persuasive have been Goodwin's counters to this position. His stance that suggests that we need a musicology of pop videos, rather than a screen-based, or iconic frame of reference, is the foundation for the subsequent research (Goodwin, 1993: 50).

Jody Berland's work into this field problematised the use of the term 'rhythm' as an editorial device in the pop video. Whilst arguing that 'the rhythm of the visual editing subsumes the larger rhythm of the song' (Berland, 1993: 38), and 'the reconstruction of sound and image has been dominated by the ... requirements of the visual media' (ibid.: 27), the writer's conclusions do offer a more persuasive and holistic summary of the form when stating that the rhythmic structure of a song is 'never contested in the video' (ibid.: 39). I take this to mean that the temporal continuity of the song remains paramount – the song unfolds in 'real time' without such devices as the equivalent of the cinematic 'flashback'. The sequential order of verses and choruses is similarly unaffected by the video form, which treats the song as the primary text on which to essentially 'build visual layers'. Thus, the whole foundation of the pop video form is musical: 'a single can exist ... without the video, but the reverse is not the case' (ibid.: 25). In other words, to extrapolate Sweeting's position, a song may be incomplete in sensory terms, but creates a complete world in symbolic terms. An incomplete video, without musical accompaniment, always connotes absence. Perhaps utilising an automotive metaphor gives the best indication of the ratio distinction. A pop video without sound is like a car without its engine running – aesthetically pleasing in many cases, yet unable to perform all of its functions. Engines work independently of cars, but cars have relatively little use or value without the invisible impetus of the engine. It is the musical dimension, in all its facets, that literally powers (and realises) the vehicle of pop video.

Simon Frith's research into value and affect drew upon important musicological models to investigate the nature of sound and musical communication (Frith, 1996). He claimed that music cannot be translated, which encourages us to construct meaning on the basis of chains of conventions and associations. Music does not resemble objects, but comes to symbolise them through cultural conventions. Thus music and sound each have a specific function as part of a cinematic experience in promoting vague emotions which visuals then help 'pin down' through ostension in causational terms. Images help objectify and anchor sounds.

The exact relationship between screen sounds and screen visuals is dependent upon each individual example's marriage of elements. As within popular song structures, there are conventions, but the form can transgress them. I have previously argued that complex historical processes have resulted in the construction of a 'specular hierarchy' (Moy, 2000) wherein sound is invariably placed beneath sight. Paradoxically, sound's 'inferior status' could be seen to bolster and ensure its importance. Within screen theory, this results in a situation where 'a sound always evokes an image' (Bresson, in Frith, 1996: 111). However, whether the images that we evoke in our imaginations are adequately objectified within pop videos is another issue. Walter Murch, sound technician on such films as *Apocalypse Now* (Coppola, 1979), claimed that in comparison to 'incomplete' sound-based media: 'film seems to be "all there" (it isn't, but it seems to be) … the metaphoric use of sound … can open up a perceptual vacuum into which the mind of the audience must inevitably rush' (Murch, in Chion, 1994: xx). What these observations help construct is the importance of symbiosis between two senses that function in different ways.

Within a cinematic experience we are placed in a precise spacial relationship to the visuals, but seem to internalise sound, or feel immersed within its general, non-specific ambience. Visuals thus have an objective status, whereas sound is more subliminal, and its importance often unacknowledged. Within a domestic environment, Ellis has argued that sound is a more crucial element in the televisual experience, as, in contrast to the engaged and sustained cinematic experience, 'The spectator glances, rather than gazes at the screen: attention is sporadic rather than sustained' (Ellis, 1988: 24). Ellis suggested that visuals are more illustrative within television texts, whereas sounds and dialogue offer more anchorage. Within this argument, television offers a bridging experience between the physical fixity of cinema and the far more mobile and 'distracted' modes of consumption offered by music and radio. This argument is certainly substantiated by the fragmentary 'multi-tasking' lifestyle of many people ('grazers', 'surfers', 'channel-hoppers') in contemporary cultural environments.

Critical debate exists around the contention that music can never be considered a purely sonic form. Goodwin argued that analysing music through an assumption of its visual lack is 'empirically unsound … [coming about] only if it has already been wrenched from its actual contexts of consumption … and analysed as something that it is not – a discrete, purely musical text' (Goodwin, 1993: 49). Perhaps many of us are therefore guilty of a mythologising process, but this does still lead to empirical realities, albeit based on 'unsound' (or is it literally 'sound') evidence. On a personal, fundamental level, consumption of recorded music is often radiophonic – there are no visuals. This leads on to a scenario where, even in the multimedia world of today, it is still perfectly possible to consume music (despite using contemporary technologies such as MP3 downloading) without having any knowledge of the visual appearance of the artists involved. Not only does this encourage the imagination, but also it frees music, possibly fleetingly and mythically, from the market-imposed stereotypes relating to age, appearance, gender and race. Radio theorist Andrew Crisell has referred to radio as an 'incomplete' or 'blind' medium (Crisell, 1996). Of course, such terms carry negative connotations, which others suggest replacing with alternative signifiers such as 'invisible' or 'magical' (Shingler and Weiringa, 1998: 174). One of mass media's earliest theoreticians, Marshall McLuhan, famously referred to radio as a 'hot' medium, as opposed to the 'cool' television form. By this he meant that a hot medium is 'one that extends one single sense in "high definition"' (McLuhan, 1987: 22). This requires imaginative participation by an audience in order to 'complete the text' in the magical sonic world.

However, despite all these varied arguments highlighting the positive dimensions of sound, or a single-sense medium, it must be recognised that such stances are swimming against the critical and empirical tide. Efforts to marginalise sound have been hegemonic. Mass culture has been 'persuaded' by both benign and interested agencies of patriarchy and global capital to accommodate an increasingly multimedia-based world-view – a society of the specular in which sound elements, whilst still significant, survive as a component within a more important audio-visual experience, rather than as the experience itself. Within popular music aesthetics this has resulted in a situation wherein something of a generation divide has been established, with younger people increasingly consuming music as part of another text – invariably visually based. At this point it is time to turn to the historical development of the form and specific examples of popular music video in order to help judge how sight and sound have been brought into close contact, and to ask what has been lost and what has been gained.

Pop Video: History and Developments

The prehistory of popular music promotion on film is long and overlooked (see Mundy, 1999). Mundy has argued for a historical approach that explicitly challenges many of the more ungrounded theories relating to the 'revolutionary' nature of pop video or its dissemination. The development of recordable videotape led to a situation whereby, during the 1970s, it became possible for an act to film an accompaniment to a track relatively cheaply and quickly. By the early 1980s, and the establishment of dedicated television programmes and networks, the form had become widespread, and certain generic conventions became apparent. Musical genres based upon 'organic' instrumentation or more traditional styles and artists tended to be presented in 'realistic' settings – not only simulations of the live concert, but in 'naturalistic' locations. More contemporary, experimental or high technology artists and recordings were given more licence to break free from such conventions.

The form did rapidly develop multiple techniques, drawing upon areas as diverse as mime, cartoon and animation, dance, cinematic references and *mise-en-scène* and various editing innovations. Certainly, in its most well-conceived and executed manifestations, it did achieve the status of a miniature work of art, but more often the form fairly rapidly became, for the most part, a standardised set of conventions and clichés. Goodwin has described his research as consisting of consuming videotexts 'with varying degrees of relish and repulsion' (Goodwin, 1993: x). Perhaps, as many would argue, the same observation can be applied to the songs that videos accompany. But this does not fully engage with the different aesthetics of sound and image that I have sought to establish. Musical clichés and sonic clichés provoke different affective states because they are expressed through profoundly different media. On a more negative level, the increasingly specular nature of pop has resulted in the marginalisation of artists who do not fit into the constraints of a commercially mediated global marketplace. The pressures placed upon mainstream pop performers to be young, beautiful and sexually provocative have never been greater. The sensuality of many pop music narratives has been sidelined by the soft-porn imperatives of much contemporary video content.

The pop video has also problematised performance codes – do musicians, or should musicians, 'act'? At what point does playing or singing become an acting rather than a musicianly performance? Or is there no distinction? In 1990 Kate Bush commented 'I don't think I ever wanted to become an actress. Acting is something that I've never had the passion for' (Bush, in Alexander, 1990). But if she is not, to an extent, acting in her videos, what is she doing? One of the issues exposed by the form is this dilemma: if the musician just 'plays' then is the video nothing more than a piece of mime? How is the relationship between the song and the video presented? Many of these questions have been explicitly manifested in the following examples.

An Overview of Kate Bush's Early Videos

'Wuthering Heights' (Director Keef)

Both the artist's dance/mime background and the backing of a major record company resulted in the comparatively unusual decision to video her very first single release in 1978. Having said that, the resulting work was low budget, consisting for the most part in a static camera filming the artist miming the song, with elements of dance and rudimentary acrobatics interspersed and repeated at points. The initial observation is that a video denies our imagination the licence to construct an iconic accompaniment to the musical narrative. Iconic knowledge was already available to the majority of the audience prior to viewing this video, but the song had already worked on the imagination, which, in a sense, the specific marriage of images to sounds then had to compete with. Those without any prior knowledge – altogether possible, particularly in that period – had their critical innocence, or imagination, 'shattered'.

On a symbolic level we are encouraged to closely identify the performer with the narrative: Kate Bush is Cathy. Videos can thus problematically conflate the author with the narrator and there can be no difference between the 'real' and 'implied' author (Goodwin, 1993: 75). Although the artist moves with grace and ease, her mime training does result in an over-exaggeration of gestures. In addition, the reinforcement of lyrical motifs with poses and movements soon becomes redundant – a grabbing gesture for 'let me grab', a clasp of the arms across the body for 'so cold'. In a sense, visual reinforcements are unnecessary as they duplicate the mood or narrative and 'close down' (as opposed to 'reinforcing') the text as a consequence. The artist's 'hamming up' her facial features in opening her eyes and mouth too wide actually detracts from the message of the song and results in an unwittingly comical edge. The literal 'melodrama' of the song becomes merely 'melodramatic' when presented visually. The art of mime and its adoption by 'silent' cinema has a long and noble lineage, but the exaggerated mime of opening the mouth too widely to simulate singing takes the style too far into parody. By the late 1970s the codes and conventions of mime were ancient history to all but a few aficionados or practitioners. To the mass audience for the video, the gestural exaggerations were brave, but misguided.

Elements that date texts can be aesthetically positive or negative. Visual motifs tend towards cliché in a way that musical elements do not. Most musical texts are 'dated' in some respect, but often escape any critical approbation. As a listening audience we actively anticipate and enjoy the prospect of the hook line or the solo, or that 'classic' guitar timbre. When similar elements are presented objectively, on screen, they do not engender the same response. The slow-motion cartwheels, visually overdubbed using rudimentary edit-suite technology, and the low-definition 'airbrushed' quality of the picture are negative in this respect, and merely render the work cheap and crude. The keynote here is that the song opens up a world for the imagination to inhabit, whereas the reductive qualities of the video do the opposite. In commercial and promotional terms the video does its job, but at the expense of the song's virtues. Of course, we might add that the artist was young and inexperienced, and the form was still in its infancy, but certainly some of these observations could also have been levelled at the artist's debut album. However, the disparity in execution and affect between the song and the video for this track remains significant.

The second single from *Kick* was granted the same kind of lo-fi treatment on video, but was a more sexualised performance, both gesturally and in terms of the artist's skin-tight costume. Again, Kate Bush 'vamping it up' added nothing to the stark sensitivity imbued by the recording of 'The Man with the Child in his Eyes', although its visual impact may have been significant upon subsequent examples (see Britney Spears's costume in 'Toxic' many years later, Jovanovic, 2005: 78). Its provocative nature, although very tame by later video standards, did at least suggest that the young artist was confident enough to visually objectify the sexual aspect of her songwriting, although, in this case, it was aesthetically misplaced.

At around the same time Kate Bush appeared on *Top of the Pops* singing and dancing to accompany 'Wuthering Heights's promotion. She commented that reviewing the performance afterwards 'was like watching myself die' (Bush, in Jovanovic, 2005: 75). This was the first of many documented responses to visual re-presentations that suggests an at least ambivalent attitude towards the medium by the artist. Does Bush's discomfort reflect upon the differences in affective response engendered by audio and audio-visual forms? When bearing in mind her perfectionist nature and *modus operandi* it may be that the lack of control and time granted visual performances is the real critical issue here. Perhaps pop video, as an entity, is similarly just too 'rushed' in comparison to the music recording process to be truly comparative in aesthetic terms; numerous examples seem to bear this observation out.

'Wow' (Director Keef)

This video, accompanying the second single from *Lionheart*, is a fascinating, possibly unwitting manifestation of the commercial efficiency and aesthetic appeal of the pop promo form. On one level, it promotes several separate aspects of the artist: her career profile; a single musical track (whose narrative concerns stages and acting); the album from which this track has been lifted and the stage show (and subsequent video) that the artist had recently undertaken. The links between the song and the visual accompaniment are complex. On one level, the visuals are a montage of filmed performances of a variety of songs, and are nothing to do with 'Wow'. However, links both intended and unintended can be made between the visuals and some elements of the song. Lack of concrete reinforcement does encourage our imaginations to construct active, fragmentary narratives, rather than just consume others' imposed and preferred readings. In actual fact, what could be viewed as a cheap exercise in 'cobbling together' a video from extant sources works surprisingly well, and far better than many other examples that attempt, often unsuccessfully, to coherently 'marry' a dedicated video text to a specific track.

The musical track features the standardised device of an understated verse juxtaposed with an 'overblown', but effective chorus. The temptation would be to duplicate this within the video *mise-en-scène* by filling the screen with visual 'explosions' or equivalents during the chorus. However, the initial chorus in this video provides no visual 'lift' to accompany the musical climax, thus reining in the temptation to 'oversell' the narrative. During a subsequent chorus, the artist merely makes circular arm movements to accompany the repetition of 'wow, wow, wow, wow'. There is thus some link and a degree of anchorage involved, but the link is not rendered too blatant, unlike within previous examples. At other points, gestures from different songs do, almost magically, coincide. The artist tugs at the brim of her trilby whilst the synth fill at the end of the chorus 'tugs' against the chords in a staccato, jerky fashion. More obviously, Bush miming the action of murdering a fellow dancer accompanies the line 'he always dies too soon'. The link is associative rather than identical – dying against killing – and denies the over-reductive potential to 'pin down meaning'. In addition, the stage sequence comes from a completely different song performance – 'James and the Cold Gun', which is an up-tempo rock track, as opposed to a slow ballad. As the song reaches its understated conclusion, the artist in close-up, gazing out reflectively across the auditorium, connoting isolation rather than mapping it out with a redundant physical reinforcement, illustrates the line 'we're all alone on the stage'. Many other examples could be given of points of departure, or partial or complete conjuncture in terms of mood, gesture and editing between sound and vision components. The significant observation is that the viewer is engendered with the creative licence to create/complete their own text. Sound and visual elements are in a constant state of movement in terms of their connections and degree of anchorage. 'Wow' is a true exemplification of the form's ability to 'choreograph' without appearing over-planned. In this it parallels the affective status of music itself, which is invariably planned to perfection, but is consumed as a simulacrum of a 'live, spontaneous' event.

What this video indicates is that in conceptual or empirical terms, cheap does not always equal nasty, and that a degree of randomness in terms of planning, editing and intended affect is no bad thing, because our interpretive imagination 'fills the vacuum'. Kate Bush's earlier excesses are reined in within 'Wow' because her stage gestures are not directly related to the musical text, but act as more of a summary, or documentary, rather than an (over) acted and obvious drama.

The video engenders a final note of poignancy in the audience. The stage performances, even in their 'silent', dislocated form, do look seriously impressive. Who knows what might have been achieved had they been the precursor to more live productions, rather than a premature hiatus?

'Army Dreamers' (Director Keef)

By the period of Kate Bush's third album, *Never for Ever*, she had secured her position as a significant and successful artist and pop star. At the same time, she had, (unbeknown to all of us) largely 'retired' from both live performance and also the type of promotional activities usually demanded of someone in her position. Thus, with more time (and money) on her hands, the videos accompanying this album's singles were made appreciably more sophisticated, ambitious and expansive, although, by later standards, they do still appear 'quaint'.

'Army Dreamers', a location production, marries literal representations of the song's narrative to some important stylistic departures. The video begins with Bush, in close-up, miming the sampled sounds of rifle bolts by blinking. This is an early, but frequently employed example of over-emphasis. The artist also cannot resist the elaborate pouts, unrealistic miming and wide-eyed stares at camera that on occasions render her performances over-dramatic and 'hammy'.

A musical and lyrical reading of this song has already been offered. Suffice it to say that although the video is not without its merits, particularly in terms of the hand-held camera work and choreography of the ensemble actors, the visual repetitions, the sub-Peckinpah slow-motion fatalities and a location that resembles a 'paintballing' wood do nothing to complement the prior text. Of course, this is merely a reading. All pop videos naturally aspire to, and achieve, polysemic status. The very amateurishness may be a skilful, oblique commentary on the naïve 'boy soldier' scenario so skilfully suggested by the musical text, but this reader remains unconvinced. One device that works effectively is the Bush character searching for a boy behind a tree to find him transformed into a soldier, but when this scene is repeated the effect is to render us too deterministically led to the intended symbolism; the subtlety of the song is swamped by the visuals. The playwright Frederic Raphael made a pertinent observation in this respect when he suggested that words have a centrality in a single-sense medium, whereas within a multimedia text their impact is lessened. They move from having 'a jewelled particularity' (to being) 'drowned in a visual soup' (Raphael, in Crisell, 1996: 155).

The video is conceptually ambitious, and clearly evidences the expenditure of time, energy and money; but this does not vouchsafe merit. Bush has often referenced a liking for this example, seeing it as: 'a complete little film, not too grand and not clouding the issue' (Bush, in Sutcliffe, 1989: 87). Conversely, for this reader, the video for 'Breathing', whilst similarly expansive and ambitious, is both truer to the spirit of the song and more creatively symbolic. The artist, trapped inside what resembles a large polythene hamster exercise ball, does chillingly portray the innocence of childhood trapped in the womb being exposed to a nuclear winter. In addition, the video utilises contrasting scenes to engender a more didactic approach to the topic. The drawn-out coda of the song is effectively complemented by the visuals, yet without being 'mirrored', by the simple device of a group of performers slowly wading through water towards the camera. Thus the doleful rhythm of the music is paralleled by the visuals. This rhythmic synchronisation exploits the differences and connections between sounds and visuals (the actors 'struggle', the music seems to) more effectively than more blatant linking devices.

'Sat in your Lap' (Director Brian Wiseman)

We must never forget that the principal driving forces behind the pop video are commercial and pleasure based; pop videos are intended to be fun. 'Sat in your Lap' is certainly pleasurable, in a skittish and fragmentary fashion, but as with so many examples of the form, the parts that work well do not intend, or succeed in adding up to a substantial aesthetic experience. The video certainly does mirror the manic activity and energy of the musical track, and the contrasting scenes do reinforce the disparate structural components of the song. In addition, humour, a not overused device in the artist's *oeuvre*, is manifested effectively with dancers in dunce caps roller-skating unsteadily towards the camera. The flamenco-style dancing that accompanies the 'when I think I'm king' section is bold and erotic, with a hint that the artist is genuinely enjoying her physical prowess as she seductively smiles at us. Bush's eyes and pouts are nevertheless detractions from the other elements that are similarly exaggerated, but the overall mood of the piece is a fitting visual embellishment for the song. The other promo video from *The Dreaming* to accompany the title track is less successful, perhaps because, as with 'Army Dreamers', a serious yet subtle political point is better suggested through lyrics and music, rather than ostended through visual equivalents. The studio *mise-en-scène* is very well constructed, but the dancers cannot effectively convey the plight of the Aboriginals, and Bush's appearance in a water-cooled 'moon suit', complete with 1980s 'big hair' and trowel-loads of make-up and lipstick, seems seriously ill-advised if the intention is for the message to remain more important than the medium.

Hair of the Hound

In 1986, following the success and acclaim of *Hounds of Love*, the four singles' video tracks were collected onto a mini-album to accompany the previous year's music release. Significantly, all the tracks were from the first side of the album, and visually re-presented individual tracks. The conceptual suite of *The Ninth Wave* remained solely as a musical entity, for several obvious reasons relating to time, money and conceptual difficulty. The artist, looking back in 1990, commented: 'Each time I've done them I've become a bit more involved … My favourite ones are when it's a story … because then it is like making a film' (Bush, in Alexander, 1990). By this point the videos were actually shot on film, improving their definition and clarity, with the artist claiming that the entire planning and shooting process for texts such as 'Running up that Hill' and 'Cloudbusting' took several weeks (Bush, 1986). The videos for 'Hounds of Love' and 'The Big Sky' marked the artist's debut as video director. The collection was a big commercial success in the UK, reaching the top of the video sales charts in 1986, perhaps reflecting both the success of the musical album and also the growing maturation of the video form in both aesthetic and market terms. As the musical album from which the videos stem forms the critical centrepiece of this book, all the accompanying videos demand close attention as a consequence.

'The Big Sky' (Director Kate Bush)

'The Big Sky' functions partly as a homage to the author's love of film. Video is often criticised as being a postmodern, intertextual 'blank parody' of previous texts. Whilst such criticism may be justified in relationship to textual, critical theory, this cannot dispel the sheer communicative pleasure imbued by a form that, in this case, pays reference to texts as diverse as *Peter Pan*, *Mary Poppins* and *Singin' in the Rain*, as well as to the modern war film in more general terms. Similarly the, by now, high production values of the artist's videos do remove them from the level of sheer kitsch or amateurism: the sets, choreography, the camera movement and the use of garish militaristic colours and costumes all impress. Bush's manner to camera is more physically restrained, and all the better as a consequence. Despite the evident amount of planning involved in such a large cast video, some of the artist's dancing does come across as relatively spontaneous and un-choreographed. This contrasts well with some of the more obviously rehearsed set pieces. In overall terms this video is a big production number, yet the enjoyment of the ensemble remains a convincing aspect, to this reader (perhaps aided by the presence of Del Palmer as a Cossack). In terms of the links between song and video, they are achieved more through the nebulous moods of energy and clutter that are found within both forms' treatments of the material. In this, they are linked less through direct 'illustration' or simple 'resemblance' and more through symbolic 'amplification' and 'disjuncture', in Goodwin's terms (1993: 86–7).

    I have previously criticised the over-extended and rather aimless run-out coda of this musical track, but the accompanying visual images actually do much to recuperate this section, rendering the visual conclusion more satisfactory than the audio version – full of movement, colour and brio. In not over-emphasising narrative parallels, the video comes to inhabit a partly detached life of its own; connected to the musical text, but not constrained by it.

'Cloudbusting' (Director Julian Doyle)

The 12-inch, or extended mix – long a feature of dance genres – had expanded into commercial pop by the mid-1980s: indeed, the longer version of 'Running up that Hill' was many people's first exposure to the startlingly different sound of the artist's move towards more rhythmic and dance-based grooves, and which the subsequent album made even more apparent. The video version of 'Cloudbusting' paralleled this trend – in its complete form, running close to 6 minutes in length. In contrast to the previous track, this video is close to a 'literal' 'retelling' of the song narrative, itself based on a prior literary text. It is also the first Bush video to incorporate a professional actor, in this case the Canadian Donald Sutherland, to play the part of Wilhelm Reich. Bush particularly admired Sutherland's performance in Nicolas Roeg's *Don't Look Now* (1971), and she was later to contribute a song to one of the director's films. Bush plays his young son, Peter. In playing the part of a male child, Bush is granted the licence to be 'childish' and exaggerated in her gestures and emotions, just as children themselves are. Her performance gains credibility as a consequence. Conversely, Sutherland seems to overstate his performance when the narrative demands dramatic gestures or strong emotions. This observation acts to bear out the previously stated finding that the pop video form often seems to function, or gravitate towards a melodramatic, mime-based terrain – the actors are almost encouraged to imitate the silent film style rather than the 'naturalism' of later screen roles. However, the effectiveness of this style of performance is, at best, partial. When Sutherland has to 'do less', his performance seems more assured and persuasive.

On a more positive level the two protagonists work well together in forming a touching and convincing familial relationship, and the sets and locations are extremely effective. 'Cloudbusting' is a big production, but expressed in a more cinematic, narrative manner than 'The Big Sky'. The disjuncture between the rhythm of the music and the rhythm of the cinematography is extensive, but the resulting hybrid work does not suffer, proving again that the video form does have the licence to become tangential to the song it illuminates without losing impact or emotional depth. The 12-inch section, built musically upon the pared-down rhythms of sawing cellos and simple, metronomic drums, is well juxtaposed by the frantic montage of the narrative 'arrest' of Wilhelm Reich that the song itself does not deal with. Thus, the video broadens and expands the narrative of the text in cinematic terms. It does not 'replace' or supersede the musical text, but rather adds more layers of interpretation. It stands as an example of what the form can achieve in narrative terms, with the child-like 'closure' of the storyline granting the audience much simple satisfaction. 'Charming' is a much underused aesthetic term, but best summarises this video.

'Hounds of Love' (Director Kate Bush)

As a musical text that is deeply metaphorical and symbolic, this track encourages a visual accompaniment that is similarly detached from an over-literal re-presentation of the lyrics. For the most part, the video successfully achieves this task by creating a kind of parallel universe that runs alongside the music, and occasionally visually 'touches base'. At points, the video does 'map out' the lyrics closely – so the protagonists run through a dark wood to accompany the line 'it's coming for me through the trees'. However, it rightly resists the temptation to throw in a few actual hounds to render redundant the openness of the song's metaphorical beasts. Neither does Kate Bush's character throw her shoes into the lake when encouraged to do so by the lyrical narrative. Rather, the underlying mood of powerful forces of desire is skilfully expressed within the relationship of Bush and her paramour, a startlingly 'chiselled' actor/dancer who resembles a young, attractive version of Anthony Hopkins. Both the main protagonists are garbed in 1940s costume, all Fair Isle jumpers, suits and tweeds, placing us within a narrative redolent of *Brief Encounter* (David Lean, 1945) or *Mrs Miniver* (William Wyler, 1942). In actual fact, Jovanovic claims that the cinematic influence came from Hitchcock's *The Thirty-Nine Steps* (1935) at Paddy Bush's suggestion, thus accounting for a 'post-postmodern' cameo from the director within the video (Jovanovic, 2005: 168). Kate Bush, with her hair tied back into a wartime bun, is lit in a high-key, over-exposed manner that results in her positively glowing out of the screen, her scarlet lipstick contrasting the white, powdered pallor of her skin. The 'party scene', including their stylised *pas de deux*, actually returns us deeper into cinema history, with echoes of a smouldering Valentino seducing his partner on the dance floor. The links between the song and the video are subtle and open to interpretation. It is both artistic in conceptual terms and pleasurable in execution and affect, demonstrating that the artist had mastered the demands and constraints of the form very early in her directorial career.

'Running up that Hill' (Director David Garfath)

This video functions very much as a companion piece to the previous example, in terms of its narrative disjuncture being occasionally countered by direct elements of anchorage. It is similarly built upon movement rather than performance or mime, but moves further into the realms of pure, balletic dance for much of the song. Whilst I do not possess the formal, critical capacity to analyse the dancing in specialist terms, Bush and partner do seem to admirably symbolise the dialectical struggles of the lyric in terms of their sinuous, coiled movements. For the most part they are free from the rhythmic and tempo constraints of the song, although a couple of sequences and gestures do anchor the visuals closely to the musical track. In contrast to the over-redundant 'literalism' of the physical gestures on early Bush videos, here the moves themselves symbolically circle around the musical text, sometimes embracing it and sometimes diverting into parallel or disconnected routes, much like the two dancers. As well as the pleasure awarded to the 'lay' audience by the athleticism and sensuality of the duo who act as the visual centrepiece of the song, the studio confines are increasingly broached as the track progresses, with the literal anchorage of 'running up that road' contrasted by the sinister imposition of the male's face on multiple female bodies, and vice versa, towards the conclusion, before we are emotionally recuperated by a return to the dancers, symbolically posing to fire 'cupid's arrow'.

Kate Bush has seemingly denigrated this video, in terms of the form it takes. Although she thought it good, she also adds, in relating it to the personally preferred 'Cloudbusting', 'the one before was really a piece of dance, so we got away easy on that one' (Bush, in Marck, 1985: 11). Many would disagree with this estimation. This video is one of the most successful of the artist's entire career. The main dance sequence, although (intentionally?) filmed in indistinct, muted tones of grey and powder blue, is given the temporal space to literally 'take off' and exemplifies the artist's physical skills, the ability of the creators and the form itself to transcend the musical foundation without superseding it.

Coming to Terms with Video

By 1985, it is fair to summarise that the video form had both explored multiple narrative discourses and, for the most part, settled into standardised conventions and modes of communication. Since her early, faltering examples, Kate Bush's videos, whilst not uniformly successful, had improved in every aspect. The four examples from *Hounds* demonstrate the flexibility of video's relationship to music and lyrics, with 'Cloudbusting' being closely anchored to the prior text, and the other three, to a large extent, offering amplification or downright disjuncture between sensory re-presentations. The exaggerated poses and mimes of the early videos have been almost completely superseded by more 'naturalistic' forms of actorly re-presentation that have credibility, adding new levels in skilfully opening up the texts to new readings. The video form allowed an artist such as Kate Bush, possessing both talents as a dancer and a conceptual imagination, to broaden the palette of her authorship into new fields. In 1985 she was beginning to direct and at least conceive of ambitions to oversee a complete filmic narrative, a project she was later to fulfil. The essentially artistic, non-linear nature of her videos reflected well on both the audience's willingness to critically participate in 'challenging work' and also on the form's licence to challenge conventions. The so-called 'MTV aesthetic' may have played its part in adversely affecting racial and gender representations: it may have 'sexualised' pop culture and mitigated against ageing or un-photogenic performers, but its championing of the form has helped to contribute to a more sophisticated visual literacy on behalf of its, mostly young, 'unsophisticated' audience. This has allowed for artists such as Kate Bush to function successfully in both commercial and aesthetic terms. *Hair of the Hound* was the artist's first work to span both these (often antagonistic) worlds.

The Sensual World: The Video

By 1990, the growing gravitas afforded the video form encouraged some artists to include accompanying documentary material with their visual albums. Along with three pop promos to accompany the album's singles – 'The Sensual World, 'Love and Anger' and 'This Woman's Work' (two of which were solely directed by Bush, and one co-directed) – the video also featured a (by then) rare filmed interview which illuminated the artist's relationship to the video form in some detail. Also included were some sequences of Bush directing, viewing camera angles, rehearsing shots and generally, not unexpectedly, being the prime creative force behind the projects. At one point she seems to rail against the dominant imperatives towards complication and saturation within video texts:

> I wanted to make the video for 'The Sensual World' as simple as possible, in that so many videos now are overloaded with effects, big sets, they look expensive. So what we wanted to do was just keep it in one set, one environment and depict what, for me, 'The Sensual World' was all about. (Bush, in Alexander, 1990).

At other points she refers to her directing style, talking about storyboarding as a way of getting the team to understand what she wants.

'This Woman's Work' (Director Kate Bush)

Despite her desire for simplicity within certain video productions, exemplified by the title track, the shoot for 'This Woman's Work' is more similar to that of earlier, more expansive narratives such as 'Cloudbusting'. Another feature it shares is the utilisation of a professional actor, in this case Tim McInnerny, well known as one of the comic foils to Rowan Atkinson in the *Blackadder* series.

The song, a sensitive depiction of the inadequacy of men during the process of childbirth, is anchored, in a literal manner, by visual imagery. As with previous video examples, some of the more physical aspects of the performances by the acting ensemble are overwrought, although Kate Bush's vocal miming is nicely restrained. McInnerny, in particular, finds it hard to avoid the pitfalls of the form when attempting to express great frustration or regret. This is strange, bearing in mind the underplaying employed by the actor within films such as *Notting Hill* (Roger Michell, 1999). On the other hand, the dramatic montage, realised in cinematic flashback in the form of one tracking shot, is extremely effective, as we are taken from the initial birth pangs, through the drive to the hospital, and culminating in the male and female hands being separated by the hospital process as the mother-to-be is taken off to carry out her 'work'. The video offers more closure than the song, but cannot be read as a wholly successful addition to the extant text, although the direction and *mise-en-scène* show great assurance. The simplicity and more symbolic anchorage offered by the video for 'The Sensual World' is a more rewarding experience in most aspects; again, giving the audience more critical space within which to fashion their own readings.

The Line, The Cross and The Curve (Director Kate Bush)

In the wake of the release of *The Red Shoes*, the artist, still mourning the death of her mother, embarked upon the ambitious video album that attempted to fashion a linear narrative out of several of the album's tracks. According to Doyle, this was advised against by some of the artist's collaborators, although their precise reasons remain unclear (Doyle, 2005: 81). The first issue raised is that *The Line* is not the visual accompaniment to the album in any coherent or sequential form; in fact, its relationship to both the album and the songs is ambivalent, if not downright confusing. The song order is rearranged from the album, and three separate versions of the title track are included. We are thus encouraged to view the work as a near-separate entity, whose narrative attempts to forge its own path. This path is notably different from that of the film *The Red Shoes*, featuring nothing of the romantic *ménage à trois*, and its fantasy narrative seems to share more common features with children's texts such as *Alice Through the Looking Glass* and, particularly, *The Wizard of Oz*. In this it may, of course, be intentionally harking back to the Andersen fairytale that was the basis for Powell's film. Rather than seeking to gain clarity and narrative closure, it is more productive to view this work as a hybrid, featuring aspects of dance, mime, speech and sequences redolent of classic Hollywood musicals. Herein lies its chief shortcoming: both the musical form and the mime technique rely on a large amount of audience suspension of disbelief. This factor, allied to the exaggerated gestures and 'magical' script and narrative, does render the film reminiscent of pantomime or juvenile drama on several occasions.

The film begins with a relatively straightforward dance-based depiction of 'Rubberband Girl'. Bush had trained hard to get back into shape during the preceding period, and her symbolically elasticated moves with a male dancer are athletic and effective. Props such as yo-yos and a straitjacket are skilfully incorporated and the backing musicians strike the only false note, moving stiffly in time with the beat whilst miming playing. After a brief linking sequence with Peter Richardson and a wind machine and Bush and partner rehearsing a move (in *cinema verité* mode), we are pushed into a more fantastic world for 'And so is Love', with Bush miming the lyric persuasively during the verses before her delivery becomes exaggerated for the chorus sections. The sequence for 'The Red Shoes' takes us into the symbolic core of the narrative, with actress Miranda Richardson, in the guise of an 'evil witch', brokering a cruel bargain with the Bush character, leaving her trapped in wearing the 'cursed' ballet shoes, unable to physically and metaphorically 'get home'. Much of the remainder of the film features her attempts to return. The sequences that do work are those that allow the artist to concentrate on dance and movement. When 'acting' in scenes with Richardson, the comparative disparity in experience between musician and actress leaves Bush cruelly exposed. This should come as no surprise, but nevertheless, the director's ambition, or possibly hubris in attempting to compete with an acclaimed and skilful professional, makes for uncomfortable viewing. In addition, the appearances of Lindsay Kemp are similarly overwrought. During 'Lily' the dialogue relating to 'singing back the symbols' is clumsy and juvenile, although the Bush character's own monologue during an instrumental sequence of the title track is more poetic in its 'heightened' use of register, and more persuasive as a consequence.

'Moments of Pleasure' is the single most successful sequence in aesthetic terms. Although it cannot match the emotional depths engendered by the musical text, the simple visual accompaniment of the artist spinning slowly against a variety of backdrops is well structured. Even the possibilities for cliché and melodrama inherent in having symbols of 'the departed' blown past the artist cannot diminish the potential to be moved by this tract of film. As with so many other video examples, simplicity and a lack of direct, anchored closure is the reason for its success. Unfortunately, the ensuing sequence draws us into an over-literal representation of 'Eat the Music', complete with smiling, exotic 'ethnics' from some kind of commercial for mango smoothies. After bursting back through the symbolic mirror the Bush character defeats the evil witch and is freed from the malevolent power of the ballet pumps, which are rendered harmless. It is difficult to render an account of this narrative without denigrating its storyline, which is essentially naïve, or even amateurish. The always self-critical artist has been particularly derogatory of both this work and her own contribution to it, going as far as referring to it as 'a load of old bollocks' (Bush, in Doyle, 2005: 81). To another interviewer, she confided:

> I shouldn't have done it … I was so tired. I'm very pleased with four minutes of it. I let down people like Miranda Richardson who worked so hard on it. I had the opportunity to do something really interesting and I completely blew it. (Bush, in Aizlewood, 2001: 95).

At around the time of the release of the film, she stated blatantly that: 'I'm no actress. I don't have the talent or the temperament' (Bush, in Maconie, 1993: 101). Unfortunately, the film project did ask her to act, and proved her self-assessment largely justified.

On several levels, we can view the project as ill-advised and over-ambitious, but the artist is too negative, and two or three sequences do work well. In its favour, the sequential nature does allow the poorer elements to be partially absorbed within the overall narrative, much as poor tracks within the artist's concept works appear less exposed than unsuccessful discrete songs on certain albums. Its 45-minute running time does not come across as excessive, but in both commercial and aesthetical terms, it was, and remains a 'vanity project' strictly for committed fans of the artist.

To conclude, Kate Bush's video work has exposed many of the pitfalls, yet also highlighted many of the creative possibilities of the form. She matured rapidly, as both a performer and then a director between 1978 and 1985. By the time of *Hounds of Love* she had tempered her physical performance excesses and was drawing more heavily upon her strengths in both dance and directorial *montage* and *mise-en-scène*. In retrospect, it is fitting to judge the video adaptations of the tracks from *Hounds of Love* to be her most successfully realised, with *Hair of the Hound* standing as an object lesson in how to combine creativity and experimentation in a commercially successful audio-visual package. They have scope and breadth, sometimes staying close to the lyrical text, but more often assuming a semi-detached life of their own. Bearing in mind the ambitions of the artist, the subsequent attempt to fashion a filmic narrative came as no surprise, but, for a variety of reasons, its successful execution eluded her. Its relative failure must have been a chastening experience for one so used to both commercial and critical success, and may have proven a contributory factor in her increasingly withdrawn career path in the years following its release.

Part Three

Her Later Work

The Whole Story

In the wake of the huge critical and commercial success of *Hounds of Love*, EMI did what any self-respecting commercial label would do to fill the anticipated gap before the next release, by issuing a compilation 'Greatest Hits' package. It was entitled, confusingly, *The Whole Story*, and released in November 1986. The package consisted of all her single hits, plus the newly recorded 'Experiment IV', whose uncompromising sound prevented it from climbing higher than 23 in the UK singles chart. It was, however, the basis for one of her most ambitious videos. The album and accompanying video collection both did extremely well, giving Bush her second chart topper(s) in succession in her home country. The album sold in excess of one million in the UK alone. The video also reached number 8 in the US charts, giving Bush her first bona fide major hit in that territory. As a 'cherry picking' exercise, the compilation refocussed our attention upon the remarkably bold and varied body of work released as singles over nearly a decade, in the process garnering the artist new, possibly younger fans unfamiliar with her pre-*Hounds* material.

The Period Leading up to *The Sensual World*

Contrary to many tabloid press tales, Kate Bush never has been 'a recluse', but instead has jealously valued her private life, and partly retreated from the glare of the public eye, usually following the release and promotion of an album. In the period between 1986 and 1989 she undertook a number of small-scale projects. Amongst these were singing on and appearing in the simple, beautiful video for Peter Gabriel's 'Don't Give Up' single – a big hit in 1986. She also re-recorded her vocal for a new version of 'Wuthering Heights', which accompanied 'Experiment IV' in October of the same year. I have never chosen to seek out or listen to this version, which would have an impossible job in replicating the perfection of the original, to my way of thinking.

Other projects included contributing live performances of songs to charitable evenings (*Utterly, Utterly Comic Relief*, April 1986 and *The Secret Policeman's Third Ball*, 28 March 1987; performing 'Running up that Hill' and 'Let It Be' with David Gilmour and Peter Gabriel) and providing the film *Castaway* (Nicolas Roeg, 1987), with an excellent song ('Be Kind To My Mistakes', March 1987). Even better was 'This Woman's Work' (which I'll return to later). This epic ballad was used in John Hughes's film *She's Having a Baby* (1988). She was also the subject of an interview disc, released in April 1987.

According to Phil Sutcliffe's 1989 *Q* interview, Bush rushed into writing and planning her next project too soon after completing the recording and promotional duties for *Hounds*:

> I was going quickly at first, thinking, nah, piece of piss! Then it all seemed like rubbish and I had to stop for a while. There's tremendous self-doubt involved. You think, Oh, God, I'll never get it finished. (Sutcliffe, 1989: 91).

Perhaps the spectre of the triumph of the previous album was bearing down on her, although the artist has never alluded to this. She confided to Len Brown in finding 'the writing very difficult on this ... I'd get to the point where I couldn't write, where I was sick of the songs' (Brown, 1988). Despite these creative blocks, recording what became *The Sensual World* took some two and a half years, on and off – not a huge amount of time by the standards of many artists. This period included collaborating with the Irish traditional act, The Chieftains, and travelling to Bulgaria to painstakingly work and record with the Trio Bulgarka, whose vocals Bush became entranced by in 1986. The album was finally released in October 1989, prefaced by the title track as its first single, released in September.

The Sensual World

'The Sensual World'

The title track announces the album in confident, if not strident or striking fashion, immediately referencing something of a return to a more organic and 'played' instrumental palette after the sonic and production experiments of the previous two albums.

Whilst not possessing the sort of standout qualities associated with her classic singles, 'The Sensual World' was a sound commercial choice, particularly effective in helping to reinsert the artist into the consciousness of the mainstream market after the three-year hiatus following *The Whole Story*. It reached number 12 in the UK chart, and was a smaller hit in several other territories. However, the track does set the tone for some of the shortcomings of the album as a whole. In particular, the mix and production seem muddy and tentative. Lead vocals are routinely under-mixed and too heavily reverbed, instrumentation lacks clarity and separation and, most tellingly, the producer was still persisting with the now outdated Gabriel/Collins 'big' snare sound that proves a near constant and intrusive presence on this album. In addition, the artist was either unable or unwilling to write consistently memorable melodies. Many of the verses on the album, this track being a prime example, are simply forgettable.

In its favour, the track is transformed by the superb instrumental breaks constructed by Davey Spillane, Donal Lunny and John Sheahan, which provide the emotive and textual highlight. We can only applaud the bravery of the artist in foregrounding the Celtic instrumentation, even to the detriment of her own contributions. The song itself, based upon the Molly Bloom character in James Joyce's *Ulysses*, and actually paraphrasing the novel (the estate of Joyce proved less than cooperative), is a brave attempt at expressing the sensuality of the literary text, in the process allowing the character to escape from the author 'out into the real world, being the real human ... stepping out of the page into the sensual world', as Bush said to Len Brown in 1988. Certainly, the lyrics themselves are rooted in desire and sensuality, but the vocals less so; perhaps the efforts are just too blatant. As so often in her career, this track would have worked better as an album track, rather than lead-off single. The album is not packed with obvious hit singles, but there were better choices than this piece.

'Love and Anger'

This track bustles along with some vitality, nicely driven by the artist's own piano work, Stuart Elliott's tribal drumming and Paddy Bush's underpinning on yet another exotic instrument from his seemingly boundless collection – in this case the valiha. The lyric, focussing on the nature of a relationship, features a strong chorus including the soaring exclamation 'What would I/we do without you?' which provides a wonderful moment of release. However, the scansion of other parts of the lyric seem particularly clumsy and forced, and the track is forced down to earth by the almost inevitable dull thud of the snare, which whilst intended to take the rhythm track to another level, actually drags it out of its skittish African terrain into something more pedestrian. In addition, the tendency to let a track fizzle out into some kind of aimless 'jam' – not uncommon in the artist's *oeuvre* – again surfaces during the latter part of 'Love and Anger'. The effect and feel is very similar to that imbued towards the end of 'The Big Sky', and about as necessary. The artist only reinforces these musical shortcomings with the confession that 'I just didn't know what I wanted to say. Really, it was a bugger, that song. And in some ways I still don't know what I'm trying to say' (Bush, in Jovanovic, 2005: 176). During this section, longstanding mentor Dave Gilmour moves away from the power chords that effectively boost the emotional charge of the chorus to provide some lead work that fails to escape from the bounds of cliché. One is left yearning for the economy of the artist's early work and her former ease with lyric and melody.

As the third track released as a single, the song reached 38 in the UK charts, which, if we can compare chart positions to the concept of 'fairness', seems about right.

'The Fog'

In both its title and the employment of spoken interludes – in this case by Bush's father (credited as 'Dr. Bush') – this song provides clear echoes with the atmospheres of *The Ninth Wave*, in particular. It is 'one of two consecutive songs addressing parent-child relationships' (Jovanovic, 2005: 176). Featuring a host of stellar contributors (classical violinist Nigel Kennedy, orchestrator Michael Kamen and Breton virtuoso Alan Stivell), this track begins engagingly with tom-toms and whistles before being augmented by Alan Murphy's jazzy chording on an acoustic guitar. Bush's vocal is higher in the mix on this track, and features the semi-constricted delivery that she has, for whatever reason, been drawn to on occasions as her career has progressed. Is it mere affectation, or a deliberate device to serve the needs of the narrative? We, the ignorant listeners, are unsure. It certainly provides an interesting texture to this track, which operates in very similar lyrical territory to the previous song.

The track slides into the orchestration of the chorus seductively, complemented by the line 'you slip into the fog'. That snare sound resurfaces, but is nicely contained by other elements, rather than brutally exposed, as on several other tracks. In all the mix is full and sympathetic to the needs of the song, with a pleasingly Chinese flavour provided by the precise strings and the subtle Celtic harp flourishes. When Bush 'opens up' her voice she provides us with evidence of a truly deep and rich vibrato that is the positive gift of vocal maturity. Occasional upward darts to her higher register provide affirmation of her continuing unique ability to switch between timbres and musical personalities in the space of one short vocal phrase. The overall melody lacks scope or originality (for Bush, the track was simply the account of 'trying to grow up') but the track as a complete entity is both well conceived and, more importantly, well produced.

'Reaching Out'

In the midst of the unfolding succession of tracks on *The Sensual World* comes this welcome curio. The whole track is redolent of the conventions and tidiness of the first album. After a short, conventional piano introduction we are eased into a lyrical terrain that is classic early Bush in its slightly precious and portentous evocation of both youthful and mature desire. The verse melody has a distinctiveness unusual on this album, and the run-up to the chorus features the welcome return of the lowly mixed choral 'yays' so typical of *Hounds of Love*.

The chorus itself, accompanied by the soaring strings of usually minimalist composer Michael Nyman, is classic transcendent pop, perhaps a little obvious in its intentions, but thrilling none the less. The vocal melody, pulling us up into the heavens, has both power and clarity and is perfectly phrased. As with another song placed later on this album, the strong impression I am given is of an artist looking back, and almost intentionally drawing upon a now superseded way of working with the sense of 'I used to do songs like this, I don't often any more'. The unusual nature of this exercise only strengthens its impact. 'Reaching Out' is a simple pop ballad that is little more than two verses and two choruses in structural terms. Like much of the artist's early classic work, it is over almost before we realise it, a conventional, yet perfectly formed jewel.

Almost inevitably, its unusual strengths and winningly commercial nature do put many of the other tracks on this album into the shade, particularly as there seems little of the musical or conceptual unity of purpose on *The Sensual World* that gave *Hounds Of Love* much of its drive and narrative breadth. So the success of 'Reaching Out' poses an enigma, one that the artist is unwilling or unable to resolve in the context of her work in this period. In being yet another song about generational relationships, based upon the straightforwardness of mother and child, it is tempting to ascribe maternal yearnings to the artist. Three songs in short succession do bear out a possible subliminal desire on the part of the now mature woman to give birth, but these must remain intentionalist assumptions on behalf of the analyst.

'Heads We're Dancing'

This track is built upon two firm bases; instrumentally it has a little of the more programmed and sequenced feel of the previous album, which makes for a welcome departure from some of the rather pedestrian 'playing' of *The Sensual World*; and secondly it takes us out of the 'realistic' terrain of many of the lyrics on the album by returning us to the more surreal and bizarre territory of *Never for Ever* and *The Dreaming*. The lyrics seem to concern the narrator engaging in a *pas de deux* with a well-known fascist dictator. In conceptual terms, the author claimed that it was based upon the anecdotal evidence of a friend who had been charmed by an individual whose true past was later discovered. This inspiration, with its scope for disguise, seduction and the exploration of schizophrenia (echoes of 'Babooshka' and 'The Infant Kiss'), provides the writer with the raw material to fashion a fascinating lyric, complete with the effective symbolism of the flip of the coin functioning on more than one level.

The musical run-out does at least move us beyond the terrain of aimless jamming by giving us some liquid bursts of bass (Robert Sandall coins the wonderful neologism 'sproingy') from that most elastic of musicians, Japan's former bassist, Mick Karn. The whole rhythm section does seem to pay tribute to one of pop music's great genre-benders – David Bowie. There are certainly echoes of his work with Nile Rodgers from *Let's Dance* on display here, particularly the title track and 'China Girl'. Although not totally breaking free from the dated feel of the backing track (Bowie's album was released in 1983, when the timbres felt fresh), the track is full of interest for its full five-minute length, with Bush the narrator and Bush the subject parting company for a brief, but welcome period.

'Deeper Understanding'

Featuring a not uncommon lyrical conceit in the computer age (to the effect that 'people don't understand me, I get more from machines'), it is tempting but rather unambitious (and ultimately too reductive) to view this track as autobiographical. A more imaginative reading would be to partly focus upon the skilful way that the lyric comments upon its own structure, just as the computer 'comments' on the narrator. This neatly foregrounds the standard verse-into-chorus shift, where the narrator presses 'Execute' and we are delivered into the soaring harmonies of the Trio Bulgarka. Upon this vocal bed John Giblin's bass plays very high melodic counterpoint melody lines whilst the piano grounds the feel in root chords. Bush's own multi-tracked melody is under-mixed; indeed, one of the most impressive facets of this track is the generosity of the 'star' to cede the sonic spotlight to her collaborators. The tribal tom-toms and tuned percussion give a light bounce to the rhythm to contrast with the washes of vocal harmonies. At two points the soloist in the Trio is pushed to the forefront of the mix. Her microtonal melisma is thrilling to western ears used to over-familiar intervals and melodies and accounted for some of the success of the constructed 'world music' genre of this period.

Throughout 'Deeper Understanding', the juxtaposition of the 'cold' world of binary codes and the 'warmth' of sonic elements is most impressive. The run-out section is also well expressed, with the ambience of the cold computer 'bleeps' being crossed with the sampled birdsong that helps bring it to a conclusion. The overall impression of technology in all its myriad positive and negative forms acts as a lyrical object lesson in how to embrace change, yet recognise its shortcomings. The importance, yet artificiality, of binary distinctions has rarely been expressed so seductively through both lyrics and sonic timbres as on this track.

'Between a Man and a Woman'

This track is another example of the many shortcomings made manifest at this point of the artist's career. After a melodically rhythmic verse that promises much, the bulk of the track falls into the over-familiar sonic terrain of dull, thudding snares, unmelodic vocals and unimaginative lyrics. Some interesting cello lines occasionally enliven the essentially droning nature of the backing track, but the song is 'album filler' at best. For a lyricist of the artist's guile and invention to state in the most straightforward of terms the mundane message that a third party should keep out of the affairs of a couple is an example of both composer and listener being 'sold short'. The exhortations and threats ('Do not interfere – you are not needed here' … 'And now I'm telling you again') are unconvincing and lack emotional gravitas or conviction. As so often, the inspiration for this track comes from cinema, in this case a quotation from Marlon Brando's character in *The Godfather* (Francis Ford Coppola, 1972), but the song never really takes flight. The strong impression given by such a track is that the artist is most suited and creatively stretched by more esoteric subject matter. The overwhelmingly literal feel of both the lyrics and the instrumental accompaniment makes this track a forgettable and very disappointing one.

'Never Be Mine'

'Never Be Mine' is essentially the second collaboration between Bush and the Trio Bulgarka, although their relationship on this track is more standardised. Rather than almost taking over the track, their contributions are more muted here, close to the manner of the 'exotic toning' more widely adopted by westerner musical 'tourists'. This implicit criticism cannot be aimed at Kate Bush if we view her career as a whole. In the context of this track, the more important ethnic contribution is made within the main body of the song by the multi-tracked uilleann pipes of the familiar Davey Spillane. However, the concluding section does reintroduce the Trio neatly.

The song itself is another structural and lyrical descendant of the artist's earliest recordings: economic, direct and proving yet again her ability to write a transcendent chorus that is life affirming and almost thrilling. I say almost as 'Never Be Mine' does not feel like much more than a skilful retread of familiar ground, albeit one that pleasingly swaps the swamping drum sounds of many of this album's tracks with a lighter and more effective skeletal sound. As on so many Kate Bush tracks, a sinuous bass provides much of the melodic impact, on this track functioning as a lead instrument at points. Unlike the previous track there is nothing to upset or annoy the long-term aficionado of her music, but the imbued feeling is one of slight ennui.

The huge legacy of *Hounds of Love* does cast its long shadow over such material, with *The Sensual World* starting to feel like a real disappointment by this point in the proceedings.

'Rocket's Tail (For Rocket)'

To dispel a lot of the anti-climactic feelings imbued by this album comes 'Rocket's Tail', an unusual track in the context of both *The Sensual World* and the artist's entire career. After some 90 seconds of intense, almost melodramatic harmonies from the Trio balanced by Bush's more restrained delivery of the lead vocal, we are abruptly hurled (fired?) into the intensity of a blues-rock rhythm track in triple time. The liveness of the feel is partly the result of the power with which Stuart Elliott hits the drums and the 'natural' resonance of the kit itself. David Gilmour contributes strangled lead lines on guitar that fit the generic mood perfectly, and we are witnessing a Bush track that feels closer to 'rocking out' than any other in her extensive *oeuvre*. It works very well, partly as it blows a few cobwebs away, in sonic terms, and also because it complements the slightly crazed imagery evoked by the lyrics, featuring the mad symbol of a firework-powered witch soaring over the River Thames. This subject matter returns us to the lyrical craziness and bravery of *The Dreaming* and *Never for Ever*, but one still grounded in the evocative reality of documentary detail (mention of Waterloo Bridge, highly symbolic to both Londoners and fans of 'little Englanders' such as the Kinks, in particular).

This burst of unhinged energy does nothing for the cohesion of what is, by now, turning into a very fragmented album – but is much needed as both a reminder of the musical and lyrical scope of the writer, and also of her wilfulness as an artist.

'This Woman's Work'

And so to this marvellous contradiction of a track, one that for a small difference in timbre in the vocals could almost seamlessly be slotted in next to any track on the first two albums. I have previously argued that this essentially backward-glancing aspect of Kate Bush's career on *The Sensual World* is not one for particular celebration, but when a ballad as thoughtful and downright beautiful as this emerges, it is impossible not to succumb utterly to its charms.

The conventional nature of the lyric should not mask its empathy, not its essential ambiguity. Again, the subject matter is a reflection upon gender roles and relations, delivered with a mixture of understanding, yearning and regret that is beguiling in its lack of clarity. The vocal range, melody and dynamic power are all simply stunning, although inevitably imbued with enigmatic issues relating to why the artist can't or won't always sing like this. Jovanovic is correct in judging the track to be 'This breath of fresh air … infuriating because a little more restraint on some of the earlier tracks could have made this a really classic album instead of just an OK one' (Jovanovic, 2005: 179). The accompaniment is back to basics: a piano accompaniment straight out of the Elton John manual of complementary lead-and-chord work, and a string arrangement by Michael Kamen strongly reminiscent of his film scores that never intrudes on the melody and message of the artist. The track was 'a really easy song to put together' (Bush, in Jovanovic, 2005: 179). 'This Woman's Work' is one of the most emotionally affecting of the artist's whole career. It deserved to be a major hit in the same way that 'The Man with the Child in his Eyes' was, but only reached number 25 in the UK.

'Walk Straight Down the Middle'

Despite strong claims to having written the classic 'album closer' with the previous track, whose emotional power would seem hard to beat, the artist chose to conclude the album with this less stand-out song. (The vinyl version did end with 'This Woman's Work', so the CD 'bonus' is nothing of the sort.) The reasons, of course, remain unknown to the listener, who only has the realities of the songs and their imbued affect as guides. The run-out section is nicely drifting and spacious on a pedal note, which suits a fade-out, but the earlier part of the track is resolutely pedestrian and underwhelming in all respects. It thus joins a few more songs on this album in that critical hinterland of 'not awful, but nothing special'. Some artists make a lucrative career out of fulfilling the needs of an undemanding public by providing just this kind of experience, but for an artist such as Kate Bush, unremarkable is unacceptable.

In comparison to its triumphant predecessor, *The Sensual World* does suffer. There are no genuinely bad songs, as found on *Lionheart*, and no sequences of substandard material, as found on *The Dreaming*. Nevertheless, despite several excellent tracks, the album, in terms of its lyrics, performances and production, does exhibit a certain degree of conservatism in terms of ambition and scope. The three tracks featuring the Trio Bulgarka, whilst all of high quality, do imbalance the album. Had the singers been featured on just one stand-out track, or conversely on the whole album, as genuine co-creators, this shortcoming could have been overcome. In addition, the constricted vocal delivery, which the artist employs from time to time, is irritating, particularly as other vocal performances show amazing power and range – again, the key term is imbalance. The ballads ('Reaching Out' and 'This Woman's Work') rank amongst the artist's finest, although they cannot hope to repeat the impact of her emergent, *ingénue* songs. It is the simple songs that work best. Several other tracks are also first-rate, particularly where the artist has a lyric that suits her essentially eccentric world-view, as on 'Rocket's Tail'.

As Jovanovic noted, when reviewing the critical reception for this album: 'Many fans were not overly impressed … It included several mid-paced, middle-of-the-road tracks that failed to sparkle' (Jovanovic, 2005: 175). Paradoxically, her desire to express herself in a way that was more intensely personal and emotional did result in songs and lyrics inhabiting a more standardised pop terrain of relationships, albeit ones without the closure and resolution of stereotypical romance narratives. The artist herself referred to it as her:

> most feminine album … On *The Dreaming* and *Hounds of Love* … I wanted to get a lot more weight and power, which I felt was a very male attitude. In some cases it worked very well, but this time I felt braver as a woman. (Bush, in Jovanovic, 2005: 175).

However, it can be argued that this bravery does not come across on the album. Some spoke of *The Sensual World* being the artist's most mature work, which perhaps encapsulates my (relative) misgivings, particularly in the light of previous, downright unhinged work. The problem with producing a classic is that all subsequent work is viewed through a false and damaging critical prism – thus, *The Sensual World*, whilst a fine album, remains a relative disappointment.

This Woman's Work

In 1990 EMI released an eight-CD box set that consisted of Bush's first six studio albums, plus two CDs of extra tracks (b-sides, 12-inch mixes, foreign-language versions of songs). Although gaining praise for its lavish packaging, the artistic reasons for its release are practically non-existent. Bush fanatics would already have owned most, if not all the extras, and more casual fans would presumably have already owned the original albums, or their CD re-releases. In addition, the package was grossly over-priced and sales would probably have reflected all the aforementioned issues. One can only assume that EMI were cashing in on an artist expected to take several years to produce any new material. Of course the music as a body of work was, and remains, hugely impressive.

The Period Leading up to *The Red Shoes*

It is fair to say that the period following the release of *The Sensual World*, in 1989, up to the release of *The Red Shoes*, in 1993, does find Ms Bush to be at her most 'low-key' in media and publicity terms. The most comprehensive of her fan websites lists 'no entries' under TV appearances for both 1991 and 1992, and scarcely any press articles in the same period. However, in 1990, after a Kate Bush convention, the artist answered questions for 45 minutes, and claimed to be planning to perform some concerts (Jovanovic, 2005: 184). Nothing ever came of these plans.

With the internet still in its infancy, the artist effectively 'disappeared' from public view for a period of around three years. However, this fact did not signal any form of retirement from the groundwork of composition and planning. The artist claimed to have put a solid two years of work into her next release in the period between the two albums (Jonssen, 1993: 34). In addition to this project, Bush recorded a cover version of Elton John's 'Rocket Man', as part of the *Two Rooms* tribute compilation. The single, whilst not matching the original, was a moderate hit in September 1991. Shortly before the release of *The Red Shoes*, the artist contributed the title song to the soundtrack album accompanying Terry Gilliam's wildly surreal and imaginative film *Brazil* (1985). In addition, the pre-planning of *The Red Shoes* also had to accommodate the process of writing and directing an accompanying short film, *The Line, The Cross and The Curve*, which starred Miranda Richardson, mime legend and early mentor Lindsay Kemp and the artist herself.

The final major demand upon her time in this period was a return to dedicated dance training, after a gap of some time. The importance to the artist of this facet of her creative life is indicated by the large photograph of Bush and her dance partner, which takes up a lot of space on the 'inner sleeve' poster of the CD for the album. In some ways the work is clearly based upon a dance/cinematic theme – *The Red Shoes* being a film about ballet.

For Bush, this period was marked by the sudden and unexpected death of her mother, Hannah, in February 1992 – a devastating blow for a family as geographically and emotionally close-knit as the Bushes. She was to make reference to the gravity of this occurrence in interviews conducted around the time of *The Red Shoes*'s release, and it is hard, with the benefit of biographical hindsight, not to view the album through a prism of loss – the album is dedicated to her mother's memory. The bereavement also delayed the recording and release of the album; she admitted 'I couldn't work for months … I had no desire to start, no desire to work at all' (Bush, in Jonssen, 1993: 33). In addition, guitarist Alan Murphy and dancer Gary Hurst also died in the period leading up to *The Red Shoes*.

Some time between *The Sensual World* and *The Red Shoes*, her romantic relationship with long-term collaborator Del Palmer also ended, although the two of them have continued to work together. As well as contributing to the Fairlight programming, Palmer is credited, somewhat vaguely, as having 'recorded' the album, as well as the more common term 'mixed'. In addition, the artist herself produces, although, strangely for one so concerned with spacial and temporal independence, she chose to go back into a commercial recording studio, EMI's Abbey Road, rather than record in her own. Another personal loss was that of the film director Michael Powell, the co-creator of the original film *The Red Shoes* (1948). Bush managed to meet Powell just once before his death, but was deeply affected by the encounter.

Kate Bush's myriad film influences have already been stated. However, with *The Red Shoes* being the artist's most high-profile and direct homage to a prior text, it is necessary to briefly talk about the film and the career of its co-creator, and one of Britain's most acclaimed film *auteurs*.

Michael Powell (and his early collaborator, Emeric Pressburger) wrote and produced many of the most imaginative British films of the 1940s and 1950s. Powell's career was effectively curtailed by the adverse reception afforded his final project, *Peeping Tom*, in 1960. This film is now accepted as a classic, along with earlier projects such as *The Life and Death of Colonel Blimp* (1943) and *Black Narcissus* (1947). *The Red Shoes*, based on a Hans Christian Andersen fairytale, concerns an intense *ménage à trois* between a ballerina, a composer and an impresario. The narrative ultimately ends in tragedy, and is remembered today for its radiant use of Technicolor, and the imaginative, almost surreal dance sequences featuring the ballerina Moira Shearer wearing the eponymous footwear. The image of the ballet pumps was to form the centrepiece of the cover for the musical album so clearly inspired by the film and its maker(s).

In addition to the CD cover and inner sleeve images already mentioned, the fold-out lyric and credits sheet is laid over a photograph of a fruit salad of exotic items: melons, mangoes, passion fruit, figs, papayas and others too difficult to identify! The image ties in closely with the text of the song 'Eat the Music', which I will return to in due course. Suffice it to say that the exotic and erotic potential of the split fruits, spilling seeds and juice in an almost tactile manner, is well expressed by the image.

This synaesthetic relationship to love and sex is a constant presence throughout the artist's career, dating back as far as tracks such as 'Feel It', from the first album.

The Red Shoes

'Rubberband Girl'

The lead-off track, and first single, announces itself in strident and ringing fashion. At last, my personal bugbear – the murky and dead drum sound of the previous album – is replaced by a livelier and more resonant sound. Whilst not 'contemporary', when bearing in mind the revolutionary shifts in drum timbres delivered by post-house dance sub-genres such as techno and rave, the bright and reverberant kit lifts the track into a terrain connoting energy and optimism. Woven into the mix are multi-tracked guitar lines, both melodic and driving, and it is obvious from the very outset that this track is probably the most overtly 'commercial' that the artist has ever released.

After the initial solo voice verse, the chorus adds bass and backing vocals. The structure hints at the simplicity of the standard 12-bar blues progression, and the lyrics only reinforce the direct energy of the backing. The main vocal line in this song is often the artist tracked in unison, rather than harmony. If the lowest notes are indeed achieved without sampling or other studio trickery, then they are astonishing tributes to the vocal range of Kate Bush, being towards the low end of male baritone range. Yet again, her voice engenders wonder and incomprehension in the listener.

Low in the mix are added grunting brass riffs and what sound like marimbas or similar (they are uncredited). The final instrumental component is some form of keyboard or sample, again uncredited, but the overall impression is of directness and simplicity in the mix – full yet essentially bright and uncluttered. At around 2:40 we are treated to some microtonal wailing from the artist that exudes freedom and a willingness to move outside of the tonal constraints of western pop. Even the (intentionally?) histrionic nature of the (guitar?) solo seems to perfectly build on the whole feel of the track. The brass riff that rises up in the mix is almost pure Stax, and the vocal yo-yoing towards the fade-out is fittingly elastic.

Of course, compared to the standard pop lyric 'Rubberband Girl' is rather eccentric in its use of metaphor, but in terms of 'market requirements', the track was an ideal reintroduction of the artist into public awareness, and deserved to be a much bigger hit than it was (number 12 in the main UK chart). More importantly, it signalled a renewed sense of sonic confidence on the part of the writer/producer, and boded well for subsequent tracks.

'And So Is Love'

Featuring subtly synthetic drum timbres and atmospheric keyboard 'pipes', this song starts moodily, with Bush's vocals deep and resonant, if slightly world-weary, reflecting the lyric 'We see that life is sad, And so is love'. Despite the final couplet 'You set me free, I set you free' this is not a redemptive lyric or musical track.

Am I also being too pedantic in noting an unnecessary amount of 'transatlantic' vocal styling creeping in? Prior to this point, it is fair to say that the vocalist has been the most English of singers in all respects, and so the hegemonic incursions of a more American register do seem puzzling, at the very least. In addition, the inclusion of the first of several 'big-name' contributions – in this case Eric Clapton impersonating Eric Clapton – does not ring true. To all but the most sonically astute of listeners, his blues fills could have been the work of any journeyman session musician, so the purpose of his contribution remains unclear.

All things considered, the track is nothing more than moderate filler, and a real anti-climax after the promise of the previous track. The 'directness' of the lyric renders it a far less personal account than many of the artist's more singular lyrics. It may be 'from the heart' but it cannot help but come across like a series of identikit phrases, and the musical backing does nothing to move the song out of the mundane.

'Eat the Music'

The opening lyric from this track, 'Split me open, with devotion', signals a prompt return to the more idiosyncratic and sexually ambiguous terrain that more accurately summarises the artist's complete *oeuvre*. Narratives linking sexual ripeness with fruit are nothing new in pop, or indeed pre-pop (blues, folk, music hall and so on) lyrics, but the sheer bravado of both lyric and musical backing do give 'Eat the Music' a certain carnivalesque vitality. As the lyric progresses we return to another fertile recurring trope, that of the nature of masculinity and femininity, although without any especially profound observations ensuing.

The track does border on tipping into the kind of clichéd Latino gestures resonant of so much western musical tourism, and certainly does linger a little too long. However, its simple infectious ascending chord pattern, driven by clipped, percussive valiha, kabossy and mariachi-style brass, is hard to resist. It is a 'fun' track, but of course, 'fun' is a mixed signifier in the world of 'serious, intellectual' music that many artists and audiences aspire to. For those of us yearning for a return to the gravitas of the sidelong concept suite, 'Eat the Music' is a little too marinated in fructose. Jovanovic goes as far as to term the song 'cringe worthy'. (Jovanovic, 2005: 188).

'Moments of Pleasure'

This 'companion track' to the previous album's 'This Woman's Work' joins the pantheon of relatively conventional, yet deeply moving songs that the artist can seemingly write at will. Alongside *Hounds of Love*'s 'The Morning Fog', this track carries a huge emotional charge, being similarly concerned with friendship and familial love. To these lyrical themes is added a mood of gravitas and loss that only ageing and the inexorable march of mortality can have upon us all. In stark terms, 'Moments of Pleasure' concerns memory and the process of grieving. The lyric focusses upon the idiosyncratic nature of remembrance – all the odd things that take us back to those who have left our physical world, but leave traces of memory. The mood is sombre, bittersweet and a little defiant, with no space for empty sentimentality or existential gloom. Particularly effective is the stark couplet 'Just being alive, It can really hurt', which sums up the process of bereavement more accurately and more economically than any florid poetic eulogy ever manages.

Instrumentally, the track is built upon the direct simplicity of piano plus orchestra, whose arrangement, by Michael Kamen – himself to die prematurely (aged 55) along with those named in the lyric – is wholly sympathetic to the imbued mood of the vocal and lyric. When the strings need to soar upward along with the melody, they do so; when they need to echo a descending piano, they do so, but just the once, as the track enters its coda for 'the fallen', amongst whom lie several musical and creative collaborators and Bush's aunt. Above all this reminiscence stands one to Hannah, her mother. The humanism, affection and grounded spirituality of this song quite overwhelmed me upon first listen. Indeed, it is one of the few songs that carry such an emotive charge that I have to be careful when I choose to listen to it. Despite the huge emotional impact that music has always had on me, relatively few songs have moved me to tears – but 'Moments of Pleasure' did, and does. In common with any process of remembrance, the nature of memory subtly changes with repetition, but the power of the musical arrangement remains strong, if always slightly changing alongside times and moods.

'The Song of Solomon'

After the emotional heights scaled by certain tracks, the dilemma posed of any composer is how to follow it. 'The Song of Solomon' neatly evades this problem by wooing us gently into a dreamy, almost soporific sonic terrain of sparse, tuned percussion, lowly mixed keyboards and acoustic guitar. As such, it skilfully shifts the album's mood without jarring the continuity. Unfortunately, its lyric and melody are more awkward and obtrusive, although this may be a deliberate ploy. The juxtaposing of the proverbial biblical poetry of Solomon with exhortations to drop the 'bullshit' is clearly a clash of registers, but to what end? Whilst the lyric is enigmatic enough to allow for a range of readings, to my mind its clumsiness only renders the musical accompaniment problematic and the whole track remains unresolved. Perhaps, as with much incomprehension about meaning, the fault lies with this reader rather than the text. Certainly, the high/low call and responses multi-tracked by Bush are as impressive as ever, rendering the reappearance of the Trio Bulgarka less than essential, but what the lyric has to say about the nature of desire and gender is nebulous, at best.

'Lily'

One of the strengths of *The Red Shoes* lies in the care devoted to continuity and running order. 'Lily' runs on the spiritual thread established by the previous track, beginning with a prayer recited by 'Lily' herself (a 'healer' visited by the artist, Jovanovic, 2005: 188). This stanza is a direct translation of the Hindu *Gayatri Mantra*, which consists of homage to Lord Savitur, the sun creator. The main narrative then develops through a call-and-response dialogue. This again suggests that personal loss has affected the composition, with the powerful line 'I feel that life has blown a great big hole through me'. Lily's response is equally dynamic, arguing that protection comes through the utilisation of a form of holy fire. The narrator is then joined in this circle of fire by angels and prophets before the remaining lyrics reinforce the message of collective defiance.

This lyric, along with the previous track's example, is unusual in terms of the artist's whole composition process by virtue of its direct referencing of a form of pantheistic religious discourse and etymology. Whether this mirrored some kind of renewal or birth of faith in the artist's own life remains unclear, but particularly in terms of this track it allows for the fashioning of an unusual and enigmatic lyric that is full of powerful imagery. If the melodic chorus is rather flat after the promise suggested by the verse melody, then this is partly offset by the punchy mix that pushes the closely melded bass and kick drum rhythm to great effect. Stuart Elliott's drum track is sprightly and dynamic, complemented by an under-mixed and nagging rhythm guitar component that is textural and distorted, rather than note-based. This was played by her regular collaborator, and soon to be romantic partner, Dan McIntosh and, when contrasted to the ringing arpeggiations of 'Rubberband Girl', provides evidence of a flexible and empathetic musical talent. As with the album's lead-off song, 'Lily' would have made a suitably energetic and commercial single.

'The Red Shoes'

The title track is another prime example of *The Red Shoes*'s by now burgeoning mood of energy and joie de vivre. As with 'Lily', the mix is skilful and sympathetic, in this case boosting the acoustic elements (mandola, valiha, guitars and whistles) at the partial expense of the bass and drum kit. Clearly, the artist-as-producer is a more confident and competent multi-tasker on this album than on previous works, which show less invention and risk-taking. This selective mix gives the track a skittish, tactile drive in triple time that builds incrementally, as the snare joins in to gradually augment the crotchet kick at half time (one beat to the bar or more intermittently) around the minute mark, before doubling up at around 2: 25. This resolution of the opening sequence's tension is abetted by the rich vocal harmonies, with Bush joined by brother Paddy and his collaborator and solo artist Colin Lloyd-Tucker on the chorus.

The lyric engages with two principal sources: the narrative of the film that directly inspires it, and also the accompanying short film *The Line, The Cross and The Curve*, which the lyric directly references and which the artist herself wrote and produced in 1993. The only shortcoming lies in the 'transatlantic' nature of the vocalising, with 'dance' and 'can't' expressed in the conventional, hegemonic manner of most mainstream pop, along with the more 'r-full' (see Upton and Widdowson, 1996: 31) accent creeping in to replace the artist's own former southern English, and unique delivery. This 'regression' comes across as something of a denial, or even an admission of defeat in cultural and linguistic terms. The imperialist march of American English has so comprehensively superseded more localised or ethnic accents in global popular music, that when those few artists to fight its dominance succumb, it is hard not to feel a slight sense of betrayal.

'The Red Shoes', as the 'follow-up' single, reached only 21 in the UK, reflecting upon her core market's preference for albums more than on the nature of the material, which was, again, highly suitable for daytime airplay on commercial pop stations.

'Top of the City'

This is another direct and at times boldly brash track that skilfully slides between its component parts whilst remaining intentionally disjointed. The fractured nature of the sonic narrative – understated, sparse verse-intros interspersed with fuller, attacking timbres for other sections – is complemented by the often negative lyrical imagery being undercut by the essentially defiant and positive mood of the whole track. This defiance in the face of adversity is by now shaping up to be one of the major underpinning themes of the album. On 'Top of the City' this fortitude is emphasised by the repetitive nature of the melody lines which, in addition to being beautifully sung, turn the lack of internal progression into an effective device. This results in each section having its own internal logic, rather than functioning as a preparation for, or relief from another section, as is so often the case within popular song. In summary, in its 'stop-go' form 'Top of the City' is an unconventionally structured track.

Reinforcing the disjointed nature of other textual aspects, the line 'Take me up to the top of the city' is emotionally transcendent whilst still being presented in an understated, sombre manner. Equally, the imbued feeling is that despite residing in 'the loneliest city in the world', the narrator will escape the physical and emotion bonds to stand on 'the angel's shoulders' – yet again, the religious metaphor surfaces, although the lyric cannot be read as 'faith-based' in any concrete sense.

Musically, the drums, on this track compressed and echoed, again predominate in the up-beat sections. The bassist, John Giblin, contributes slippery, rubato lines, although his contributions do remain almost ambient, deep in the mix. Other instrumental contributions remain very sparse, with classical virtuoso Nigel Kennedy's contribution all but irrelevant. However, the very presence of so many stellar contributors to this album, if sometimes problematic, does at least bear evidence to the wide-ranging respect and influence wielded by the artist amongst her peers.

'Constellation of the Heart'

This is an odd track for the artist in a several ways. Firstly, it pays explicit lyrical reference to other Kate Bush tracks ('The Big Sky', 'Moments of Pleasure') and secondly, it pays more implicit reference to another artist, Prince, who in fact appears elsewhere on the album. This stylistic influence extends from the title (rather reminiscent of Prince's 'Condition of the Heart', from 1985's *Around the World in a Day*) to the musical style, featuring resonant 'rock' drum sounds underpinned by funk-style slap bass and 'chicken-scratch' guitar. The artist herself plays the sort of fat synth-stab chords reminding the listener of 1980s Prince tracks such as '1999', (1982). In short, the track itself lacks its own clear identity. Whilst efficient as a pastiche of a number of generic timbres, it remains fatally compromised by its derivative nature. The chorus employs a clever lyrical conceit wherein reversing the view through a telescope will allow one to look within, but it is over-employed to the point of irritation and the track drags long before the end.

'Constellation of the Heart', being the third essentially up-tempo track in succession (surely a first in the artist's career), at least has vitality and an element of funk in its favour. In particular, the two interwoven rhythm guitar tracks have a vibrancy and invention often lacking in 'classic' funk, and the bass track is given its rightful prominence in the mix; but the song itself, as a result of resurrecting some of the 1980s less vital sounds, cannot be considered successful, either in its own right or in the overall context of the album. As Jovanovic concludes, 'If this was an attempt to break into the US funk scene it failed miserably. If it wasn't such an attempt it failed anyway' (Jovanovic, 2005: 189).

'Big Stripey Lie'

If ever a track cries out 'experimental track best left as a b-side', then 'Big Stripey Lie' fits the bill. Firstly, its inclusion is a strange decision, bearing in mind that tracks accompanying hit singles (in this case 'Rubberband Girl') rarely find their way onto the artist's albums. Secondly, the jarring nature of guitar and some of the violin components seems explicitly designed to irritate the vast majority of the artist's following. If we also mention that the track features the artist herself singing in her 'strangled voice' and playing electric guitar and bass – not her usual instruments of choice – then its choice as an album track becomes even more perplexing. Despite all these damning criticisms, the guitar work is certainly impressive within its own atonal avant-garde terms of reference, although very out of place on a Kate Bush album. CD programming and skip functions – widely employed by the period of this album's release – do certainly lessen the linear impact of a track such as this.

In exposing the minor, but significant limitations of the Bush voice, the artist does herself a great disservice in much the same manner that this track detracts from the album in which it functions as a noisy hiatus.

'Why Should I Love You?'

The influence of the stellar guest Prince, as co-arranger and multi-instrumentalist, is almost overwhelming on this track. On a positive note guests are, or should be, included on tracks to make a real difference. Elsewhere on this album it can be argued that they do not, but 'Why Should I Love You?' has Prince's imprint indelibly stamped, whether it be in the jazz-funk style guitar solos, the backing vocals or particularly in the melodic cadence of the chorus (redolent of tracks such as 'Around the World in a Day'). In addition, many would argue that Prince, particularly during his purple patch (excuse the pun) in the decade between 1982 and 1992, was one of the most influential and talented of composers, players and performers. Nonetheless, the influence is so overbearing as to render Kate Bush as the guest, rather than the musical host – clearly an issue on her own album!

The track itself is not without its merits. As well as the aforementioned contributions, the Trio Bulgarka harmonise beautifully to reinforce the organ riff that subsequently powers the whole rhythm track, and the bass track (again by Prince) punctuates the flow in a delightfully syncopated and sinuous manner. However, leaving the chorus to one side the rest of the track's melodies are dull, the lyrics merely reproduce the kind of soul/gospel 'a is for apple' style mapping that is clichéd and the other guest, comedian Lenny Henry, whilst an adequate singer, is far from a vital addition – the phrase 'old pal's act' springs to mind.

A more damning criticism lies in the fact that this track is the third mediocre song in a row, making *The Red Shoes* yet another Kate Bush album (after *The Dreaming* and, to a lesser extent, *The Sensual World* and *Never for Ever*) that loses impetus towards its close. In terms of its diegesis, this is much more of an aesthetical problem than an album that starts poorly, or 'dips' before making a strong recovery.

'You're the One'

A fine, if generic choice for an album-closer, this track is a slow and stately bluesy ballad, grounded by the warm Hammond chords of Gary Brooker. It is skilfully enlivened by a shift in rhythm and pace at the end of the verses. In addition 'You're the One' features well-pitched contributions from Jeff Beck, particularly in his second solo, whose 'crying' tone takes us back to late-1960s timbres. This is an era little visited within the Bush *oeuvre*, and all the more effective as a result.

The lyric is a difficult one to bring originality to, being the standardised tale of a broken relationship, and one party's emotional inability or desire to move on. The hackneyed nature of the narrative does render most of the lyrics little more than retreads of other songs. In particular, the simple repetition of the line 'You're the only one I want' cannot escape engendering a certain element of tedium to the proceedings. And although for the most part the artist's accent remains firmly on this side of the Atlantic, the 'strangled' voice does intrude in this sparse mix.

The track cannot be judged an unqualified success, but within the context of the whole album, and in particular the three preceding tracks, it concludes the album in an affirmative and worthwhile fashion.

Taken as an entity, *The Red Shoes* is of variable quality. The almost inevitable consequence of the CD format has been the extension of album durations. At 55 minutes, *The Red Shoes* is fully ten minutes longer than *The Sensual World*. But within this new expansionist world, a good 40 minutes of this album's music is very pleasurable, which compares favourably to earlier works such as *The Dreaming*. However, it must be said that *The Dreaming* packs more innovation and mostly successful experimentation into its more economic running order than the artist's post-*Hounds* output. In retrospect, the artist much later honestly admitted that 'It's much too long and it goes on and it gets boring' (Bush, in Doyle, 2005: 86).

In its favour, the production on *The Red Shoes* is uniformly sympathetic and extremely competent. The intention to work (relatively) quickly and to give a more live feel to the proceedings than the previous few albums is largely achieved. On 'Rubberband Girl' 'the bass, drums and basic keyboards were all done together' (Palmer, in Jovanovic, 2005: 187). It achieves the difficult goal of appearing neither dated nor desperate in its desire to be 'of the moment'. The drums are particularly well presented (with two drummers sometimes playing in real time, simultaneously, Jovanovic, 2005: 186), if sometimes the bass lines do seem under-mixed and lacking in ambition. Mike Brocken has spoken of the influence of digital dance music on the whole pop scene in the 1990s. He rightly identifies the decline of melody and modulation in bass lines, with their partial replacement by frequencies (Brocken, 2003b: 240). This can certainly be felt in Bush's first two post-*Hounds* albums.

The impact of the guest stars is sometimes positive, sometimes irrelevant and on occasions smacks of musical 'cronyism'. Prince, somewhat unsurprisingly bearing in mind his huge global influence during the album's preceding period, does cast a shadow over more than the one track he is actually concerned with. Unfortunately, this influence does draw Kate Bush into musical genres and timbres that stretch her talents out of the 'comfort zone'. Neither her voice nor her musical sensibility suits the world of funk. Musicians, regardless of ability, normally work most effectively within certain parameters. In particular, the tracks towards the end of this album merely make us aware as to precisely where those parameters end.

The majority of songs work well, albeit in the more limited melodic and lyrical terrain adopted by the late-period artist – and by extension, the whole world of pop – in the more recent period of commercial songwriting and mainstream albums. That most ambiguous of terms – mainstream – is certainly applicable to *The Red Shoes*, particularly when considering the overall up-beat nature of both the tracks and the lyrical content. However, the mainstream nature of this album is less disappointing than the form it takes on the previous album, which exhibits a certain downbeat and 'middle-aged' mood of playing it safe. Irvin summarises this and the previous album as 'spotty collections with frequent flashes of staggering beauty' (Irvin, 2005: 96). Jovanovic states that 'If you took the best tracks from *The Sensual World* and *The Red Shoes*, you'd have a great album instead of two average ones' (Jovanovic, 2005: 191). This is being churlish and wise after the event. One could make the same claim for most consecutive albums by any artist. Where the biographer is right is in comparing these albums adversely with previous work. However, in its favour, of the two albums *The Red Shoes* is the better work and a worthy addition to the *oeuvre* of the artist.

The Period Leading up to *Aerial*

The ever-extending periods between the artist's later albums over the past 20 years are unusual, but certainly not without precedent in the world of popular music. The 12 years between *The Red Shoes*, in 1993, and *Aerial*, in 2005 is excessive by the standards of, say, the average 'indie' band. However, if we compare the hiatus with an artist such as Stevie Wonder, similar in terms of status, we find that his 2005 release was the first for a decade. Vashti Bunyan produced her first album in 1969, effectively disappeared from the public gaze and released a critically acclaimed follow-up as late as 2005, a gap of 36 years. In actual fact, the gap between Kate Bush albums had the effect of keeping the artist in the public eye, almost as an inadvertent marketing device, as release dates came and went from 2003 onwards. Thus, almost by default, *Aerial* could not but fail to carry 'a genuine sense of occasion' (Petridis, 2005: 12).

By one of those bizarre coincidences, *Aerial* emerged at around the same time as another album by a 47-year-old pop legend – in this case Madonna's *Confessions on a Dance Floor*. However, as Stephen Troussé rightly judges: 'while Madonna's presence in the last decade has diminished, a consequence of her sheer ubiquity. In the same period, without releasing a single record, Kate Bush's reputation has grown' (Troussé, 2005: 98).

The artist re-emerged in late 2005 to promote the new album with her customary select few interviews. According to the *Gaffaweb* chronology, many years between the two albums see no press or media interviews to directly feature the artist – Kate Bush (again) became a private person. The best summation of her life over the previous 12 years comes within Tom Doyle's extended article.

According to Doyle, after the release of *The Red Shoes* and the accompanying video album *The Line, The Cross and The Curve* (Kate Bush attended the premieres in London and Ontario), the artist took two years off. In 1996, the composition process resulted in a new song, 'King of the Mountain', followed by another quiet period. In 1998, another song is written whilst pregnant. After the birth of Albert (Bertie, in July 1998, around the time of his mother's 40th birthday), the happy couple (Kate and guitarist Dan McIntosh), despite feeling 'completely shattered for a couple of years' (Doyle, 2005: 81), move house and oversee the building of a home studio. During the same period the artist forms a new production company, Noble and Brite, which licenses material to her parent company, EMI. In 2003, the London Metropolitan Orchestra, under Michael Kamen, recorded string accompaniments to tracks just prior to his early death in November (Jovanovic, 2005: 204).

Perhaps unsurprisingly, to those students of her biography, Kate Bush, as a mature mother, devotes herself whole-heartedly to parenthood without the help of nanny or housekeeper. She commented that the feeling was 'totally incomparable with anything else ... I don't want to miss a minute of him. It's so much fun, by far the best thing I've ever done' (Bush, in Jovanovic, 2005: 201). During this period rumours begin to circulate regarding the forthcoming album, provisionally entitled *How to be Invisible*. Very slowly the subsequent (double) album comes together, 'two years of more concentrated effort ... the album is complete. You look up from the mixing desk and it is 2005' (Doyle, 2005: 81).

The parallels between *Aerial* and *Hounds of Love*, in conceptual and sequential terms, are very evident. Each album is effectively split into two halves, with the first half featuring discrete songs, and the second using a linked 'suite' of tracks that give it the status of a conceptual work. The chief distinction comes about as much through changing times and technologies as through artistic choice – *Hounds of Love* is a two-sided vinyl album whereas *Aerial* is a two-disc CD album. In terms of duration this is reflected in the 1985 release, whose running time of nearly 50 minutes exceeds the norm by an appreciable, but not unique percentage. Similarly, the 2005 album, totalling some 80 minutes, is very long by contemporary standards, but not without precedent. However, 80 minutes of music is still very ambitious, in both conceptual and empirical terms. The question as to how to experience *Aerial* is one for the individual listener to grapple with. From my own point of view, it functions best as an 'either/or' experience, with the two discs functioning as near-separate entities.

In terms of the album package, *Aerial* is the first Kate Bush album not to feature an image of the artist on the external cover. The reasons for this are open to conjecture. The two sides of the effectively gatefold sleeve give us the tonal simplicity of a dark brown series of shapes in silhouette, backlit by a sun. On one level, this image literally symbolises the titles of the two albums, *A Sea of Honey* and *A Sky of Honey*. However, the images are ambiguous, even polysemic, representing both topographical features yet also optical sound wave patterns, familiar to all those who have produced digital music. Similarly, the word aerial is plural, representing both an ancient messenger from mythology (whose statue stands naked above the main entrance to the BBC's Broadcasting House, in London) and also the aerial by which we receive sound waves. The inner images feature a simple building and its courtyard, which contains a breeze-blown washing line, clothing and some doves in flight. The photography and images within the lyric booklet mostly repeat or complement those on the CD package, and include the painting *Fishermen*, an old image showing a group of men hauling a boat called 'Aerial'. There is also one small solo portrait of the artist showing half her face and her hands (and looking enigmatic and rather furtive, to my way of thinking), and other shots featuring Bertie alone and with his mother. In overall terms it is a sumptuous package, although considerably less controversial or disturbing than earlier album covers. On a negative note, although individual musicians are rightly credited, individual track credits are not included – a strange exclusion by an artist who had almost always vouchsafed this important information on past albums. Perennial contributors Stuart Elliott and brother Paddy are present, as are many other long-standing collaborators.

Aerial: A Sea of Honey

'King of the Mountain'

In customary fashion, the first single from the album is also the lead-off track. The lyric, for the most part, is a direct musing on the nature of celebrity as personified by Elvis Presley. In addition, the image of 'the king' 'in the snow with Rosebud' also makes clear connection with the cinematic figure of Charles Foster Kane, from Orson Welles's *Citizen Kane* (1941).

Musically, a torpid, cross-faded synth line rises and falls whilst couching the rhythm track between its ambient fingers (Irvin refers to the track's 'pleasingly spare … opaque membrane … the baggage which spoilt *The Red Shoes* … has left the building', 2005: 96). Atmospheric synth strings are augmented by what becomes a recognisably reggae-textured 'skank' stroke. This element, combined with a very 'live' sounding drum kit that is played in a gloriously excessive fashion – with double cymbal crashes and extravagant rolls – gives the track much of its vitality. Although not overtly 'commercial' in terms of timbres or musical structure – the drum kit does not enter until 1: 20 – the melody is distinctive and the whole track has a winning dynamism. Particularly effective are the lyric-less vocal representations of the wind that sweep in using ethereal harmonies at 3: 42. This pushes the track to its affective plateau in an unusual manner. The track gave the artist her biggest hit single for 20 years, peaking at number 4 in the UK charts. However, in tune with the times, the song disappeared as rapidly as it had risen, indicating its limited appeal to singles' buyers in the 2005 marketplace, yet re-emphasising her continuing relevance to the 'adult' market.

'π'

Built upon a bed of lowly mixed tom-toms and a (possibly) sequenced organ tone that punctuates the triplet-feel of the rhythm, this track develops into a jazzy waltz. Melodically innovative and lyrically brave, the Bush voice switches between clear tones without a hint of vibrato to near-murmured sections for the chorus, which feature the recitation of the mathematical equation of π – an uncommon device, even for a 'mere' album track. Possibly she is 'testing the critical cliché that she could sing the telephone directory and have grown men swoon' (Troussé, 2005: 98). The lack of clarity in the enunciation that results from what sounds like the artist's top lip being held stationary is quite thrilling in its repression of oral power. A wash of acoustic guitars adds sprightliness to the mix, and the interplay between voices and the counterpointed 'muddy' bass line is a delight. The interest is sustained for its full six minutes and the track manages to cleverly oppose the jollity of the rhythm track with a low-key melody that sometimes meanders uncertainly between tones (numbers), and at other times just settles on one pedal note for a protracted period.

'Bertie'

Aural equivalents of the 'family snapshot' are often problematic for the listener. For her devoted 'lovehounds' a lyric extolling the artist's maternal love is clearly an acceptable conceit. But for the more detached (and emotionally English) observer, the subject matter cannot help but feel rather sentimental and mawkish. Probably most parents have felt the same emotions for their children: but it is one thing to feel emotions, and quite another to broadcast them to millions of listeners.

Despite this churlish caveat, the song is full of charm. Its 'gorgeous, effulgent lullaby' does give 'ample testament to the bliss Bush has clearly found in motherhood' (Troussé, 2005: 98). I do doubt that it is the 'real heart of the record' (ibid.), but its emotional impact upon some reviewers must be recognised.

In its favour, renaissance instruments do admirably echo the simplicity and innocence of the lyric. Clever sequencing on *Aerial* presents a second successive track that is again predominantly in triple time, although it breaks out of this home metre with subtlety towards the end of the song. The melody is a melismatic jig that trips up and down the scale. It is hard not to hear the 'dancing' in the vocals that gives each section in a short and modest track a huge timbral scope. The first verse even sounds a little transatlantic before an almost baroque rigour asserts itself in the section beginning 'sweet kisses'. Richly redolent of an ancient historical period, the lyrical sentiments are placed in a most suitable and sympathetic context.

'Mrs. Bartolozzi'

This track presents the artist as solo performer. Apart from one small refrain featuring multi-tracked vocals the whole six-minute track is built upon nothing more than a single voice accompanied by a piano. The lyric is a simple contemplation of a domestic task that develops into a more sexualised narrative that drifts between reality and fantasy. Particularly in the opening verse many of the phrases scan very poorly, in syllabic terms, although the melody is much smoother and generally very elegant. The piano accompaniment is simple, yet subtle and varied. Particularly effective is the transposition up the keyboard to accompany the harmony section towards the end of the track. Its evocation of childhood and nursery rhymes takes us back to earlier similar sequences in tracks such as 'In Search of Peter Pan' and 'Kite', issued a full quarter of a century earlier.

The artist's voice, when hitting its highest notes within this track, is a little thin and exposed by the sparseness of the setting. But devices such as the extended pauses between the lines in the refrain section do work exceedingly well in engendering tension and anticipation. 'Mrs. Bartolozzi' is the track seized upon by reviewers eager to revisit the 'artist as unhinged crank' that have beset Kate Bush throughout her career. In reality, a repeated refrain of 'Washing machine' is totally suited to the needs of both lyric and melody. The track is charming, whilst not possessing the erotic charge found elsewhere in her creative *oeuvre*.

'How to be Invisible'

In terms of its bass and drum components, this track is one of the simplest of the artist's entire career, featuring a simple common time crotchet beat given a slight kick by a 'locomotive' shuffle on the snare. This prosaic base allows for multi-layered electric guitars to provide the main instrumental focus, and again demonstrates the impeccable taste and eclecticism of Bush's contributors. As well as playing countrified licks reminiscent of Mark Knopfler or Chet Atkins, the guitarist (in all probability Dan McIntosh) employs echo, offbeat reggae strokes and atonal arpeggiations that mesh and meld in an understated, yet virtuoso fashion.

'How to be Invisible' features a cunningly metaphorical lyric, building lines such as 'take a pinch of keyhole' and 'eye of Braille, hem of anorak' into a spell-like narrative that encourages us to reflect upon both the singularity of celebrity identity and upon more general issues of visibility in all its physical and emotional 'manifestations'. It is thus at once autobiographical yet universal, with this profundity cleverly disguised within a rhythm that is jolly and understated, rather than portentous. On tracks such as this, the artist's arrangement manages to retain interest for over five minutes. The song feels easy and unforced, without any of the strained or tedious 'run-outs' that characterise several earlier tracks of this length.

'Joanni'

Although it is difficult to be certain, given the lack of specific track information on players and instrumentation, this track does appear to return us to the *modus operandi* of album such as *Hounds of Love*. The rhythm section utilises programmed components such as sequenced synths to give the verses a 'cold' but not unfunky feel (for Troussé, 'dense, atmospheric trip-hop', 2005: 98), before played percussive and melodic elements take the choruses into a different timbral and emotional terrain. The lyric is direct in its re-telling of the legend of Joan of Arc, but the melody murmurs and meanders along in a peculiar, yet oddly accessible manner, before bursting outward and upward in two stages during the pre-chorus and chorus proper.

'Joanni' also features a beautiful guitar solo that enters at 3: 30 and soars upon a few sustained tones high above the washes of synth strings that ebb and flow like waves throughout most of the track. The whole song is both melodically seductive and rhythmically driving. In particular, the vocal track, for the most part single-tracked, exudes confidence. Earlier in the artist's career, the temptation would have been to overdub elaborate harmonies at certain points, but restraint, experience and plain good taste guide the simplistic rationale here, as elsewhere on *A Sea of Honey*.

'A Coral Room'

This track stands as the latest example of one of the artist's most enduring and fulfilling staples – the mainly solo piano and vocal performance. Past examples include 'This Woman's Work' from *The Sensual World* and *The Red Shoes*'s 'Moments of Pleasure'. As with the last-mentioned example, 'A Coral Room' is about loss and how we trigger memories. For one reviewer it is the 'shiver-inducing stand-out track' (Doyle, 2005: 86), perhaps influenced by the artist's own admission that, in dealing directly with the death of her mother it was almost 'considered to be too personal for release' (Bush, ibid.).

It is certainly a moving and consummately conceived piece of work, with the artist employing three distinct rhythm-plus-melody sections to express herself. As so often, the narrative is concerned with bringing contrasting emotions into close contact, in this case the 'frontier where love and grief embrace' (Irvin, 2005: 96). Particularly effective is the torpid, melismatic section beginning with 'moving and glistening' at 1: 25 where one gets the real sense of drifting at a submarine pace. The metaphoric filters – webs, nets, water – through which memories re-present themselves to us seem perfectly judged (Troussé talks of the 'flooded city of memory … the calcified chamber of the heart', 2005: 98), as does the plaintive repeated refrain that frames the whole song: 'Put your hand over the side of the boat, and what do you feel?'. This leaves us all aware of the open-ended nature of reminiscence and existence, and concludes this economic (38-minute) collection of songs with a suitably enigmatic question.

For this writer, the track cannot match up to the sheer torrent of emotions and memories unleashed on 'Moments of Pleasure', which offers catharsis, melodrama and a certain amount of 'closure'. But 'A Coral Room' is a worthy closing track, giving what is essentially only the first half of the album its own individual identity. Even without *A Sky of Honey*, this CD stands alone as a brilliantly conceived and well-executed album of songs.

A Sky of Honey

For one reviewer, *Aerial*'s first album functions to mirror Blake's sombre *Songs of Experience*, whereas the second 'is one vast rolling Song of Innocence, responding to desolation with a world brimful of laughter, sunlight and birdsong' (ibid.). Equally, echoes of the English pastoral style of Vaughan Williams (mention of 'the Lark Ascending' on one track) and Delius (linking us back to *Never For Ever*) do resonate through the suite of songs and textures.

Alex Petridis offers a précis of *A Sky of Honey* in terms of the chronology of a day, which of course, to an extent, echoes the time passage elements of *The Ninth Wave*: 'the sun comes up, birds sing, Bush watches a pavement artist at work, it rains, Bush has a moonlight swim and watches the sun come up again' (Petridis, 2005: 12). Of course, almost any text or work can be stripped down to such skeletal components. The craft and impact lie in the way that the skeleton is fleshed out. In musical terms there are textural and temporal aspects to this process – both of which are most skilfully executed as the suite unfolds.

'Prelude'

At less than 1: 30, this track is an atmospheric vignette built upon simple piano, which doubles the sampled birdsong with subtlety towards its conclusion. Bertie provides suitably awed comments relating to birds and speech, expressed in the understated, innocent terms of childhood.

'Prologue'

Built upon a repetitive drone rhythm element and sampled birdsong, this track makes great use of simple piano chords and melody lines that ripple up and down between the verses. The lyric is all giggly anticipation of the unfolding day. Its very English evocation of the elements is only emphasised by the received pronunciation of 'What a lovely afternoon'. The tension engendered by this waiting strategy is never fully dissipated, despite other musical elements leisurely adding themselves – bass lines, strings and, some 4: 40 into the track, percussive elements. As the track segues into 'An Architect's Dream', birdsong returns, and is it combined with the artist's leitmotif whale cries, returning us to 'Moving' and 1978?

As its title indicates, 'Prologue' exploits the advantages of not having to be judged as a discrete song, but rather as part of an unfolding suite of tracks that build a conceptual narrative. Thus the lack of resolution becomes its strength rather than a shortcoming. If the artist's command of Italian lacks the accuracy required by this most precise of languages, then this is a minor concern. The ability to combine an air of repose with the yearning for what is yet to unfold is a difficult dilemma, but within this track it is beautifully solved.

'An Architect's Dream'

Built on the synaesthetics of the media of paint and graphic design, this sequence reintroduces Rolf Harris to a Kate Bush track after a gap of some 23 years. He provides the *sotto voce* commentary on the painter's craft upon which the narrator then comments. As with 'Prelude' the instrumental track has a mainly 'live, played' feel augmented by a widely panned bongo-and-conga-based drum rhythm so repetitive as to suggest it has been looped. This lends the track a certain clinical drive that is much needed to counter the rather overly 'tasteful' work of the bass, keyboards and strings.

The overall feel imbued is slightly less stilted and robotic than some of the artist's earliest attempts to combine played and programmed elements (*Never for Ever*'s 'Delius'), although it lacks the positive experimental dimension of such 'primitive' recordings. The most notable contribution is a seductive and softly strummed guitar motif that slides between two chords before resolving itself with an ascending conclusion. This figure emerges at 1: 48 and repeats on four further occasions. The vocal is wonderfully carefree and at ease with this lyric, although the overall track does not quite build on the promise of its predecessor.

'The Painter's Link'

As suggested by the title, at 1: 35, this segment is barely a track in its own right, but does provide an effective bridge between what precedes and what follows. Rolf Harris's sung verse demonstrates that imprecise pitching does not invariably prove an obstacle in the world of pop, before Kate Bush's richly soaring multi-track melodies provide a necessary and effective contrast with the other 'artist'.

'Sunset'

In its employment of stopped piano chords and languid double bass, this track edges into the genre of jazz – one almost totally bypassed in the artist's extant *oeuvre*. Over a very easy instrumental feel the vocal metre slides from ululating melisma to clipped, precise syllables within the same verse. The chorus is subtle in its phrasing, and culminates in a protracted pause that connotes a great sense of confidence. As the next verse unfolds, the drum kit, barely audible, emerges from the sea and sky of honey referenced in the lyric. The words deal with the temporal passage of time evoked through texture, colour and the forces of nature.

The complete track oozes reflectivity, yet allied to an intense sense of close observation. And then quite suddenly, almost four minutes in, a most unexpected eruption of flamenco-style guitars occurs, linked to a doubling of tempo. This coda, complemented by an urgency in vocal phrasing, is both a surprise and a delight, before the last few seconds return us to the pace and repose of the earlier section.

'Aerial Tai'

At around one minute, this segment is one of the shortest tracks of the artist's career. Constructed upon the simplest circular three-note piano motif, the vocalising consists of the artist imitating birdsong. This is obviously not to everyone's taste. Petridis lauds Bush for constructing a work 'filled with things only Kate Bush would do' before adding the caveat 'Some of the things you rather wish she wouldn't, including imitating bird calls and doing funny voices' (Petridis, 2005: 12); but such quirks and foibles strike me as brave, and usually well executed. If critics are to praise the artist for being avant-garde, then they must accept what transpires from such a term. On 'Aerial Tai' I am reminded of scat singing, and more specifically Sheila Chandra's impersonations of tablas on tracks such as 'Speaking in Tongues' (1992). In general all the interludes on *Aerial* serve their atmospheric and sequential purpose admirably.

'Somewhere in Between'

A track of sunset moods and sights that takes us towards a night of sleep is built upon two pattering tuned snares reminiscent of the methods employed in ambient drum'n'bass. Again, the feel is relaxed and jazzy; this track best exemplifies the conceptual album wherein, at times, 'virtually nothing happens, albeit very beautifully' (ibid.) The liminal dimension is skilfully enforced by impressionistic lyrics such as 'dancing and skipping/Along a chink of light' and 'the waxing and the waning wave'. The main vocal is doubled an octave down by an (unaccredited) male voice before the Bush vocal is doubled as the song recedes into the twilight – the one voice holding its pitch, whilst the other slides downward into the metaphorical murk.

'Nocturn'

The mood of repose continues in the early section of 'Nocturn', with slightly, intentionally sleepy vocal melodies slipping between the tones. This mood is unsurprising, bearing in mind its connection to sleep and moonlight. However, at 1: 38 a very solid drum kit and bass rhythm reminiscent of classic Tamla Motown emerges out of the strings and atmospheric samples. The vocal melody stays relaxed, even torpid on 'We tire of the city/we tire of it all' but the contrast between the vocals and the rhythm, which is politely soulful and 'danceable', is well maintained. The insistent, but simple bass line drops in and out of the mix, rendering its presence (and absence) high in terms of our appreciation. This is much needed, with bass lines on later Kate Bush albums often being rather peripheral to the overall ambience.

As the tentative nature of the lyric intimates, this narrative 'could be a dream'. Troussé describes the track as a 'euphorically pounding dream sequence' (2005: 98), which is to over-emphasise its connoted energy; but it is certainly naggingly insistent, although in the mode of Marvin Gaye's *What's Going On* (1971) rather than a rave track. Lines such as 'The sky's above our heads/The sea's around our legs' again return us to the narrator of *The Ninth Wave*, as do the many other references to sea and surf. The phrase 'we become panoramic' in particular carries echoes of 'Hello Earth', in lyrical, if not musical terms.

The track takes its time. Instrumental textures like a funky guitar scratch join the mix as we are pulled along. Plural acoustic guitars augment, but shift the textural base after six minutes before highly pitched harmonies making great use of vibrato shift the terrain further. The final vocal sequence, featuring a chorus of half-spoken lines, shifts the mood into a more urgent territory before the abrupt transition into the next track is effected. At over 8: 30, 'Nocturn' is the longest single track of the artist's career, but uses every second and every instrumental component to great effect.

'Aerial'

Sequenced string lines in triple time strike a contrast with the groove-based insistency of the previous track. The sun rises along with the energy of the narrator, which has already been rising for the previous few minutes. But this now takes the form of the energy of sentience and reality rather than the dream world. After 48 seconds one of the most pounding and 'metallic' backing tracks of Bush's career bursts in as the rhythmic feel switches to four-beat. The backing track draws upon the standardised but effective device of guitar and keyboard chords circling around a bass pedal note rooted to the crotchet beat. When the verse returns the overlaying of triple-time vocals over steady crotchet kick drums is a wonderful mesh of rhythmic feels, giving the drive of 'fours' to the actuality of 'sixes'. After the space offered by a birdsong-and-laughter interlude, we are hurled back into the main rhythm track at 3: 34. The break lasts too long, but increases the tension and the power of its (partial) resolution as a consequence. Use of echo and the highly pitched melodies add to the feeling of transcendence and space.

From 4: 40 that great rarity in the Bush canon, the guitar solo, emerges. In the main it takes the form of a distorted funk solo, built upon fast, chopping partial chords rather than solo notes. The reliance upon percussion and kick drum without the comforting resolve of the snare pulse adds to the latent, rather than actual energy. This is abetted by the vocals, almost incoherent in terms of narrative, that use echo to deny the closure of linear meaning. The abrupt breakdown of the rhythm track to birdsong for the final 50 seconds does provide much of the resolution denied for the previous several minutes and gives us the circularity of a 'homecoming' after some 42 minutes of mainly seamless music.

Individually and collectively, *Aerial* has to be seen as something of a triumphant return to form by an artist after two relatively disappointing previous albums. Bearing in mind the impetus of popular music towards connotations of 'youth' and 'craziness', the album takes us some way back down the road towards the unbridled ambition and bizarre elements of *Hounds of Love* and *The Dreaming*. Bearing in mind its 80-minute running time, it is also a remarkably consistent piece of work without the pitfalls that such an observation would normally assume. Although not selling in the huge quantities of some past releases, *Aerial* remained in the UK top-75 album charts for 15 weeks, selling over 300,000 copies in the process.

The guitar work (all playing credited to Dan McIntosh) is consistently varied and effective, the vocals are assured and the production has removed itself from the shackles of fashion or outdated sounds found on previous albums. Petridis criticises the work as, at times, 'dated', drawing upon 'lumpy funk' and a 'preponderance of fretless bass' (Petridis, 2005: 12), but for this writer, these are not issues, unlike on the two previous albums. The album generally was particularly well received ('madly ambitious' ... 'Goofily exuberant', Troussé, 2005: 98, and one to which you 'willingly succumb', Petridis, 2005: 12), garnering the artist nominations in Brit Awards categories (which she did not win, although this may have been influenced by her probable refusal to perform at the ceremony). Irvin was right to describe the album as 'consistently engrossing in the manner of *Hounds of Love*' (Irvin, 2005: 96). If this consistency does result in a levelling out of some of the extreme peaks of *jouissance* or troughs of failed experimentation then it is, in the main, a price worth paying. Age should not be an issue for creative artists, but in popular music it always will be. For a 47-year-old mother to produce her best work for over 20 years is doubly impressive as a result. Irvin refers to the album as containing 'something middle-class ... slightly fusty; something arcane glimpsed through a leaded window, but also something bizarrely avant-garde, refreshingly out of step with the booty-proffering noughties' (ibid.). It is thus resolutely the expressive property of its originator, not made with the market, or even any market in mind. And now, we assume, comes another long wait ...

Coda: We Become Panoramic

How to sum up Kate Bush's body of work, and in particular *Hounds of Love*? As I stated at the outset of this book, music is a slippery beast. It seduces us into thinking that the sounds themselves are what is being scrutinised, whereas, to an extent, it is ourselves that we study, articulated by this most nebulous of sign systems. Music helps define us all: temporally, spacially, empirically and socially.

Hounds of Love happened at the right time – in terms of the temporal shift in production and technology, as well as for this writer, the artist herself and the 'marketplace' for popular music as a whole. With great commercial success and critical acclaim comes an often unwelcome legacy – how to transcend or, at best, live up to its impact. It took Kate Bush a further 20 years to release an album that was not, at best, a qualified success (as with *The Sensual World* and *The Red Shoes*), with *Aerial*. The fact that it shares with *Hounds* a 'half conceptual' structure is surely a contributory factor in its success.

During the final stages of working on this text, I read Kevin Holm-Hudson's illuminating account of the connections between cinematic and sonic structures and editing devices (Holm-Hudson, 2005). Within this scenario, techniques developed within film, such as dissolves, fades and cut-ins, are later adopted within music recording (ibid.: 74–6). He argued that such procedures as segues, superimpositions and overlaps between tracks actually function to transform collections of separate songs into unified works which can be compared to 'fine art' experiences such as those found within classical music or cinema. Bearing in mind Kate Bush's love and extensive referencing of film, the connection seems particularly appropriate in this case. His particular focus was upon Pink Floyd's *Dark Side of the Moon* (1973), an acclaimed album that is one of the biggest selling musical works in the history of music, and one which took up almost permanent residence in the US and UK album charts in the years following its release. Mention of Pink Floyd does, fittingly, return us to David Gilmour, whose influence upon Kate Bush stretches between her adolescence, right up to her most recent (and possibly final?) live performance, accompanying Gilmour during 'Comfortably Numb' on 18 January 2002 (Mallet, 2002). Other projects to operate in a similar fashion include Marvin Gaye's *What's Going On* (1971), The Who's *Tommy* (1969) and many albums, or 'song suites' by progressive rock acts.

Not all such albums gain the success and status of *Dark Side of the Moon*, but in a few instances they do assume the mantle of 'great works', or 'seminal texts' and transcend the 'popular' limitations imposed upon commercial music by establishment critical hegemony. I am arguing for *Hounds of Love* to be granted such status. Whilst I am not in the least prejudiced against 'low-culture' music or albums that are collections of songs, it must be recognised that the concept album does, in its best manifestations, allow many of us the interpretive breadth and imaginative scope that elevates its status: it asks more of us, and the resulting rewards can be greater as a consequence. It becomes a seamless journey that opens up the imagination. In the process, as Kate Bush puts it in 'Nocturn', 'we become panoramic'. In looking back over her career, it seems that the artist's (*auteur*'s) boundless ambition and huge talent have been best served by this 'bigger canvas'.

It is by no means certain that Kate Bush will continue, or resume her recording career in the future, although her manifest love of music does suggest that she will not 'retire' just yet. But if no more new material is issued, *Aerial* does at least provide us with a degree of 'closure'. Its double album form allows Bush the space to provide us with a conventionally structured collection of songs on *A Sea of Honey*, whose individual strengths return us to the very first album, *The Kick Inside*. My own impression is that, particularly within *A Sky of Honey*, the artist revisits the towering achievement of *Hounds of Love* and *The Ninth Wave*, at least in conceptual and structural terms. She does this not to compete with or outdo the previous work, but because she recognises that this is how she best works.

Her triumphs are manifold: not only in the works themselves (both musical and audio-visual), but also in the manner that she has balanced her productive life between the contrasting demands of creativity and stardom whilst never compromising the musical works. She has succeeded in structuring her own career, as an independent, empowered female *auteur* (but never an autocrat), in a field that continues to contrive to discriminate against her gender in so many ways. She has expressed herself in a particularly British, and southern English manner in a direct challenge to the forces of globalised, North American hegemony. And so much of her music is nothing short of ravishing. Certain tracks have an emotional impact upon me unequalled by any other artist. Her breadth of achievement is unique.

Bibliography

Print Sources

Aizlewood, J. (2001),"The Big Sleep", in *Q*, December, pp 92–6.

Alexander, J. (1990),'The Sensual World of Kate Bush', interview conducted as part of *The Sensual World: The Video* (PMI).

Banks, J. (1996), *Monopoly Television: MTV's Quest to Control the Music*, Oxford: Westview.

Banfield, S. (ed.) (1995), 'England, 1918–45', in *Twentieth Century (Blackwell History of Music in Britain)*, Oxford: Blackwell.

Barkham, P. (2005), 'After 12 Years of Silence Kate Bush is Back', in *The Guardian*, 28 September 2005, p. 5.

Barthes, R. (1972). *Mythologies*, London: Cape.

Barthes, R. (1977), *Image, Music, Text*, London: Fontana.

Battersby, C. (1989), *Gender and Genius: Towards a Feminist Aesthetics*, London: Women's Press.

Berland, J. (1993), 'Sound, Image and Social Space: Music Video and Media Reconstruction', in Frith, S., A. Goodwin and L. Grossberg (eds), *Sound and Vision: The Music Video Reader*, London: Routledge, pp. 25–44.

Borthwick, S. and R. Moy (2004), *Popular Music Genres: An Introduction*, Edinburgh: Edinburgh University Press.

Bracewell, M. (1997), *England is Mine: Pop life in Albion from Wilde to Goldie*, London: HarperCollins.

Brocken, M. (2003a), *The British Folk Revival 1944–2002*, Aldershot: Ashgate.

Brocken, M. (2003b), *Bacharach: Maestro! The Life of a Pop Genius*, New Malden: Chrome Dreams.

Brown, L. (1988), 'In the Realm of the Senses', *New Musical Express*, 7 October, accessed from rocksbackpages, 24 June 2004.

Bryson, B. (1990), *Mother Tongue: The English Language*, London: Penguin.

Buckley, D. (2006), Personal interview, 6 January.

Buckley, D. (2006), Personal interview, 18 March.

Burgess, R. (1997), *The Art of Record Production*, London: Omnibus.

Burns, L and M. Lafrance (2002), *Disruptive Divas: Feminism, Identity & Popular Music*, London: Routledge.

Bush, K. (1982), Interview in *Electronica & Music Maker*, interviewer unknown, accessed from gaffaweb, 6 April 2006.

Bush, K. (1985), 'The Private Kate Bush', interview in *Hot Press*, November, interviewer uncredited, accessed from gaffaweb, 7 April 2006.

Bush, K. (1986), 'An Interview with Auntie Hetty', in Kate Bush Club Fan letter no. 20, accessed from gaffaweb, 7 April 2006.

Buckley, D. (2000), *Strange Fascination. David Bowie: The Definitive Story*, London: Virgin.

Cann, K. and S. Mayes (1988), *Kate Bush: A Visual Documentary*, London: Omnibus.

Chion, M. (1994), 'Wasted Words', in Altman, R. (ed.), *Sound Theory Sound Practice*, London: Routledge, pp. 104–12.

Colls, R. (2002), *Identity of England*, Oxford: Oxford University Press.

Clarke, S (1978), 'Kate Bush City Limits', *New Musical Express*, March, accessed from gaffaweb, 30 June 2004.

Costa, M. (2005), 'The Queen of Drama', in *The Guardian*, 28 September, p. 5.

Crisell, A. (1996), *Understanding Radio*, London: Routledge.

Cunningham, M. (1998), *Good Vibrations: A History of Record Production* (2nd edn), Chessington: Castle.

Dickinson, K. (ed.) (2003), *Movie Music: The Film Reader*, London: Routledge.

Doherty, H. (1978a), 'The Kick Outside', *Melody Maker*, June 3, accessed from rocksbackpages, 16 June 2004.

Doherty, H. (1978b), 'Enigma Variations', *Melody Maker*, November, accessed from rocksbackpages, 24 June 2004.

Doyle, T. (2005), 'Weak? Frail? Mentally Unstable? Fuck Off!', in *Mojo* 145, December, pp. 76–92.

Ellis, J. (1988), *Visible Fictions*, London: Routledge.

Elmes, S. (2001), *The Routes of English*, London: BBC.

Fabbri, F. (1982), 'A Theory of Musical Genres: Two Applications', in Horn, D. and P. Tagg (eds), *Popular Music Perspectives: Papers from the First International Conference on Popular Music Research*, Exeter: IASPM.

Fielder, H. (1984), *The Book of Genesis*, London: Sidgwick & Jackson.

Fraser, P. (2005), *Teaching Music Video*, London: BFI.

Freeborn, D. (1998), *From Old English to Standard English*, Basingstoke: Macmillan.

Frith, S. (1996), *Performing Rites*: *Evaluating Popular Music*, Oxford: Oxford University Press.

Frith, S., A. Goodwin and L. Grossberg (eds) (1993), *Sound and Vision*: *The Music Video Reader*, London: Routledge.

Gardam, T. (2006), 'Thinking Outside the Box', in *Guardian Review*, 11 March, p. 10.

Gilbert, J. and E. Pearson (1999), *Discographies: Dance, Music, Culture and the Politics of Sound*, London: Routledge.

Goodwin, A. (1993), *Dancing in the Distraction Factory: Music Television and Popular Culture*, London: Routledge.

Grossberg, L. (1993), 'The Media Economy of Rock Culture: Cinema, Post-Modernity and Authenticity', in Frith, S., A. Goodwin and L. Grossberg (eds), *Sound and Vision*: *The Music Video Reader*, London: Routledge, pp. 185–209.

Guilbert, G.-C. (2002), *Madonna as Postmodern Myth: How One Star's Self-Construction Rewrites Sex, Gender, Hollywood and the American Dream*, London: McFarland & Company.

Halstead, J. (1997), *The Woman Composer*, Aldershot: Ashgate.

Harris, J. (2006), 'Talking Lovelorn Left-Wing Electric Troubadour Blues', in *Mojo* 149, April, pp. 58–63.

Hawkins, S. (2002), *Setting the Pop Score: Pop Texts and Identity Politics*, Aldershot: Ashgate.

Hawkins, S. (2004), 'On Performativity and Production in Madonna's "Music", in Whiteley, S., A. Bennett and S. Hawkins (eds), *Music, Space and Place: Popular Music and Cultural Identity*, Aldershot: Ashgate, pp. 16–24.

Himes, G. (2002), 'I Smell the Blood of a Half-Englishman: Billy Bragg', in *Harp*, May, accessed from rocksbackpages, 15 February 2006.

Hinton, Brian (2000), *Joni Mitchell: Both Sides Now*, London: Sanctuary.

Holm-Hudson, K. (2005), 'Worked out within the Grooves': the Sound and Structure of *The Dark Side of the Moon*', in Reising, R. (ed.), *Speak to Me: The Legacy of Pink Floyd's* The Dark Side of the Moon, Aldershot: Ashgate, pp 69–86.

Holm-Hudson, K. (ed.) (2002), *Progressive Rock Reconsidered*, London: Routledge.

Hyder, R. (2004), *Brimful of Asia: Negotiating Ethnicity on the UK Music Scene*, Aldershot: Ashgate.

Inglis, I. (ed.) 2003),*Popular Music and Film*, London: Wallflower.

Irvin, J. (2005), 'And is there honey still for tea?', in *Mojo* 145, December, pp 96–7.

Jones, A. (1986), 'Chartfile', in *Record Mirror*, June, accessed from gaffaweb, 30 June 2004.

Jonssen, M. (1993), 'Rubber Souls', in *Vox*, November, pp. 32–4, 172.

Jovanovic, R. (2005), *Kate Bush: The Biography*, London: Piatkus Press.

Juby, K. (1988), *Kate Bush: The Whole Story*, London: Sidgwick & Jackson.

Kaplan, E.A. (1987), *Rocking Around the Clock: Music Television, Postmodernism and Consumer Culture*, London: Methuen.

Kruse, H. (1990), 'In Praise of Kate Bush', in Frith, S and A. Goodwin (eds), *On Record: Rock, Pop and the Written Word*, London: Routledge, pp. 450–65.

Lambert, P. (1985), 'Pop: Music for a New Year', in *The Wall Street Journal*, 30 December, accessed from gaffaweb, 30 June 2004.

Leblanc, L. (2001), *Pretty in Punk: Girls' Gender Resistance in a Boy's Subculture*, New Jersey: Rutgers University Press.

Macan, E. (1997), *Rocking the Classics: English Progressive Rock and the Counter-Culture*, Oxford: Oxford University Press.

Maconie, S. (1993), 'Little Miss Can't Be Wrong', in *Q* 87, December, pp. 98–104.

Marck, J. (1985), 'Kate Bush Breaks Out: Bush's Bridges', interview in *Now: Toronto Weekly*, 28 November, accessed from gaffaweb, 7 April 2006.

Mayhew, E. (2004), 'Positioning the Producer: Gender Divisions in Creative Labour and Value', in Whiteley, S., A. Bennett and S. Hawkins (eds), *Music, Space and Place: Popular Music and Cultural Identity*, Aldershot: Ashgate, pp 149–62.

McClary, S. (1991), *Feminine Endings: Music, Gender & Sexuality*, Oxford: University of Minnesota Press.

McClary, S. and R. Walser (1990), 'Start Making Sense! Musicology Wrestles with Rock', in Frith, S. and A. Goodwin (eds), *On Record: Rock, Pop and the Written Word*, London: Routledge, pp. 277–92.

McLuhan, M. (1987), *Understanding Media: the Extensions of Man*, London: Ark.

McRobbie, A. (1991), *Feminism and Youth Culture: From Jackie to Just Seventeen*, London: Macmillan.

McRobbie, A. (1999), *In the Culture Society: Art, Fashion and Popular Music*, London: Routledge.

Mendelssohn, J. (1971), 'Faces: Long Player', album review from *Rolling Stone*, 18 March, accessed from rocksbackpages, 15 February 2006.

Mendelssohn, J. (2004), *Waiting For Kate Bush*, London: Omnibus.

Moy, R. (2000), *An Analysis of the Position and Status of Sound Ratio*, Lampeter: Edwin Mellen.

Mundy, J. (1999), *Popular Music on Screen: From Hollywood Musical to Music Video*, Manchester: Manchester University Press.

Negus, K. (1990), Personal interview, 18 October.

Negus, K. (1993), *Producing Pop: Culture and Conflict in the Popular Music Industry*, London: Edward Arnold.

O'Brien, K. (1995), *Hymn to Her: Women Musicians Talk*, London: Virago.

O'Brien, L. (2002), *She-Bop II: the Definitive History of Women in Rock, Pop and Soul*, London: Continuum.

Owens, D. (2004), Online review, 23 June, accessed from Amazon.co.uk: Music: Lionheart, 30 June 2004.

Palmer, D. (1989), 'A Soft Landing in the Sensual World', from the Kate Bush Club Newsletter, issue 23, Fall 1989, accessed from gaffaweb, 22 February 2006.

Petridis, A. (2005), 'Domestic Goddess', in *The Guardian Film & Music*, 4 November, p. 12.

Phillips-Oland, P. (2001), *The Art of Writing Great Lyrics*, New York: Allworth.

Pringle, D. (1980), Television interview in *Profiles in Rock*, CITY-TV, Toronto, December, accessed from gaffaweb, 7 April 2006.

Raphael, A. (1995), *Never Mind the Bollocks: Women Rewrite Rock*, London: Virago.

Reimers, J. (1983), Interview from *Voc'l* magazine, accessed from gaffaweb, 7 April 2006.

Reynolds, S. (1993), 'Kate Bush', *Pulse*, December, accessed from rocksbackpages, 24 June 2004.

Reynolds, S. and J. Press (1995), *The Sex Revolts: Gender, Rebellion And Rock'n'Roll*, London: Serpent's Tail.

Rule, G. (1999), *Electro Shock: Groundbreakers of Synth Music*, London: Backbeat.

Sandall, R. (1989), 'Wiggly', in *Q38*, November, p. 110.

Sarris, A. (1968), *American Cinema: Directors and Directions*, New York: Dutton.

Scott, P. (2005), 'Wuthering Frights', in *Daily Mail*, 17 September, pp. 34–5.

Shingler. P. and C. Weiringa (1998), *On Air: Methods and Meanings of Radio*, London: Arnold.

Silverman, K. (2003), 'The Female Authorial Voice', in Wexman, V. (ed.), *Film and Authorship*, New Jersey: Rutgers University Press, pp. 50–75.

Straw, W. (1993), 'Popular Music and Post-Modernism in the 1980s', in Frith, S., A. Goodwin and L. Grossberg (eds), *Sound and Vision: The Music Video Reader*, London: Routledge, pp. 3–24.

Stump, P. (1997), *The Music's All That Matters: A History of Progressive Rock*, London: Quartet.

Sutcliffe, P. (1989), 'Iron Maiden', in *Q* 38, November, pp. 84–92.

Sutcliffe, P. (2003), 'Season of the Witch', in *Mojo* 111, February, pp. 72–80.

Swales, P. (1985), Interview in *Musician*, Fall 1985, accessed from gaffaweb, 17 February 2006.

Sweeting, A. (1994), 'Flop of the Pops', in *The Guardian G2*, 19 December, p. 5.

Toop, D. (1995), *Ocean of Sound: Aether Talk, Ambient Sound and Imaginary Worlds*, London: Serpent's Tail.

Troussé, S. (2005), 'The Arc Ascending', in *Uncut* 103, December, pp. 98–9.

Upton, C. and J. Widdowson (1996), *An Atlas of English Dialects*, London: BCA.

Vermorel, F. (1983), *The Secret History of Kate Bush: And the Strange Art of Pop*, London: Omnibus.

Vermorel, F. and J. Vermorel (1979), *Kate Bush Biography*, London: Target.

Wall, M. (1985), Review in *Kerrang!*, September, accessed from gaffaweb, 30 June 2004.

Warner, T. (2003), *Pop Music, Technology and Creativity: Trevor Horn and the digital Revolution*, Aldershot: Ashgate.

Wexman, V. (ed.) (2003), *Film and Authorship*, New Jersey: Rutgers University Press.

White, C. (2005), 'Kid Adorno', in Tate, J. (ed.), *The Music and Art of Radiohead*, Aldershot: Ashgate, pp. 9–14.

Whiteley, S. (ed.) (1997), *Sexing the Groove: Popular Music and Gender*, London: Routledge.

Whiteley, S. (2000), *Women And Popular Music: Sexuality, Identity and Subjectivity*, London: Routledge.

Whitelely, S. (2005), *Too Much Too Young: Popular Music, Age and Gender*, London: Routledge.

Wollen, P. (1998), *Signs and Meanings in the Cinema*, London: BFI.

Young, J. (1978), 'Kate Bush Gets Her Kicks', in *Trouser Press*, July, accessed from gaffaweb, 30 June 2004.

Internet Sources

http://www.Amazon.co.uk: Reviews: Music
http://homepage.eircom.net/~twoms/katenews.htm
http://homevideo.about.com
http://gaffaweb.org
http://www.popular-musicology-online.com
http://www.rocksbackpages.com

Music Sources

Amos, Tori (1992), *Little Earthquakes*, EastWest.
Björk, selected albums:

(1993), *Debut*, One Little Indian.
(1995), *Post*, One Little Indian.
(1997), *Homogenic*, One Little Indian.
(2001), *Vespertine*, One Little Indian.
(2003), *Medulla*, One Little Indian.
Bragg, Billy (2002), *England, Half-English*, Cooking Vinyl.
Bowie, David (1983), *Let's Dance*, EMI.
Bush, Kate, selected albums:
(1978), *The Kick Inside*, EMI.
(1978), *Lionheart*, EMI.
(1980), *Never For Ever*, EMI.
(1982), *The Dreaming*, EMI.
(1985), *Hounds of Love*, EMI.
(1989), *The Sensual World.*, EMI.
(1993), *The Red Shoes*, EMI.
(2005), *Aerial*, EMI
Butterworth, George (2001), *George Butterworth*, Decca.
Chandra, Sheila (1992), *Weaving My Ancestors' Voices*, Real World.
Elgar, Edward (1987), *Sea Pictures. The Music Makers*, EMI.
Madonna, selected albums:
(1984), *Like A Virgin*, Sire.
(1992), *Erotica.* Maverick
(1998), *Ray of Light*, Maverick.
(2000), *Music*, Maverick.
(2003), *American Life*, Maverick.
(2005), *Confessions on a Dance Floor*, Maverick.
Mitchell, Joni (1972), *Court and Spark*, Asylum.
Roxy Music, selected albums:
(1972) *Roxy Music*, Island.
(1974) *Stranded*, Island.
Vaughan Williams, Ralph (2005), *The Lark Ascending. Fantasia on a Theme by Thomas Tallis*, HMV.

Video, Film and Radio Sources

Bush, Kate (1994), *The Line, The Cross and The Curve*, PMI.
Keshishian, A. (1991), *In Bed With Madonna: Truth or Dare*, MGM.
Lloyd, A.L. (1971), *The Folk Virtuoso*, BBC Radio 4 broadcast.
Mallet, D. (2002), *David Gilmour – In Concert*, EMI.
Skinner, R. (1992), *Classic Albums: Hounds of Love*, BBC Radio 1, originally broadcast 25 January.
Walker, C. (1997), *The South Bank Show: Björk*, ITV, broadcast 9 November.
Various (1986), *Kate Bush: The Whole Story*, PMI.
Various (1990), *The Sensual World: The Video*, PMI.

Index